Information Technology Certified Associate

CYBERSECURITY
FUNDAMENTALS
Study Guide, 3rd Edition

Part of the ITCA Stackable
Certificate Program
www.isaca.org/itca

ISACA.

About ISACA

For more than 50 years, ISACA® (www.isaca.org) has advanced the best talent, expertise and learning in technology. ISACA equips individuals with knowledge, credentials, education and community to progress their careers and transform their organizations, and enables enterprises to train and build quality teams. ISACA is a global professional association and learning organization that leverages the expertise of its 145,000 members who work in information security, governance, assurance, risk and privacy to drive innovation through technology. It has a presence in 188 countries, including more than 220 chapters worldwide.

Disclaimer

ISACA has designed and created *Cybersecurity Fundamentals Study Guide, 3rd Edition* (the "Work") primarily as an educational resource for professionals. ISACA makes no claim that use of any of the Work will assure a successful outcome. The Work should not be considered inclusive of all proper information, procedures, and tests or exclusive of other information, procedures, and tests that are reasonably directed to obtaining the same results. In determining the propriety of any specific information, procedure, or test, professionals should apply their own professional judgment to the specific circumstances presented by the particular systems or information technology environment.

ISACA acknowledges The Open Group® for permission to include text/figures derived from its copyrighted source, *Introduction to the TOGAF® Standard*, Version 9.2, April 2018, Tables 1 and 2. TOGAF is a registered trademark of The Open Group in the United States and other countries.

Reservation of Rights

ISACA

1700 E. Golf Road, Suite 400
Schaumburg, IL 60173, USA
Phone: +1.847.660.5505
Fax: +1.847.253.1755
Contact us: https://support.isaca.org
Website: www.isaca.org

Provide Feedback: To comment, please visit https://support.isaca.org.
Participate in the ISACA Online Forums: https://engage.isaca.org/onlineforums

Twitter: http://twitter.com/ISACANews
LinkedIn: www.linkedin.com/company/isaca
Facebook: www.facebook.com/ISACAGlobal
Instagram: www.instagram.com/isacanews/

ISBN 978-1-60420-751-4
Cybersecurity Fundamentals Study Guide, 3rd Edition
Printed in the United States of America

Acknowledgments

The *Cybersecurity Fundamentals Study Guide, 3rd Edition* reflects the collective effort of many developers and volunteers. Special thanks go to:

Expert Reviewers

Ehab Badawi, CISA, CISM, CISSP, SAC Wireless, USA
Abigail L. Deras, CISSP, GCFE, Qualcomm, USA
Michael A. Gioia, CISM, CISSP, GSLC, PCIP, Bentley University, USA
Clyde Hague, CRISC, CISM, CISSP, NCAA, USA
Matthew A. Shabat, JD, CRISC, CISM, Native American Industrial Solutions LLC, USA
Jo Stewart-Rattray, CISA, CRISC, CISM, CGEIT, FACS CP(Cyber), IP3P, BRM Advisory, Australia
Ilker Tutu, CISA, CRISC, CISM, CGEIT, CCSP, CIA, CISSP, PCI ISA, ISO 27001, ITIL, PayPal Europe, Luxembourg
Koby Zvirsh, CISM, Trigo Vision, Israel

Board of Directors

Tracey Dedrick, Chair, Former Chief Risk Officer, Hudson City Bancorp, USA
Rolf von Roessing, Vice-Chair, CISA, CISM, CGEIT, CDPSE, CISSP, FBCI, Partner, FORFA Consulting AG, Switzerland
Gabriela Hernandez-Cardoso, Independent Board Member, Mexico
Pam Nigro, CISA, CRISC, CGEIT, CRMA, Vice President–Information Technology, Security Officer, Home Access Health, USA
Maureen O'Connell, Board Chair, Acacia Research (NASDAQ), Former Chief Financial Officer and Chief Administration Officer, Scholastic, Inc., USA
David Samuelson, Chief Executive Officer, ISACA, USA
Gerrard Schmid, President and Chief Executive Officer, Diebold Nixdorf, USA
Gregory Touhill, CISM, CISSP, President, AppGate Federal Group, USA
Asaf Weisberg, CISA, CRISC, CISM, CGEIT, Chief Executive Officer, introSight Ltd., Israel
Anna Yip, Chief Executive Officer, SmarTone Telecommunications Limited, Hong Kong
Brennan P. Baybeck, CISA, CRISC, CISM, CISSP, ISACA Board Chair, 2019-2020, Vice President and Chief Information Security Officer for Customer Services, Oracle Corporation, USA
Rob Clyde, CISM, ISACA Board Chair, 2018-2019, Independent Director, Titus, and Executive Chair, White Cloud Security, USA
Chris K. Dimitriadis, Ph.D., CISA, CRISC, CISM, ISACA Board Chair, 2015-2017, Group Chief Executive Officer, INTRALOT, Greece

Page intentionally left blank

Table of Contents

Chapter 3:

Securing Assets **83**

Chapter 4:

Security Operations and Response...**155**

Page intentionally left blank

LIST OF FIGURES

Chapter 3. Securing Assets

Cybersecurity Fundamentals Study Guide, 3rd Edition
ISACA. All Rights Reserved.

Chapter 4. Security Operations and Response

Page intentionally left blank

Cybersecurity Fundamentals Study Guide, 3rd Edition

Introduction

The *Cybersecurity Fundamentals Study Guide, 3rd Edition* is a reference guide designed to assist individuals in acquiring a base-level knowledge of cybersecurity. It helps individuals prepare for the ISACA® Cybersecurity Fundamentals certificate, one of the components of the ISACA Information Technology Certified Associate™ program.

Topics in this guide are presented at a foundational level and include basic terminology, concepts, examples, general practices and explanations of cybersecurity principles. The *Cybersecurity Fundamentals Study Guide, 3rd Edition* provides the IT or business professional with knowledge in the following main content areas:

- Types of security
- Security governance
- Business continuity and disaster recovery
- Recovery
- Privacy vs. security
- Threat landscape
- Cyberrisk
- Cyberattacks
- Securing assets
- Security operations and response
- Vulnerability management
- Penetration testing
- Incident response
- Monitoring

Every chapter contains the following:

- **Learning objectives**—Knowledge that learners should understand after reading the chapter
- **Sections**—Knowledge content
- **Knowledge Checks**—Quiz on the chapter knowledge

Page intentionally left blank

Chapter 1:

Security Fundamentals

Security Fundamentals

Security Fundamentals

1.1 Learning Objectives

After completing this chapter, learners will be able to:

1. Identify and explain cybersecurity concepts.
2. Identify main components of telecommunications technologies.
3. Differentiate types of security.
4. Identify differences between information technology systems and specialized systems.
5. Discuss enterprise cybersecurity roles and responsibilities.
6. Define governance, risk management and compliance (GRC).
7. Identify and discuss common causes of enterprise service disruption.
8. Explain business continuity planning.
9. Describe the relationship between business continuity planning (BCP) and disaster recovery (DR).
10. Explain the objectives of information security.
11. Distinguish between privacy and security.

1.2 Overview

The need for cybersecurity professionals continues to increase. The protection of information is a critical function for all enterprises, industries and societies, regardless of size or location. Cybersecurity is a growing and rapidly changing field, largely because of its criticality to business survival, job stability and national security. Therefore, cybersecurity demands skilled professionals who possess the knowledge, skills and ability to confront the difficulties that accompany constant technological change. An evolving threat landscape, adapting to new and emerging technologies, and a myriad of regulations require cybersecurity professionals to be skilled not only in technology but also increasingly in business-related functions. The security implications of information and communications technology (ICT) cannot be overlooked or underestimated. Safeguarding information has been a priority for as long as people have needed to keep information secure and private. Even Julius Caesar used an encryption cipher to ensure message confidentiality. But as time and technology move forward, so do the demands of security—especially in a global market.

Cybersecurity plays a significant role in the ever-evolving information security global market. New trends in mobility and connectivity present a broad range of challenges as new attacks surface for emerging technologies. To combat and manage a dynamic threat landscape, cybersecurity professionals must remain informed and flexible. As has long been the case for IT professionals, cybersecurity requires the need for lifelong learning.

To successfully protect their systems and information, cybersecurity professionals must demonstrate a high degree of situational awareness. This takes time to cultivate, because it usually develops through experience. Each enterprise has its own distinct culture, which means that conditions may vary widely from one enterprise to another. Therefore, it is critical for cybersecurity professionals to have a detailed understanding of the environment in which they operate and a broader ongoing awareness and understanding of threats affecting other enterprises and industries to ensure relevant knowledge is maintained.

1.3 What is Security?

The technology industry is laden with terms such as IT security, information security and cybersecurity. Often, these terms are used interchangeably, which is not always correct.

The word security is broadly used when referring to protection of individuals, enterprises, and objects. Security can be used to reference people, places, or things, which sometimes creates confusion—especially when referencing types of security. To illustrate this, following are definitions of security from two well-known dictionaries:

- *[T]he quality or state of being secure...something given, deposited, or pledged to make certain the fulfillment of an obligation...an instrument of investment in the form of a document (such as a stock certificate or bond)...something that secures*[1]

- *[P]rotection of a person, building, organization, or country against threats such as crime or attacks...the group of people responsible for protecting a building...the fact that something is not likely to fail or be lost...property or goods that you promise to give to someone if you cannot pay what you owe them*[2]

Security can also imply physical security (i.e., points of entry) or logical security, which is synonymous with cybersecurity. Security is sometimes used as a shorthand term for either information security or cybersecurity, for those working in this industry. For example, the European Network and Information Security Agency (ENISA) glossary defines security as "all aspects relating to defining, achieving, and maintaining data confidentiality, integrity, availability, accountability, authenticity, and reliability."[3] The US National Institute of Standards and Technology (NIST) glossary lists many variants depending on source documents; however, one definition is similar to the ENISA definition:

> *Protecting information and information systems from unauthorized access, use, disclosure, disruption, modification, or destruction in order to provide—(A) integrity, which means guarding against improper information modification or destruction, and includes ensuring information non-repudiation and authenticity; (B) confidentiality, which means preserving authorized restrictions on access and disclosure, including means for protecting personal privacy and proprietary information; and (C) availability, which means ensuring timely and reliable access to and use of information.*[4]

Both referenced definitions overlook the fact that security in practice is a process. Moreover, security is a state of mind that requires iterative work to continually evaluate surroundings and make decisions that minimize harm. It is this premise that drives risk management, discussed in Chapter 2.

It is important to learn that all types of security (physical, information, cybersecurity, network, etc.) serve to minimize risk. No piece of technology can ever be 100-percent secure. Comprehensive enterprise security strategies require cooperation among parties responsible for people, processes and technology (**figure 1.1**).

---

[1] Merriam-Webster, Incorporated; *Dictionary*, 2020, www.merriam-webster.com/dictionary/security
[2] Cambridge University Press; *Cambridge Dictionary*, 2020, https://dictionary.cambridge.org/us/dictionary/english
[3] European Union Agency for Cybersecurity, "Glossary: Published under Risk Management," www.enisa.europa.eu/topics/threat-risk-management/risk-management/current-risk/risk-management-inventory/glossary
[4] National Institute of Standards and Technology, "Glossary," https://csrc.nist.gov/glossary/term/security

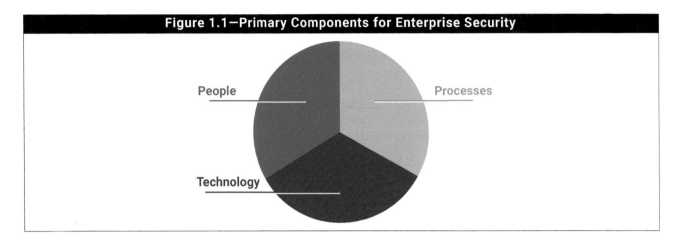

Figure 1.1—Primary Components for Enterprise Security

1.4 Types of Security

This section delineates the several types of information technology (IT) security and their components. The professional security opportunities within IT are abundant. Security opportunities and work scope vary largely by industry, enterprise size and geographic size.

1.4.1 Information and Communications Technology Security

Information and communications technology (ICT) security is the protection of telecommunications and transmission technologies.[5] ICT security is broader than either IT security or cybersecurity as it includes the protection of telecommunications technologies, such as radio, telephone and microwave. Telecommunications technologies include three main components:[6]

- **Transmitter**—device that originates communication
- **Medium**—atmosphere or cables over which the transmission takes place
- **Receiver**—end point of transmission

As traditional telephone networks disappear, ICT security continues to evolve to capture any technology and transmission line that carries data. ICT includes the components shown in **figure 1.2**.

---

[5] Techopedia. "Information and Communications Technology (ICT)," 30 August 2019, www.techopedia.com/definition/24152/information-and-communications-technology-ict
[6] Ace project, "Telecommunications Technology,"http://aceproject.org/ace-en/topics/et/eta/eta01/default

Figure 1.2—Information and Communications Technology (ICT) Components

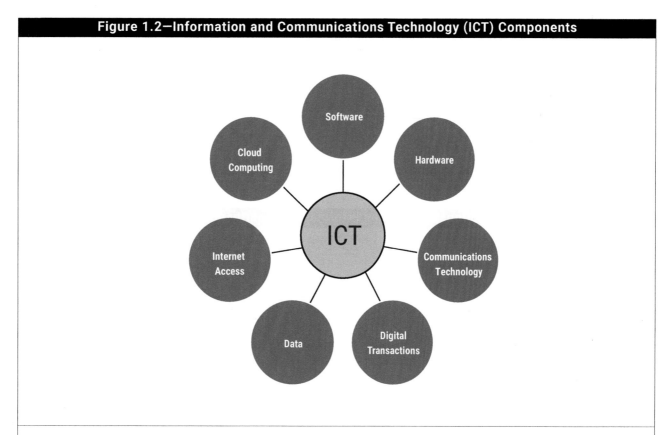

Source: Adapted from Rouse, M.; "ICT (information and communications technology, or technologies)," Tech Target, https://searchcio.techtarget.com/definition/ICT-information-and-communications-technology-or-technologies

1.4.2 IT Security

IT security refers to the protection of the hardware, software, communication and facilities used to input, store, process, transmit and output data in whatever form. IT security is synonymous with older terminology including automated information systems (AIS) security, computer security and information systems security and may be incorrectly interchanged with information security or cybersecurity. IT security includes the physical components of data processing and storage facilities—which overlap with information security and physical security.[7]

1.4.3 Information Security

The goal of information security is to keep data safe from unauthorized access, modification and theft during processing, storage and transmission. Information security deals with all formats of information—paper documents, digital assets, intellectual property in people's minds, and verbal and visual communications.

1.4.4 Cybersecurity

Cybersecurity is a component of information security (**figure 1.3**). Cybersecurity is the protection of information assets by addressing threats to information processed, stored and transported by internetworked information systems.

---

[7] Lynch, K.; "Understanding the Difference Between IT and Cyber Security," Security Boulevard, 31 July 2019, https://securityboulevard.com/2019/07/understanding-the-difference-between-it-and-cyber-security/

Cybersecurity is concerned with protecting digital assets—everything encompassed within network hardware, software and information that is processed, stored within isolated systems, or transported by internetworked information environments (**figure 1.4**). Information security encompasses all formats of information; cybersecurity focuses on only digital information assets.

Cybersecurity addresses internal and external threats to enterprise digital information assets by focusing on critical electronic data processes, transaction processing, risk analytics and information system security engineering. Cybersecurity usually addresses an entity initiating threats due to the existence of a global cyberspace (i.e., Internet).

Unlike information security, cybersecurity responsibility does not include natural hazards, human error, or physical security. Information security and cybersecurity controls are discussed in greater detail in Chapter 3.

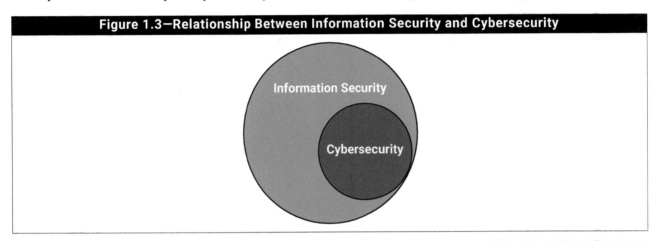

Figure 1.3—Relationship Between Information Security and Cybersecurity

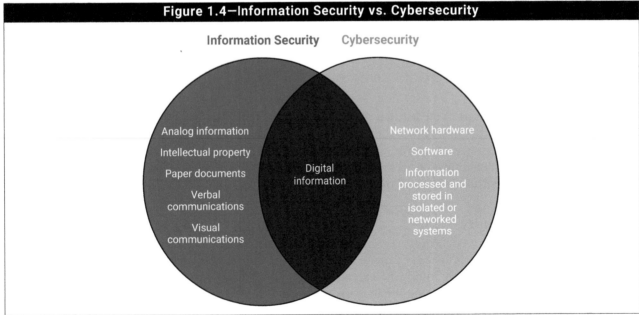

Figure 1.4—Information Security vs. Cybersecurity

1.4.5 Physical Security

Physical security is that part of security concerned with physical measures designed to safeguard personnel; to prevent unauthorized access to equipment, installations, material, and documents; and to safeguard against espionage, sabotage, damage, and theft.[8]

---

[8] GlobalSecurity.org, *Physical Security*, Field Manual 3-19.30, 8 January 2001, www.globalsecurity.org/military/library/policy/army/fm/3-19-30/index.html

Information security overlaps with the human component of physical security, which also aims to safeguard property and physical assets (**figure 1.5**).

Physical security is often overlooked, given the sensationalist reporting associated with cyberattacks; however, the expansion of wireless technologies and Internet-based surveillance components has made the physical security market a multibillion-dollar business that is forecast to grow to US $119.4 billion by 2023.[9, 10] Nonetheless, recent research overwhelmingly shows that chief executive officers "prioritize cyber over physical security with regard to importance, budget, personnel allocation, and overall strategy"[11] (**figure 1.6**).

Physical security has evolved exponentially beyond guard duty and loss prevention. The layered security concept within physical security represents a complex interdependence on technology, as shown in **figure 1.7**. The evolution of access controls, surveillance and climate controls has intertwined physical security and information security so much that cooperation is imperative for a unified security strategy. Beyond protection, physical security also includes deterrence, detection and response to aforementioned threats. Physical security controls are discussed in greater detail in Chapter 3.

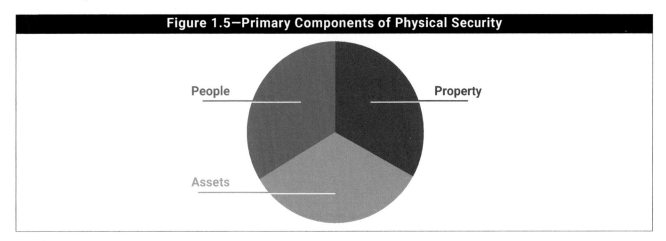

Figure 1.5—Primary Components of Physical Security

[9] Swinhoe, D.; "What is physical security? How to keep your facilities and devices safe from on-site attackers," CSO, 4 December 2018, www.csoonline.com/article/3324614/what-is-physical-security-how-to-keep-your-facilities-and-devices-safe-from-on-site-attackers.html?upd=1586460306648

[10] Shepard, S.; "Physical Security Market Projected to Grow to $119.4 Billion by 2023," SecurityToday, 22 February 2019, https://securitytoday.com/articles/2019/02/22/physical-security-market-projected-to-grow-to-119.4-billion-by-2023.aspx

[11] Center for Cyber and Homeland Security and International Security Management Association, Cyber and Physical Security: Perspectives from the C-Suite, May 2019, http://cchs.auburn.edu/_files/isma-survey-paper.pdf

Figure 1.6—CEO Prioritization of Cyber vs. Physical Security

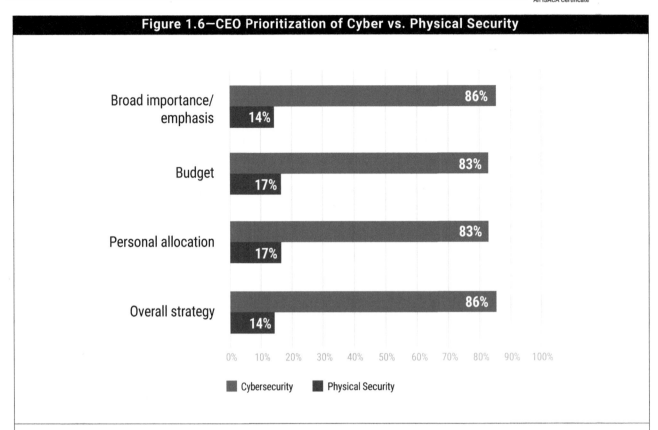

Source: Center for Cyber and Homeland Security (CCHS) and International Security Management Association (ISMA), *Cyber and Physical Security: Perspectives from the C-Suite*, May 2019, http://cchs.auburn.edu/_files/isma-survey-paper.pdf

Figure 1.7—Layers of Physical Security

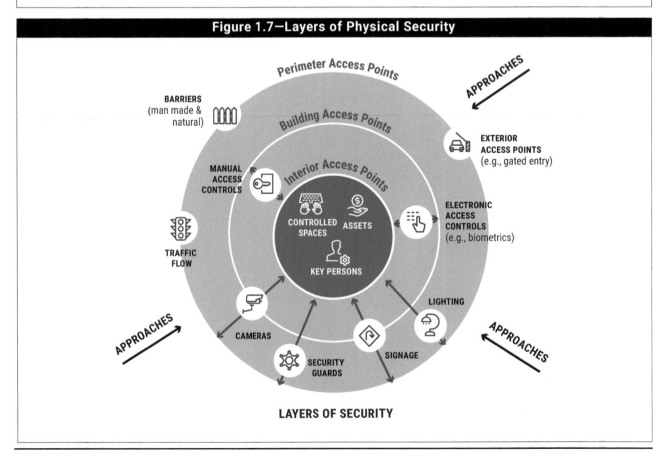

1.4.6 Cybersecurity Focus Areas

Cybersecurity has specific areas of focus, including network security and application security, which also have subcomponents.

Network security entails protecting computer networks. Computer networks come in different shapes and sizes that may use physical cabling or wireless technologies. As such, network security is concerned with protecting all relevant physical and logical parts of a network. Network security—once limited to on-premise networks—continues to evolve in response to expansion of wireless networks, bring your own device (BYOD), cloud adoption and an increasingly mobile workforce. As a result of the expanding network architecture, industry is trending towards the use of the term infrastructure security, rather than the term network security, but ISACA discourages the use of the broad term infrastructure security in the context of network security. Network infrastructure security is a better alternative term. Chapter 3 discusses network security in greater detail.

Application security is another focus area (i.e., component) of cybersecurity that focuses on making applications secure. This cybersecurity focus area continues to be extremely important despite its scope. According to the 2019 Veracode *State of Software Security X* report, 83 percent of applications have one security flaw on an initial scan.[12] Remember that security is not an end goal but, rather, an iterative process. Vulnerabilities are continually discovered, so it is extremely important to continually review and remediate application security flaws. Application security is discussed in greater detail in Chapter 3.

---

[12] Veracode; *State of Software Security X*, 2019, www.veracode.com/state-of-software-security-report

1.5 Specialized Systems

Some computer systems and applications are very specialized[13] and may have unique threats and risk, requiring distinct types of controls. An industrial control system is a type of operational technology (OT) that monitors and controls physical equipment and processes that are typically found in critical infrastructure sectors, such as utilities and defense systems. Operational technology controls the physical world while IT systems manage data.[14]

An industrial control system (ICS) resides in industrial and manufacturing environments, e.g., energy production, transportation and power management. These systems are also known as operational control systems in some parts of the world. It was not until the early 21st century that attempts were made to standardize operational technology terms, such as process control system (PCS), distributed control system (DCS) and supervisory control and data acquisition (SCADA) system. Before that, the terms were used interchangeably.[15] Following are definitions of ICS from the United States and Europe:

- The European Union Agency for Network and Information Security (ENISA) describes ICS as those systems "used to control industrial processes such as manufacturing, product handling, production, and distribution."[16]
- The US National Institute of Standards and Technology (NIST) adds specificity, defining ICS as "a general term that encompasses several types of control systems, including supervisory control and data acquisition (SCADA) systems, distributed control systems (DCS), and other control system configurations such as skid-mounted Programmable Logic Controllers (PLC) often found in the industrial sectors and critical infrastructures."[17]

SCADA systems are the more widely known class of control systems to those not working in OT; however, industrial control systems encompass far more. This class of systems also includes programmable automation controllers (PACs), human-machine interface (HMI), industrial automation and control systems (IACSs), and remote terminal units (RTUs).[18] Other specialized systems include air traffic control systems, building management systems (i.e., HVAC, fire suppression, backup power, etc.) and defense systems.

Historically, a vast number of these specialized systems were not intended to be connected to the Internet, but, over time, technological advancements in ICS components facilitated convergence of OT onto IT systems. Unfortunately, industrial control systems and components are often plagued with poor or no security mechanisms. Because of the importance of these systems on critical operations, these systems can be targeted by many adversaries, and the impact of a successful attack can be catastrophic or even life threatening. The advent of technology continues to push convergence of IT and OT, which is problematic for many, given that the design or deployment of most industrial control systems did not consider security. Although vendors are improving security, ICSs are highly vulnerable and often need special controls to compensate for their inherent weaknesses. Additionally, ICSs are expensive to replace, so they often remain in service far beyond their recommended lifespan. Aspiring IT and security professionals must be aware of OT and the security challenges it presents, because IT and OT continue to converge.

[13] ISACA, *Industrial Control Systems: A Primer for the Rest of Us*, 2015, www.isaca.org/bookstore/bookstore-wht_papers-digital/whpicsys
[14] Virtual Armour, "Operational Technology vs. Information Technology: Differences, Similarities, & How the Intermix With Industrial Control Systems," Networking & Cybersecurity Blog, 15 November 2019, www.virtualarmour.com/operational-technology-vs-information-technology-differences-similarities-how-the-intermix-with-industrial-control-systems/
[15] Macaulay, T.; B. L. Singer; *Cybersecurity for Industrial Control Systems: SCADA, DCS, PLC, HMI, and SIS*, CRC Press, USA, 2012
[16] Pauna, A.; K. Moulinos; M. Lakka; J. May; T. Tryfonas; *Can we learn from SCADA security incidents?*, ENISA, 9 October 2013, www.enisa.europa.eu/activities/Resilience-and-CIIP/critical-infrastructure-and-services/scada-industrial-control-systems/can-we-learn-from-scada-security-incidents
[17] Stouffer, K.; J. Falco; K. Scarfone; *Guide to Industrial Control Systems (ICS) Security*, Special Publication 800-82, NIST, USA, 2011
[18] MWES Engineered Systems, "Types of Industrial Control Systems," www.mwes.com/types-od-industrial-control-systems

1.6 Roles and Responsibilities

Cybersecurity is the responsibility of the entire organization at every level. This section outlines some of the specific roles in managing cyberrisk within most organizations. These practitioners work within the direction, policies, guidelines, mandates and regulations set by the board of directors, executives and cybersecurity management. Cybersecurity roles are shown in **figure 1.8**.

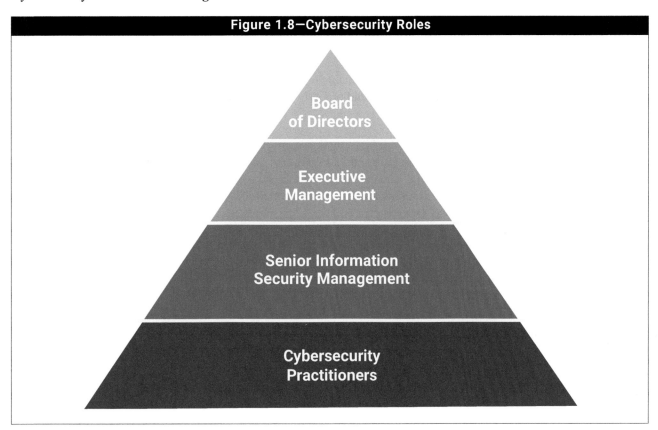

Figure 1.8—Cybersecurity Roles

1.6.1 Board of Directors

Cybersecurity governance requires strategic direction and inputs. It depends on commitment, resources and responsibility for cybersecurity management, and it requires a means for the board to determine whether its intent has been met. Effective governance also requires executive management and senior management involvement and support, through activities such as policy inputs and approval, appropriate monitoring and metrics, and reporting and trend analysis.

Members of the board need to be aware of the information assets of the organization at a high level and their criticality to ongoing business operations. The board should periodically be provided with the high-level results of comprehensive risk assessments and business impact analyses (BIAs), which identify how quickly essential business unit systems and processes should return to full operation following a disaster event. As a result of these activities, board members should identify the key assets they want protected and verify that protection levels and priorities are appropriate to a standard of due care. These tasks may be assigned to committees (e.g., Audit and Risk Committee) rather than the entire board.

The tone at the top must be conducive to effective security governance. It is up to senior management to set a positive example in this regard, because employees are much more likely to abide by security measures when they see their superiors respecting the same measures. Executive management's endorsement of security requirements

ensures that security expectations are met at all levels of the enterprise. Penalties for noncompliance must be defined, communicated and enforced from the board level down.

Beyond these requirements, the board has an ongoing obligation to provide oversight for activities related to cybersecurity. Senior management has an ethical responsibility, and in many cases a legal obligation, to exercise due care in protection of the organization's key assets, including its confidential and critical information. Therefore, board involvement and oversight are required.

1.6.2 Executive Management

An organization's executive management team is responsible for ensuring that needed organizational functions, resources and supporting infrastructure are available and properly utilized to fulfill the directives of the board, regulatory compliance and other demands.

Generally, executive management looks to the chief information security officer (CISO) or other senior cybersecurity manager to define the information security program and its subsequent management. Often, the cybersecurity manager is also expected to provide education and guidance to the executive management team. The manager's role in this situation is often constrained to the presentation of options supported by key, actionable information. In other words, the cybersecurity manager acts as an advisor.

Executive management sets the tone for cybersecurity management within the organization. The level of visible involvement and the inclusion of information risk management in key business activities and decisions indicate to other managers the level of importance that they are also expected to apply to risk management for activities within their organizations.

1.6.3 Senior Information Security Management

The exact title for the individual who oversees information security and cybersecurity varies from organization to organization. One of the most common titles is chief information security officer (CISO), but some organizations prefer chief security officer (CSO) to denote responsibility for all security matters, both physical and digital. Likewise, the responsibilities and authority of information security managers vary dramatically between organizations.

Generally, the cybersecurity manager is responsible for:

- Developing the security strategy
- Overseeing the security program and initiatives
- Coordinating with business process owners for ongoing alignment
- Ensuring that risk and business impact assessments are conducted
- Developing risk mitigation strategies
- Enforcing policy and regulatory compliance
- Monitoring the utilization and effectiveness of security resources
- Developing and implementing monitoring and metrics
- Directing and monitoring security activities
- Managing cybersecurity incidents and their remediation, and incorporating lessons learned

1.6.4 Cybersecurity Practitioners

In most organizations, cybersecurity is managed by a team of and experts and cybersecurity practitioners that may include security architects, administrators, digital forensics engineers, incident handlers and vulnerability researchers, to name a few. Together, they design, implement and manage processes and technical controls and respond to events and incidents.

The cybersecurity practitioner's duties include analysis of policy, trends and intelligence. Using problem solving and detection skills, these practitioners strive to better understand how an adversary may think or behave. The inherent complexity of cybersecurity practitioner work requires them to possess not only a wide array of technical IT skills, but also advanced analytical capabilities. A cybersecurity practitioner may also be a part of senior management.

1.7 Governance, Risk Management and Compliance

Within the realm of IT, the term governance refers to the way enterprises are directed and managed at the highest level.[19]

Governance ensures that:[20]

- Stakeholder needs, conditions and options are evaluated to determine balanced, agreed-on enterprise objectives.
- Direction is set through prioritization and decision making.
- Performance and compliance are monitored against agreed-on direction and objectives.

In most enterprises, governance is the responsibility of the board of directors, under the leadership of the chairperson. Specific governance responsibilities may be delegated to special organizational structures at an appropriate level, particularly in larger, complex enterprises.

Management plans, builds, runs and monitors activities, in alignment with the direction set by the governance body, to achieve enterprise objectives. In most enterprises, management is the responsibility of the executive management under the leadership of the chief executive officer (CEO).

Proper governance requires structure, which varies, because no two businesses or groups are the same. Each enterprise has its own mission (business), size, industry, culture and legal requirements. However, all enterprises have a responsibility and duty to protect their assets and operations, including their IT infrastructure and information. At the highest level, this is generally referred to as governance, risk management and compliance (GRC). Some entities implement these three areas in an integrated manner, while others may have fewer comprehensive approaches. Regardless of the actual implementation, every enterprise needs a plan to manage governance, risk management and compliance.

Risk management is the coordination of activities with the objective to identify, assess and respond to risk. Risk management requires the development and implementation of internal controls to manage and mitigate risk throughout the organization, e.g., strategic, compliance, financial, operational and reputational risk.

Compliance is the act of adhering to, and the ability to *demonstrate* adherence to, mandated requirements defined by laws and regulations. Compliance also includes voluntary requirements resulting from contractual obligations and internal policies.

---

[19] *Op cit* Cambridge University Press
[20] ISACA, COBIT 2019 Information Security Focus Area, 2020, https://www.isaca.org/bookstore/bookstore-cobit_19-print/cb19is

1.8 Cybersecurity Governance

Cybersecurity plays a significant role in the ever-evolving global market. New trends in mobility and connectivity present a broad range of challenges as new attacks surface for emerging technologies. Cybersecurity governance is a subset of enterprise governance and provides a strategic direction for security activities to maintain effective risk and resource management for enterprises.

The protection of assets from threats is a primary goal for security in general. Threats, in turn, must be categorized related to the likelihood (i.e., probability) that they will impact protected assets. In security, threats related to malicious or other human activities are often given greater attention. **Figure 1.9** illustrates these security concepts and relationships.

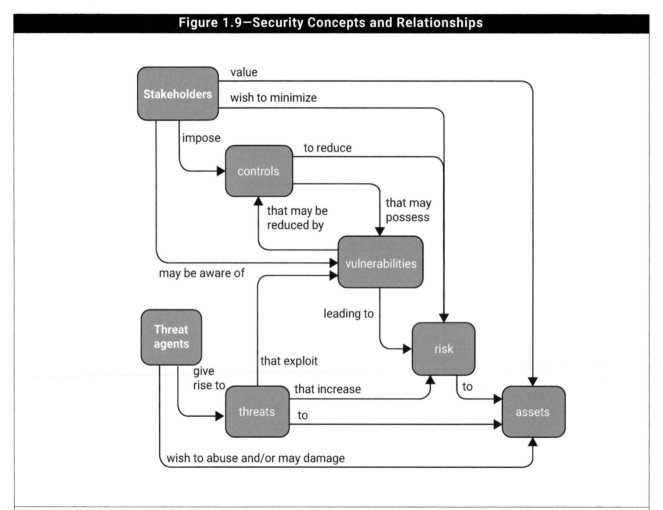

Figure 1.9—Security Concepts and Relationships

1.9 Resilience

Resilience[21] refers to the ability of an enterprise to recover quickly from difficulties.[22] Resilience is the ability to return to normal after any level of business disruption. Disruptions may stem from any of the following:

- Disaster
- Emergency
- Hazard
- Risk
- Vulnerability

Disasters are emergency events of such great magnitude that they overwhelm the capacity to respond and take considerable time to recover. Most importantly, disasters require recovery efforts to restore operational status.

An emergency is an event resulting from one or more hazards that requires the dedication of police, fire, or emergency medical services (EMS). An emergency is not inherently a disaster, because emergencies occur daily and are usually managed without difficulty.

Hazards are sources of potential harm to a community's population, environment, property (public and private), infrastructure and/or business. There are many categories of hazards;[23] however, for the scope of this study guide, the discussion is limited to natural, technological and terrorism.

- Natural hazards are hazards resulting from an adverse interaction between a natural process and human society or its man-made environment. Specific categories of natural hazards can include:
  - **Tectonic (seismic)**—Earthquakes, volcanoes, tsunamis
  - **Mass-movement**—Avalanches, landslides, sinkholes
  - **Hydrologic**—Foods, drought, coastal/soil erosion
  - **Meteorological**—Tropical cyclones, monsoons, tornadoes, ice storms, wildfires, thunderstorms, other winter storms, extreme hot or cold, fog
  - **Biological/Health-related**—Human, animal, agricultural epidemics and other uncategorized natural hazards
- Technological or man-made hazards are often attributed to technological innovation or failures of existing technologies. Specific categories include:
  - **Transportation**—Transportation-related accidents, system failures or shutdowns, travel impediments
  - **Infrastructure**—Failures of power, telecommunications, utilities, fuel, etc.
  - **Industrial**—Hazardous materials, raw material extraction, structural fires and failures
- Terrorism hazards include disasters and emergencies resulting from conscious anti-social and anti-establishment acts of individuals or groups of individuals. Terrorism hazards include:
  - Chemical
  - Biological
  - Radiological/nuclear
  - Explosives
  - Cyber (computer-related) attacks

---

[21] The material in this section is from the Corporation for National & Community Service, National Service Knowledge Network Online Learning Center, www.nationalservice.gov/sites/default/files/olc/moodle/ds_online_orientation/view0a56.html?id=3139&chapterid=898

[22] Oxford University Press, *Oxford Learner's Dictionary*, 2020, www.oxfordlearnersdictionaries.com/us/definition/english/resilience?q=resilience

[23] United Nations Office for Disaster Risk Reduction, "Hazard," www.undrr.org/terminology/hazard

A risk refers to the combination of the probability of an event (hazards produce events) and its impact. Risk is an unavoidable part of life. We discuss risk in greater detail in Chapter 2.

A vulnerability refers to the propensity of an individual, enterprise, or system to incur damage from a disaster. Note that a vulnerability does not indicate the likelihood of exposure but rather how the affected would fare should a potential disaster or hazard strike.

It is necessary to understand that disruptions of any kind may cause vital information resources to be inoperative for a period of time, adversely impacting enterprise operations. Disruptions may only last a few minutes or carry on for an extended period of time—depending on the extent of damage to the enterprise.

Disasters may be caused by natural calamities, such as earthquakes, floods, tornadoes and fire, or a disaster may be caused by events precipitated by humans, such as terrorist attacks, hacker attacks, viruses, or human error. Many disruptions start as minor incidents. Normally, if the enterprise has a help desk or service desk, it will act as an early warning system to recognize the first signs of an upcoming disruption. Often, such disruptions (e.g., gradually deteriorating database performance) go undetected. Until these creeping disasters strike (e.g., the database halts), they cause only infrequent user complaints.

A cybersecurity-related disaster may occur when a disruption in service is caused by system malfunctions, accidental file deletions, untested application releases, loss of backup, denial of service attacks, intrusions, or viruses. These events may require action to recover operational status to resume service. Such actions may necessitate restoration of hardware, software, or data files.

Enterprises can reduce their vulnerability and, therefore, increase their resilience by performing disaster preparedness and mitigation activities.

1.10 Business Continuity and Disaster Recovery

The purpose of business continuity planning (BCP)/disaster recovery planning (DRP) is to enable a business to continue offering critical services in the event of a disruption and to survive a disastrous interruption to activities. Rigorous planning and commitment of resources are necessary to adequately plan for such an event.

BCP and DRP are commonly confused. BCP is how the business continues to operate during a significant event; disaster recovery relates only to the recovery and restoration of the technology components of the business.

BCP is primarily the responsibility of senior management because they are entrusted with safeguarding the assets and the viability of the enterprise, as defined in the BCP/DRP policy. The BCP is generally followed by the business and supporting units, to provide a reduced but sufficient level of functionality in the business operations immediately after encountering an interruption, while recovery is taking place. The BCP process is shown in **figure 1.10**.

Figure 1.10—BCP Planning Process

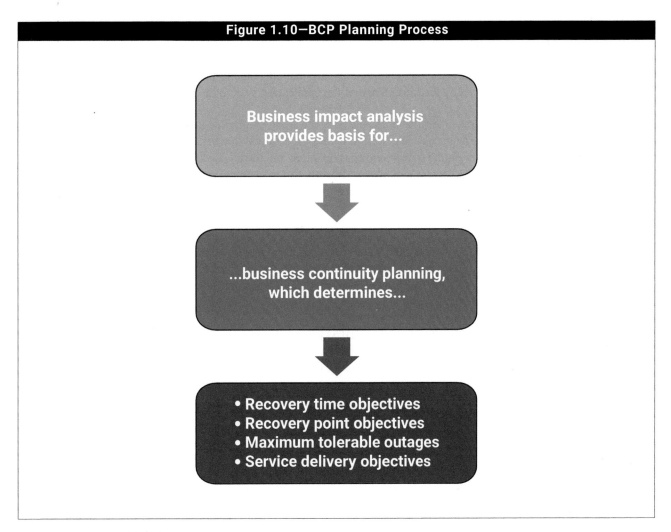

BCP takes into consideration:

- Critical operations necessary to the survival of the enterprise
- The human/material resources supporting these critical operations
- Disaster preparedness covering incident response management to address all relevant incidents affecting business processes
- Evacuation procedures (These may also fall under an emergency management plan, depending on the business.)
- Procedures for invoking the BCP (escalation procedures)
- The clear identification of the responsibilities in the plan
- The clear identification of the persons responsible for each function in the plan
- The clear identification of contract information
- The step-by-step explanation of the recovery process to return the business to normal operations
- The clear identification of the various resources required for recovery and continued operation of the enterprise

Information is of strategic importance and is a critical component because most key business processes depend on the availability of key systems, infrastructure components and data. Many enterprises may have multiple plans that address various aspects of BCP and DRP; however, smaller businesses may opt for one integrated plan. Enterprises employing multiple plans must ensure consistency to be viable.

The criticality of the various application systems deployed in the enterprise depends on the nature of the business and the value of each application to the business. The value of each application to the business is directly proportional to the role of the information system in supporting the strategy of the enterprise. The components of the information system (including the technology infrastructure components) are then matched to the applications (e.g., the value of a computer or a network is determined by the importance of the application system that uses it).

Even if similar processes of the same enterprise are handled at different geographic locations, the BCP and DRP solutions may be different for different scenarios. Solutions may be different due to contractual requirements (e.g., the same enterprise is processing an online transaction for one client and the back office is processing for another client). A BCP solution for the online service will be significantly different from one for the back-office processing.

1.11 Business Impact Analysis

The first step in preparing a new BCP is to identify the business processes of strategic importance—those key processes that are responsible for the permanent growth of the business and for the fulfillment of the business goals. Ideally, the BCP/DRP should be supported by a formal executive policy that states the overall target for recovery for the enterprise and empowers those people involved in developing, testing and maintaining the plans.

Based on the key processes, a business impact analysis (BIA) process should begin to determine timeframes, priorities, resources and interdependencies that support the key processes. Business risk is directly proportional to the impact on the enterprise and the probability of occurrence of the perceived threat. Thus, the result of the BIA should be the identification of the following:

- The human resources, data, infrastructure elements and other resources (including those provided by third parties) that support the key processes
- A list of potential vulnerabilities—the dangers or threats to the enterprise
- The estimated probability of the occurrence of these threats
- The efficiency and effectiveness of existing risk mitigation controls (risk countermeasures)

Information is collected for the BIA from different parts of the enterprise that own key processes/applications. To evaluate the impact of downtime for a particular process/application, the impact bands are developed (i.e., high, medium, low) and, for each process, the impact is estimated in time (hours, days, weeks). The same approach is used when estimating the impact of data loss. If necessary, the financial impact may be estimated using the same techniques, assigning the financial value to the particular impact band. In addition, data for the BIA may be collected on the time frames needed to supply vital resources—how long the enterprise may run if a supply is broken or when the replacement has arrived.

The BIA should answer three important questions:

1. What are the critical (and different) business processes?
2. What are the critical information resources related to the critical business processes of the enterprise?
3. What is the critical recovery time period for information resources in which business processing must be resumed before significant or unacceptable losses are suffered?

The core source of data used in BCP is the BIA, which identifies the critical timelines for services and products associated with value creation and business risk tolerance. The BIA also establishes the recovery point objective (RPO) and recovery time objective (RTO) for a process, which respectively defines how much data can be lost in recovery and how quickly recovery must be accomplished. Because the BCP is based on the BIA, the practitioner must review the process used to determine the BIA to validate that it is accurate and considers all the risk factors. In enterprises that have adopted a comprehensive business continuity management system (BCMS), the risk practitioner may benefit from having direct access to BCPs for review and reference in the context of risk management.[24] Note that the BIA should also inform the DRP.

1.12 Recovery Concepts

Data recovery is the process of restoring data that has been lost, accidentally deleted, corrupted, or otherwise made inaccessible for any reason. Recovery processes vary depending on the type and amount of data lost, the backup method employed and the backup media. An enterprise DRP must provide the strategy for how data will be recovered and assign recovery responsibilities.

1.12.1 Backups

Backup procedures are used to copy files to a second medium, such as a disk, tape, or the cloud. Backup files should also be kept at an offsite location in the event of disaster at the operating site, which could destroy backups. Backups are usually automated using operating system commands or backup utility programs. Most backup programs compress the data so that the backups require fewer media.

There are three types of data backups: full, incremental and differential. Full backups provide a complete copy of every selected file on the system, regardless of whether it was backed up recently. This is the slowest backup method, but the fastest method for restoring data. Incremental backups copy all files that have changed since the last backup was made, regardless of whether the last backup was a full or incremental backup. This is the fastest backup method, but the slowest method for restoring data. Differential backups copy only the files that have changed since the last full backup. The file grows until the next full backup is performed.

1.13 Information Security Objectives

Ideally, cybersecurity requires business owners be active in security, beyond the protection of their own assets. They should be prepared to identify and address emerging risk and challenges to keep assets protected. Cybersecurity works with information security and is beyond merely Internet, network and/or application security. It requires working with all of these components in order to keep the cyberspace reliable and trustworthy.

Today, the objective of information security is threefold, involving the critical components of confidentiality, integrity and availability (**figure 1.11**). Typically referred to as the CIA triad, all three components are concerned with the protection of information. Confidentiality means protection from unauthorized access, while integrity means protection from unauthorized modification, and availability means protection from disruptions in access.

---

[24] ISACA, *CRISC Review Manual 6th Edition*, USA, 2015, www.isaca.org/bookstore/crisc-exam-resources/crr6ed

Figure 1.11—CIA Triad

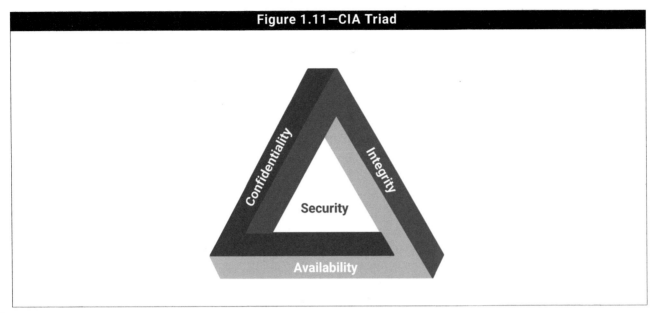

① Confidentiality is preserving authorized restrictions on access or disclosure, including means for protecting privacy and proprietary information. Different types of information require different levels of confidentiality, and the need for confidentiality can change over time. Personal, financial and medical information require a higher degree of confidentiality than the minutes of a staff meeting, for example. Similarly, some enterprises need to protect information on competitive future products before their release but may need to make the same information public afterward. Data must be protected from improper disclosure according to its sensitivity and applicable legal requirements. The confidentiality of digital information can be maintained using several means, including access controls, file permissions and encryption.

② Integrity is the guarding against improper information modification or destruction and includes ensuring information nonrepudiation and authenticity. For example, if a bank transfers $10,000 to another financial institution, it is important that the amount does not change to $100,000 during the exchange. The concept of integrity also applies to electronic messaging, files, software and configurations. Any violation of integrity is significant, because it may be the first step in a successful attack against system availability or confidentiality. Contaminated systems and corrupted data must be dealt with immediately to assess the potential for further violation or damage. The integrity of digital assets (to include data tampering) can be controlled and verified by logging, digital signatures, hashes, encryption and access controls.

③ Availability ensures the timely and reliable access to and use of information and systems to the right people. This includes safeguards to make sure data are not accidentally or maliciously deleted. This is particularly important with a mission-critical system because any interruptions in its availability can result in a loss of productivity and revenue. Similarly, the loss of data can impact management's ability to make effective decisions and responses. Availability can be protected by the use of redundancy, backups and implementation of business continuity management and planning.

Nonrepudiation is the assurance that a party cannot later deny originating data; nonrepudiation furthermore entails proof of the integrity and origin of data, which proof can be verified by a third party—i.e., that the information is genuine. This is an important consideration in cybersecurity. When information is sent, it is important to verify that it is coming from the source that it says it is coming from. Nonrepudiation provides a means so that the person who sends or receives information cannot deny that they sent or received the information. It is implemented through digital signatures and transactional logs.

Need-to-know and principle of least privilege (PoLP) are two extremely important foundational tenets of security that help inform the types of security controls needed in an enterprise. Need-to-know is a principle by which employees are only given access to data, systems, or spaces that are necessary to do their job. In this regard, it is a principled approach of controlling what someone can *see*.

Some may be inclined to believe that this principle only applies to those working in or with a military or government agency that handles classified information—however, that is not true. Need-to-know equally applies to all industries and enterprises. An example of need-to-know that does not involve security clearances is restricting access to payroll files outside of the Human Resource department. The principle of least privilege is an extension of need-to-know which limits what individuals can *do;* therefore, individuals are only granted the least amount of system access necessary to perform their job. Examples of this include not allowing non-IT employees administrator access to laptops and not automatically granting Windows system administrator superuser privileges to Linux servers.

It is worth stating that an individual granted superuser privileges does not infer free reign over information. Those actively seeking out or misusing information, for which there is not a legitimate business need, calls into question their integrity which undermines security programs and may be grounds for disciplinary action, up to and including dismissal. Implementation of these two principles are covered in Chapter 3.

The impacts, potential consequences and methods of control of confidentiality, integrity and availability are shown in **figure 1.12.**

Figure 1.12—Confidentiality, Integrity and Availability Model and Related Impacts		
Requirement	**Impact and Potential**	**Methods of Control**
Confidentiality—The protection of information from unauthorized disclosure	Loss of confidentiality can result in the following consequences: • Disclosure of information protected by privacy laws • Loss of public confidence • Loss of competitive advantage • Legal action against the enterprise • Interference with national security • Loss of compliance	Confidentiality can be preserved using the following methods: • Access controls • File permissions • Encryption
Integrity—The accuracy and completeness of information in accordance with business values and expectations	Loss of integrity can result in the following consequences: • Inaccuracy • Erroneous decisions • Fraud • Failure of hardware • Loss of compliance	Integrity can be preserved using the following methods: • Access controls • Logging • Digital signatures • Hashes • Backups • Encryption

Figure 1.12—Confidentiality, Integrity and Availability Model and Related Impacts *(cont.)*		
Requirement	**Impact and Potential**	**Methods of Control**
Availability—The ability to access information and resources required by the business process	Loss of availability can result in the following consequences: • Loss of functionality and operational effectiveness • Loss of productive time • Fines from regulators or a lawsuit • Interference with enterprise's objectives • Loss of compliance	Availability can be preserved using the following methods: • Redundancy of network, system, data • Highly available system architectures • Data replication • Backups • Access controls • A well-designed disaster recovery plan or business continuity plan

1.14 Privacy

Privacy[25] is a subjective term, for which a universally accepted definition does not exist. Privacy must be considered within the context of personal information that is being collected, used, stored or otherwise accessed, and includes examining the rights, values and interests of individuals. The related characteristics, descriptive information, and labels, activities and opinions of individuals are just a few of the applicable privacy considerations.

Privacy means many things to different individuals, depending on a variety of historical, social, cultural, and political factors. Privacy also has different meanings to different enterprises and governments, and to nonprofit and global associations, such as ISACA, throughout the world. At its most rudimentary definition, privacy can be the right to be left alone.[26]

For the benefit of common understanding and application by its members, ISACA defines privacy as:

> *The right of an individual to trust that others will appropriately and respectfully use, store, share and dispose of his/her associated personal and sensitive information within the context, and according to the purposes for which it was collected or derived.*[27]

What is appropriate depends on the associated circumstances, laws and the individual's reasonable expectations. An individual also has the right to reasonably control and be aware of the collection, use and disclosure of his/her associated personal and sensitive information.

Privacy requirements are not simply the specifications that are provided within laws and regulations. Laws and regulations historically have trailed information usage and creation innovations, especially in the last five decades, due to the exponential growth of online services and the new ways that technologies use and create information. Current laws, even in the most technologically advanced regions in the world, address only a small fraction of privacy risk.

The need for privacy must be understood, even if laws and regulations are not yet imposing requirements on the enterprise. Every enterprise that collects, stores, processes, or accesses personal information needs to establish the meaning of privacy to their enterprise, employees, customers, patients and all others whose personal information the enterprise is using in some way. In addition, each enterprise must also understand how those associated individuals view privacy within their own culture and associated geographic areas, privacy concepts across geographic areas due to international trade and commerce and privacy as defined by applicable laws and regulations.

[25] ISACA, *Privacy Principles and Program Management Guide*, USA, 2016, www.isaca.org/bookstore/cobit-5/ipp
[26] Warren, S.D.; L.D. Brandeis; "The Right to Privacy," *Harvard Law Review*, Vol. IV, No. 5., 15 December 1890, groups.csail.mit.edu/mac/classes/6.805/articles/privacy/Privacy_brand_warr2.html
[27] ISACA, "Glossary," www.isaca.org/resources/glossary

1.15 Privacy vs. Security

Security, confidentiality and privacy[28] are not the same thing; they are closely related, but they are distinct concepts. Safeguarding information has been a concern for as long as people needed to maintain information confidentiality. In 1900 B.C., Egyptian scribes used nonstandard hieroglyphics to create secret messages, but perhaps the best known example of safeguarding information is the creation of the Caesar cipher, which was used by Julius Caesar in 50 B.C. to maintain the confidentiality of military and government communications. The Caesar cipher was used to encrypt text by shifting the letters of the alphabet by three places.[29] The need for information security evolved as people's need for integrity and availability of personal information evolved.

Confidentiality, integrity and availability (CIA) are characteristics that provide value to information and comprise the information security triad. The CIA triad model is critical in addressing the evolving and growing threats that are posed by the digital world; however, people's need to safeguard personal information has evolved further to the need for additional protections, including privacy.

A common misunderstanding is to assume that information security is the same as privacy, because confidentiality is at the core of the information security function. However, confidentiality is not the same as privacy—privacy is a possible outcome of security. **Figure 1.13** is a visual comparison of confidentiality and privacy, as defined by ISACA.

Figure 1.13—Confidentiality and Privacy

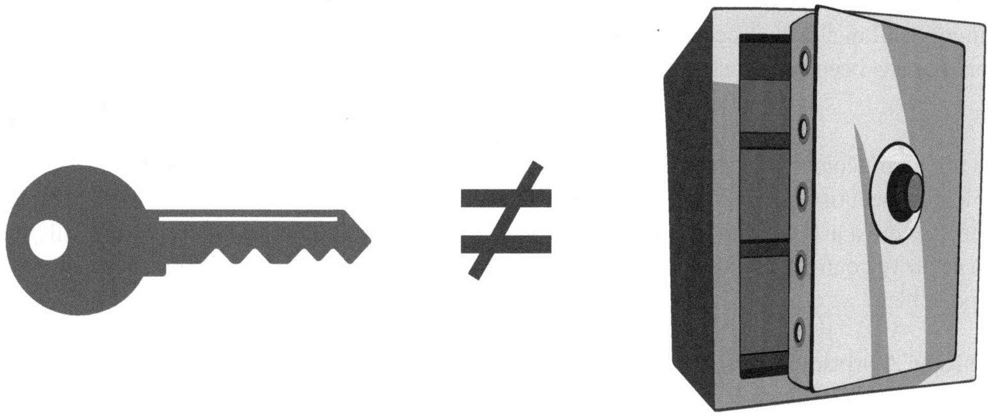

Confidentiality is preserving authorized restrictions on access and disclosure, including means for protecting privacy and proprietary information.

Privacy is the right of an individual to trust that others will appropriately and respectfully use, store, share and dispose of the individual's personal and sensitive information within the context, and according to the purposes, for which it was collected or derived.

Source: ISACA, *Privacy Principles and Program Management Guide*, USA, 2016, figure 3, https://www.isaca.org/bookstore/cobit-5/ipp

---

[28] *Op cit* ISACA, *Privacy Principles and Program Management Guide*
[29] Whitman, M.E.; H.J. Mattord; *Principles of Information Security*, 2nd Edition, Thomson Course Technology, USA, 2005

This common mistake can lead to potentially devastating public press, irreversible damage to personal lives and huge fines and lawsuits. The published privacy notices on websites and through other direct communication between enterprises and consumers are a contract with the individuals from whom the enterprise collected personal information. The privacy notices are often the first and main point of contact between the public and the enterprise. If an enterprise privacy notice tells customers that the enterprise is performing certain activities to ensure customer privacy, the enterprise must ensure that its employees know the privacy notice commitments, whether or not the employees were involved with the privacy notice creation.

The worldwide privacy laws and regulations allow individuals to make informed choices, such as choices about how their medical information is used and shared by the enterprises with which they do business. Privacy protections in many parts of the world stipulate that privacy is a human right. As such, enterprises dealing with personally identifiable information must afford a high standard to protecting that data; for example, enabling patients to find out how their information may be used and how their personal information has been disclosed to others or the right for the consumer/end user to "be forgotten" in an information system.

International privacy protections also enable consumers to find out how financial information is protected and to know that the people who are handling their information have been properly trained to protect consumer privacy. Various privacy protections throughout the globe limit the release of personal information to the minimum reasonably needed for the purpose of the disclosure. Privacy protections in many countries give people the right to examine and obtain a copy of their personal records and request corrections.

Security for legal and regulatory protections includes the reasonable and prudent internal enterprise policies, processes, safeguards, controls, steps and tools that are used to maintain CIA and support privacy protection. Security activities involve all methods, processes and technology that are used to ensure the CIA and safety of the personal information that has been entrusted to a third party by the consumer, customer, patient, or any other type of individual.

Although privacy is not an outcome of security alone (an enterprise can have great security but have no privacy), the enterprise must implement security as one of the components of a privacy management program to ensure privacy protections. An enterprise must use security as a means to obtain privacy protections and controls. An enterprise without information security controls cannot protect the privacy of the individuals for whose personal information the enterprise is responsible.[30]

In the context of the ISACA privacy principles, the following analogies are helpful to see the relationship between information security and privacy (**figure 1.14**):

Figure 1.14—Security vs. Privacy	
Security	**Privacy**
• Is a process	• Is a consequence
• Is action	• Is a result of successful actions
• Is the strategy	• Is the outcome
• Is the state of being free from danger	• Is a state of being free from unsanctioned intrusion[31]
Source: ISACA, *Privacy Principles and Program Management*, USA, 2016, page 14, www.isaca.org/bookstore/cobit-5/ipp	

---

[30] Herold, R.; "What Is The Difference Between Security and Privacy?," Mafiadoc, https://mafiadoc.com/what-is-the-difference-between-security-and-privacy-rebecca-_5a0e89171723dd236f155f4e.html

[31] *Op cit* Whitman

1.16 Chapter 1 Knowledge Check

REVIEW QUESTIONS

1. Which of the following is the best definition for cybersecurity?

    A. The protection of information from unauthorized access or disclosure

    B. Protecting information assets by addressing threats to information that is processed, stored or transported by internetworked information systems Pg 22

    C. The protection of paper documents, digital and intellectual property, and verbal or visual communications

2. Which of the following cybersecurity roles is charged with the duty of managing incidents and remediation?

    A. Board of directors

    B. Cybersecurity management Pg 28

    C. Executive management

3. Which of the following common controls protect the availability of information:

    A. Access controls, file permissions, encryption

    B. Access controls, backups, redundancy

    C. Access controls, logging, encryption

4. Match the following predicates (left) to the appropriate respective subjects (right).

a. is a process.	Privacy or Security
b. is action.	Privacy or Security
c. is the strategy.	Privacy or Security
d. is the state of being free from danger.	Privacy or Security
e. is a consequence.	Privacy or Security
f. is the result of successful actions.	Privacy or Security
g. is the outcome.	Privacy or Security
h. is a state of being free from unsanctioned intrusion.	Privacy or Security

5. Which of the following are foundational tenets of security that inform security controls?

    A. Availability, integrity

    B. Confidentiality, nonrepudiation

    C. Need-to-know, principle of least privilege

Answers on page 42

Chapter 1 ANSWER KEY

Review Questions

1. A. The protection of information from unauthorized access or disclosure

    B. Protecting information assets by addressing threats to information that is processed, stored or transported by internetworked information systems. Refer to page 22.

    C. The protection of paper documents, digital and intellectual property, and verbal or visual communications

2. A. Board of directors

    B. Cybersecurity management. Refer to page 28.

    C. Executive management

3. A. Access controls, file permissions, encryption

    B. Access controls, backups, redundancy. Refer to page 36.

    C. Access controls, logging, encryption

4. Match the following predicates (left) to the appropriate respective subjects (right). **Refer to page 40.**

a. is a process.	Security
b. is action.	Security
c. is the strategy.	Security
d. is the state of being free from danger.	Security
e. is a consequence.	Privacy
f. is the result of successful actions.	Privacy
g. is the outcome.	Privacy
h. is a state of being free from unsanctioned intrusion.	Privacy

5. A. Availability, integrity

    B. Confidentiality, nonrepudiation

    C. Need-to-know, principle of least privilege. Refer to page 37.

Threat Landscape

Threat Landscape

Threat Landscape

2.1 Learning Objectives

After completing this chapter, learners will be able to:

1. Define cyberrisk.
2. Define key terms associated with risk.
3. Identify and describe threats to enterprises.
4. Identify common types of vulnerabilities.
5. Identify common threat agents.
6. Identify attributes of cyberattacks.
7. Explain the cyberattack process.
8. Identify cybersecurity attack models.
9. Identify common cyberattacks.
10. Describe the IT risk management life cycle.

2.2 Cyberrisk

The core duty of cybersecurity is to manage risk, which includes identifying and mitigating technical risk—also called cyberrisk—to enterprise digital assets. Cyberrisk is that portion of overall risk management that solely focuses on risk that manifests in the cyber (interconnected information environments) domain. Although most people have an inherent understanding of risk in their day-to-day lives, it is important to understand risk in the context of cybersecurity, which means knowing how to determine, measure and reduce risk effectively.

Assessing risk is one of the most critical functions of any security organization. Effective policies, security implementations, resource allocation and incident response preparedness are dependent on understanding the risk and the associated threats an enterprise faces. Using a risk-based approach for information security and cybersecurity allows more informed decision making to protect the enterprise and to apply limited budgets and resources effectively. If controls are not implemented based on awareness of actual risk, then valuable enterprise assets will not be adequately protected while other assets will be wastefully overprotected.[32]

Too often, cybersecurity controls are implemented with little or no assessment of risk. Although one might argue that at least enterprises are doing *something*, the fact remains that assessing a situation without follow-up action is wasteful. The whole premise behind a risk assessment is to take inventory of enterprise surroundings and analyze the likelihood and impact of risk, keeping in mind that risk assessments represent a moment in time and, therefore, are most effective when periodically or continuously updated.

To that end, the following statement from former US Secretary of Defense Donald Rumsfeld best summarizes cybersecurity:

> [Reports] that say something hasn't happened are always interesting to me, because as we know, there are known knowns; there are things we know we know. We also know there are known unknowns; that is to say we know there are some things we do not know. But there are also unknown unknowns—the ones we don't know we don't know.[33]

Therefore, understanding risk and risk assessments are critical requirements for any security practitioner.

---

[32] Anderson, K.; "A Business Model for Information Security," *Information Systems Control Journal*, vol. 3, 2008
[33] The Rumsfeld Papers, "Known and Unknown: Author's Note," https://papers.rumsfeld.com/about/page/authors-note

Cybersecurity Fundamentals Study Guide, 3rd Edition

2.2.1 Key Terms and Definitions

There are many potential definitions of risk—some general and others more technical. It is important to distinguish between a risk and a threat. Although many people use the words threat and risk synonymously, they have different meanings. As with any key concept, there is some variation in definition from one enterprise to another. For the purposes of this guide, the following definitions apply:

- **Asset**—Something of either tangible or intangible value that is worth protecting, including people, information, infrastructure, finances and reputation.

- **Capability**—The knowledge and skill set required by a threat to carry out an event.[34]

- **Impact**—An adverse effect that results from an event occurring.[35]

- **Intent**—An actor or event with the potential to adversely impact an information system.

- **Likelihood**[36]—The probability of something happening.

- **Opportunity**—The resources and positioning required by a threat to carry out an action.[37]

- **Probability**—Synonym for likelihood.

- **Risk**—The combination of the probability of an event and its impact.[38] Risk is mitigated through the use of controls or safeguards.

- **Threat**—Anything (e.g., object, substance, human) that is capable of acting against an asset in a manner that can result in harm. ISO/IEC 13335 defines a threat broadly as a potential cause of an unwanted incident. Some enterprises make a further distinction between a threat source and a threat event, classifying a threat source as the actual process or agent attempting to cause harm, and a threat event as the result or outcome of a threat agent's malicious activity.

- **Vulnerability**—A weakness in the design, implementation, operation, or internal control of a process that could expose the system to adverse threats from threat events. Although much of cybersecurity is focused on the design, implementation and management of controls to mitigate risk, it is critical for security practitioners to understand that risk can never be eliminated. Beyond the general definition of risk provided previously, there are other, more specific types of risk that apply to cybersecurity.

Figure 2.1 depicts the factors involved in assessing risk, and **figure 2.2** illustrates one example of how many of these key terms come into play when framing an approach to risk management.

---

[34] United States Naval Academy, *SY110, Introduction to Cyber Security*, www.usna.edu/CyberDept/sy110/calendar.php?load=home
[35] *Ibid.*
[36] *Op cit* ISACA, *CRISC Review Manual 6th Edition*
[37] *Op cit* United States Naval Academy, *SY110*
[38] *Op cit* ISACA, " Glossary"

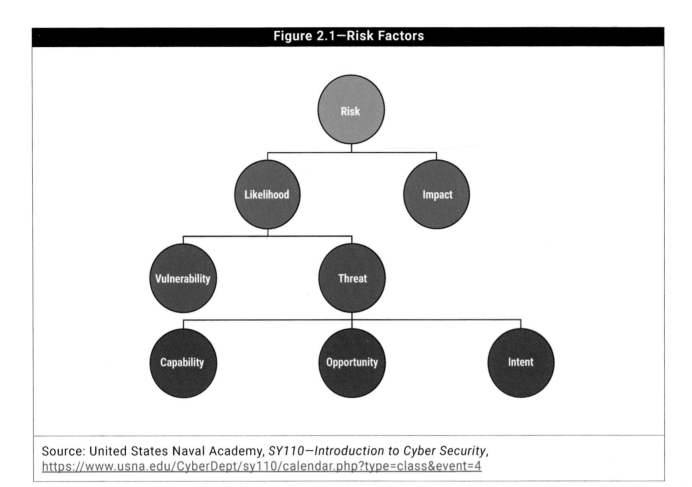

Figure 2.1—Risk Factors

Source: United States Naval Academy, *SY110—Introduction to Cyber Security*,
https://www.usna.edu/CyberDept/sy110/calendar.php?type=class&event=4

Threat events are caused by threat sources. A threat source is characterized as:

- The intent and method targeted at the exploitation of a vulnerability
- A situation and method that may accidentally exploit a vulnerability

In general, types of threat sources include:

- Hostile cyber or physical attacks
- Human errors of omission or commission
- Structural failures of enterprise-controlled resources (e.g., hardware, software, environmental controls)
- Natural and man-made disasters, accidents and failures beyond the control of the enterprise

Although most attacks are the result of a coordinated effort, there are other events that can pose various types of risk to an enterprise and can aid an adversary in a possible cyberattack. Some of the most common nonadversarial threat events are:

- Mishandling of critical or sensitive information by authorized users
- Incorrect privilege settings
- Fire, flood, hurricane, windstorm, or earthquake at primary or backup facilities
- Introduction of vulnerabilities into software products
- Pervasive disk errors or other problems caused by aging equipment

Figure 2.2—Influencing Risk Factors

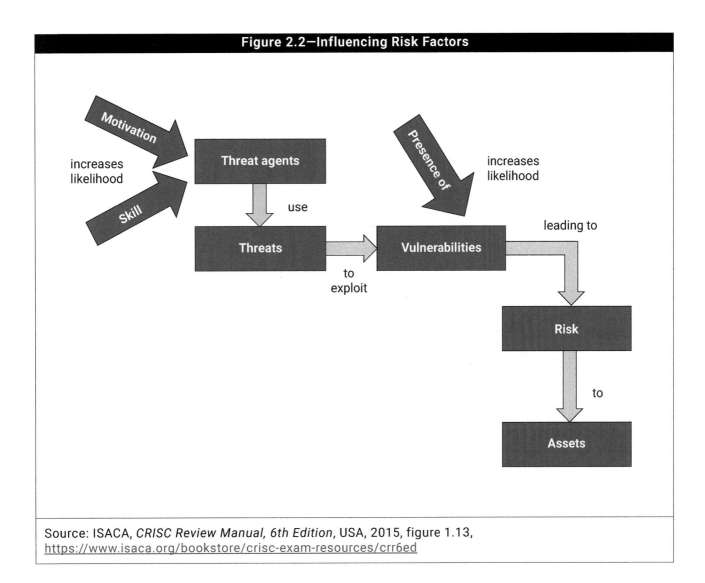

Source: ISACA, *CRISC Review Manual, 6th Edition*, USA, 2015, figure 1.13,
https://www.isaca.org/bookstore/crisc-exam-resources/crr6ed

2.2.2 Likelihood and Impact

Likelihood[39] (also called probability) is the measure of frequency of which an event may occur. This depends on whether there is a potential source for the event (threat) and the extent to which the particular type of event can affect its target (vulnerability), taking into account any controls or countermeasures that the enterprise has put in place to reduce its vulnerability. In the context of risk identification, likelihood is used to calculate the risk that an organization faces based on the number of events that may occur within a given time period (often an annual basis).

The risk faced by an enterprise consists of some combination of known and unknown threats, directed against systems that have some combination of known and unknown vulnerabilities. A vulnerability assessment that identifies no vulnerabilities does not mean that the system is invulnerable in the absolute sense. It means only that the types of vulnerabilities that the assessment was intended to detect were not detected.

Failure to detect a vulnerability may be the result of its absence, or it may be a false negative arising from misconfiguration of a tool or improper performance of a manual review. In the case of a zero-knowledge penetration test that fails to identify opportunities to exploit a system, it may be that the team was unlucky or lacked imagination, which may not be true of an outside attacker. Even if no known vulnerabilities exist within the system, the system

---

[39] *Op cit* ISACA, *CRISC Review Manual 6th Edition*

may still remain vulnerable to unknown vulnerabilities, more of which are discovered every day (and some of these are stored or sold for future use as zero-day exploits). The likelihood of an attack is often a component of external factors, such as the motivation of the attacker, as shown in **figure 2.3**.

Given the combination of unknown threat and unknown vulnerability, it is difficult for the cybersecurity professional to provide a comprehensive estimate of the likelihood of a successful attack. Vulnerability assessments and penetration tests provide the cybersecurity practitioner with valuable information on which to partially estimate this likelihood, because:

- Although the presence of a vulnerability does not guarantee a corresponding threat, the all-hours nature of information systems and the rapid speed of processing make it much more likely that an information system will come under an assortment of attacks in a short time than would be true of a physical system.

- A vulnerability known to an assessment tool is also knowable to threat agents, all but the most elite of whom tend to build their attacks to target common vulnerabilities.

- The presence of one or more known vulnerabilities—unless these have been previously identified and the risk is accepted by the enterprise for good reason—suggests a weakness in the overall security program.

When assessing a threat, cybersecurity professionals often analyze the likelihood and impact of the threat to rank and prioritize it among other existing threats.

In some cases where clear, statistically sound data are available, likelihood can be a matter of mathematical probability. This is true with situations such as weather events or natural disasters. However, sometimes accurate data are simply not available, as is often the case when analyzing human threat agents in cybersecurity environments. Some factors create situations where the likelihood of certain threats is more or less prevalent for a given enterprise. For example, a connection to the Internet will predispose a system to port scanning. Typically, qualitative rankings such as "High, Medium, Low" or "Certain, Very Likely, Unlikely, Impossible" can be used to rank and prioritize threats stemming from human activity. When using qualitative rankings, however, the most important step is to rigorously define the meaning of each category and use definitions consistently throughout the assessment process.

For each identified threat, the impact or magnitude of harm expected to result should also be determined. Impact assessments focus on the resulting damage if a vulnerability is exploited. A single vulnerability may have multiple impacts within the cyber domain, both technological and nontechnological.[40]

The impact of a threat takes many forms, but it often has an operational consequence of some sort, whether financial, reputational, or legal. Impacts can be described either qualitatively or quantitatively, but as with likelihoods, qualitative rankings are most often used in cybersecurity risk assessment. Likewise, each ranking should be well-defined and consistently used. In cybersecurity, impacts are also evaluated in terms of confidentiality, integrity and availability.

The cybersecurity professional must adequately research vulnerability assessment findings and use sound judgement when reporting findings and potential impacts to the CISO or designee. Further, the cybersecurity professional must temper expectations if vulnerability assessments and penetration tests fail to find vulnerabilities.

---

[40] *Op cit* United States Naval Academy, *SY110*

Figure 2.3—Generic Risk Model

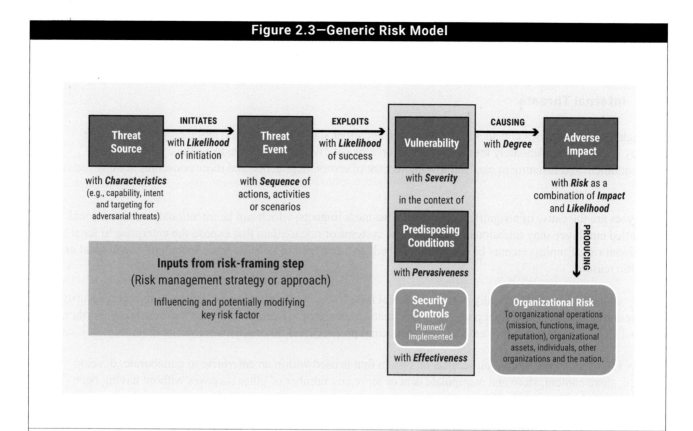

Source: National Institute of Standards and Technology (NIST), "Generic Risk Model," *Guide for Conducting Risk Assessments*, SP 800-30 Rev 1, 17 September 2012, figure 3

2.3 Threats

Threats[41] can be external or internal, intentional (adversarial) or unintentional (nonadversarial). They may be caused by natural events or political, economic, or competitive factors. Threats always exist and are typically beyond the direct control of the security practitioner or asset owner. Not all conceivable threats need to be considered by every enterprise. For example, an enterprise that operates in a region with a seismic rating of zero does not have to document exposure to volcanoes or earthquakes. However, it is important to identify the various types of threats that do apply and may be used to compromise systems or otherwise affect the enterprise.

Threats may be divided into multiple categories, including:[42]

- Physical
- Natural events
- Loss of essential services
- Compromise of information
- Technical failures
- Unauthorized actions
- Compromise of functions

---

[41] *Op cit* ISACA, *CRISC Review Manual 6th Edition*

[42] International Organization for Standardization/International Electrotechnical Commission (ISO/IEC); *ISO/IEC 27005:2018 Information Technology—Security Techniques—Information Security Risk Management*, Switzerland, 2018, www.iso.org/standard/75281.html

Threats may be the result of accidental actions, intentional/deliberate actions, or natural events. Threats may originate from either internal or external sources, and actual attacks may leverage a combination of internal and external sources.

2.3.1 Internal Threats

Although many enterprises consider their employees and other staff to be their best asset, employees may be unhappy if they are inadequately trained, treated poorly, or not given enough time to do their jobs properly. Disillusionment and resentment can lead to a higher risk of errors, negligence and more conscious actions such as theft.

Employees are the cause of a significant number of business impacts, which can be intentional or unintentional. A disgruntled employee may intentionally compromise systems or release data that expose the enterprise to legal or reputational risk. Employees may be convinced, bribed, or threatened to disclose trade secrets for ideological or economic reasons.

Employees may also unintentionally put enterprises at risk. Users are the first line of defense; therefore, security awareness training is an important part of any information security program to minimize their mistakes. Further, shadow IT is a perpetual threat to enterprises, intellectual property and other sensitive information.

Shadow IT[43] is an application, tool, service, or system that is used within an enterprise to collaborate, develop software, share content, store and manipulate data or serve any number of other purposes without having been reviewed, tested, approved, implemented, or secured by the enterprise IT and/or information security functions, in accordance with written policies and procedures. Shadow IT can drive disruption and innovation, but also has the potential to expose an enterprise to significant risk. Enterprises that fail to manage the upside and downside of shadow IT do so at their own peril. Common examples of shadow IT include collaboration tools for meetings and/or teams, task management tools and solutions for file transfer and/or data exchange.

Many employees have a level of access to systems and data that far exceeds their actual job requirements, which can be exploited in an attack. The solution to the employee problem, therefore, lies at least in part in the application of need-to-know and least privilege, but it is an imperfect solution. Any system has trusted insiders, and one of them choosing to violate trust is difficult to either predict or prevent.

2.3.2 External Threats

In a networked environment where data are stored offsite or hosted by cloud service providers, threats to information systems from outside of the enterprise can originate from anywhere and may take a number of forms, including, but not limited to, the following:

- Espionage
- Theft
- Sabotage
- Terrorism
- Criminal acts
- Software errors
- Hardware flaws
- Mechanical failures
- Lost assets

---

[43] ISACA, *Shadow IT Primer*, 2017, www.isaca.org/bookstore/bookstore-wht_papers-digital/whpshad

- Data corruption
- Facility flaws (freezing pipe/pipe burst)
- Fire
- Supply chain interruption
- Industrial accidents
- Disease (epidemic)
- Seismic activity
- Flooding
- Power surge/utility failure
- Severe storms

Natural events, such as a flood, storm, earthquake, or tornado, are unpredictable and may be extremely damaging. The use of governmental data and weather monitoring services may identify the threats associated with natural events and allow the risk practitioner to take necessary steps to be prepared.

An external human threat includes a highlight skilled hacker, a thief, or an opportunist taking full advantage of a wealth of online information.

Most breaches are the result of targets of opportunity, not determined attacks. As seen in the annual reports from Verizon and other organizations, many enterprises are breached because they were discovered to be easy targets and threat agents took advantage of their vulnerabilities.

2.3.3 Emerging Threats

Indications of emerging threats may include unusual activity on a system, repeated alarms, slow system or network performance, or new or excessive activity in logs. In many cases, compromised enterprises have evidence of emergent threats in their logs, well in advance of the actual compromise, but the evidence is either not noticed or acted on. Lack of effective monitoring, when coupled with a threat, is a combination that can lead to a breach.

Most technologies are built with an emphasis on function and purpose without due consideration for the security implications. As a result, new technology can be a source of new vulnerabilities and may even be a threat agent within an information system. The security practitioner must be alert to the emergence of new technologies and prepare for their introduction into the enterprise, particularly if these technologies promise cost savings or competitive advantage. As a result, consumer demand for cyberthreat information or threat intelligence is high.

Threat intelligence refers to the systematic gathering of evidence about the threat environment (indicators of compromise, behaviors, motivations, etc.), analysis of the evidence as it relates to a specific enterprise and ultimately the utilization of that analysis to minimize risk. Threat intelligence increases situational awareness as it helps enterprises understand current and future threats to their digital assets. Threat intelligence is discussed further in Chapter 4.

Bring your own device (BYOD) is an example of a revolution in how enterprises view technology assets, one whose risk is self-evident but that has tempted a wide variety of enterprises by promising to greatly reduce the cost of initial procurement of IT assets and the rate at which they need to be refreshed. A threat strategy that emphasizes rejection of new technology is unlikely to remain in place long beyond the point at which something gains executive sponsorship.

2.3.4 Threat Modeling

Threat modeling refers to the process of proactively identifying potential risk and threats. The increasingly dynamic threat landscape makes threat modeling imperative. The fundamental principle underlying threat modeling is that there are always limited resources for security, and it is necessary to determine how to use those limited resources effectively.[44] Threat models are systematic and structured.[45] The activity of threat modeling creates threat models that are guided using any number of methodologies including, but not limited to:

- Attack trees
- Security cards
- Spoofing–Tampering–Repudiation–Information–Disclosure–Denial of Service–Elevation of Privilege (STRIDE)
- Operationally Critical Threat Asset and Vulnerability Evaluation (OCTAVE)
- Trike

Specific details and implementation exceed the scope of this publication, but readers interested in learning more are encouraged to read *Threat Modeling: A Summary of Available Methods* published by Carnegie Mellon University Software Engineering Institute.[46]

The types and focus of threat-modeling methodologies continue to evolve, but they all generally require that enterprises take a step back and look at their specific defenses through an adversarial lens.

With regard to datacentric threat modeling, the process involves:[47]

- Identifying subcomponents, dependencies and interaction points
- Discovering, inventorying and evaluating threats
- Mitigating risk brought about by threats

Threat modeling is equally important to security engineering programs. With regard to software development, threat modeling helps enterprises address the following project questions:[48]

- What are we working on?
- What can go wrong?
- What are we going to do about it?
- Did we do a good job?

Regardless of the methodology used or intended purpose (e.g., data, software, etc.), threat modeling involves four steps that help to answer these questions:[49]

- Decompose the application or infrastructure
- Determine the threats
- Determine countermeasures and mitigations
- Rank the threats

[44] NIST, Draft NIST Special Publication 800-154, "Guide to Data-Centric System Threat Modeling," 2016, https://csrc.nist.gov/CSRC/media/Publications/sp/800-154/draft/documents/sp800_154_draft.pdf

[45] Fruhlinger, J.; "Threat modeling explained: A process for anticipating cyber attacks," *CSO Magazine*, 15 April 2020, https://www.csoonline.com/article/3537370/threat-modeling-explained-a-process-for-anticipating-cyber-attacks.html

[46] Shevchenko, N.; T. Chick; P. O'Riordan; T. Scalon; C. Woody; "Threat Modeling: A Summary of Available Methods," Software Engineering Institute, July 2018, https://resources.sei.cmu.edu/asset_files/WhitePaper/2018_019_001_524597.pdf

[47] ISACA, *Continuous Assurance Using Data Threat Modeling*, 2018, https://www.isaca.org/bookstore/bookstore-wht_papers-digital/whpcad

[48] ISACA, "ISACA Perspective: Security Engineering, the Who, What, Why and How," 19 March 2018, https://www.isaca.org/why-isaca/about-us/newsroom/press-releases/2018/isaca-perspective-security-engineering-the-who-what-why-and-how

[49] *Op cit* Fruhlinger

2.4 Vulnerabilities

Vulnerabilities are weaknesses, gaps, or holes in security that provide an opportunity for a threat or create consequences that may impact the enterprise.[50] The method used to take advantage of a vulnerability is called an exploit. Vulnerabilities can occur in many forms and at different architectural levels (e.g., physical, operating system, application). Vulnerabilities are continuously being discovered and enterprises must be constantly vigilant in identifying them and quickly remediating. **Figure 2.4** provides a list of common types of vulnerabilities.

Enterprises need to identify and assess vulnerabilities to determine the threat and potential impact and to determine the best course of action in addressing each vulnerability. Vulnerabilities can be identified by information provided by software vendors (e.g., through the release of patches and updates) and by utilizing processes and tools that identify known vulnerabilities in the specific enterprise environment. Vulnerability scanning and penetration testing are discussed further in Chapter 4.

Figure 2.4—Common Types of Vulnerabilities		
Type of Vulnerability	**Cause**	**Cybersecurity Examples**
Technical	Errors in design, implementation, placement or configuration	• Coding errors • Inadequate passwords • Open network ports • Lack of monitoring
Process	Errors in operation	• Failure to monitor logs • Failure to patch software
Organizational	Errors in management, decision, planning, or from ignorance	• Lack of policies • Lack of awareness • Failure to implement controls
Emergent	Interactions between, or changes in, environments	• Cross-organizational failures • Interoperability errors • Implementing new technology

2.5 Cyberattacks

A threat landscape, also referred to as a threat environment, is a collection of threats. The cybersecurity threat landscape is constantly changing and evolving as new technologies are developed and cyberattacks and tools become more sophisticated. Enterprises are becoming increasingly dependent on digital technologies that can be susceptible to cyberrisk. Cloud computing, social media, mobile computing and Internet of Things (IoT) are changing how enterprises use and share information. These technologies provide increased levels of access and connectivity, which create larger openings for cybercrime.

Attack vectors and methodologies continue to evolve, which represents a significant threat on the client side. Although some attacks are made at random with no particular target (opportunistic attacks) in mind, targeted attacks are made against recipients who have been researched and identified as useful by attackers.

Phishing attacks are often directed toward recipients who have access to data or systems to which the attacker wishes to gain access. In other cases, malware is deployed in widespread attacks with the hope that it will hit as many vulnerable systems as possible, though these situations are not likened to cyberattacks. It is essential for cybersecurity professionals to be able to identify threats to manage them appropriately. The time between evidence of initial compromise and when it was detection is called dwell time.

[50] Op cit ISACA, CRISC Review Manual 6th Edition

Cybercriminals are usually motivated by one or more of the following:

- Financial gains
- Intellectual property (espionage)
- Politics (hacktivism)

The cyberthreat landscape is ever changing, making it important to remain aware of broad industry trends but also industry specific ones. Recent trends in the cyberthreat landscape include:

- Threat agents are increasingly sophisticated in their attacks and use of tools.
- Nation states have the capabilities to infiltrate government and private targets (cyberwarfare).
- Cloud computing results in large concentrations of data within a small number of facilities, which are likely targets for attackers.
- Social networks have become a primary channel for communication, knowledge collection, marketing and dissemination of information. Attackers can misuse social networks to gain personal data and promulgate disinformation.
- Attack patterns are now being applied to mobile devices. This is of particular concern for mobile and other small digital devices that are interconnected and often have poor security controls.

New and aspiring security professionals are encouraged to immerse themselves in reputable reports. Annual reports, such as ISACA, *State of Cybersecurity;* ENISA, *Threat Landscape (ETL);* and Verizon, *Data Breach Investigations Report (DBIR),* have been reporting since at least 2015, and are useful sources of year-over-year insights from their respective reporting.

2.5.1 Threat Agents

Figure 2.5 is a good illustration of threat agents.

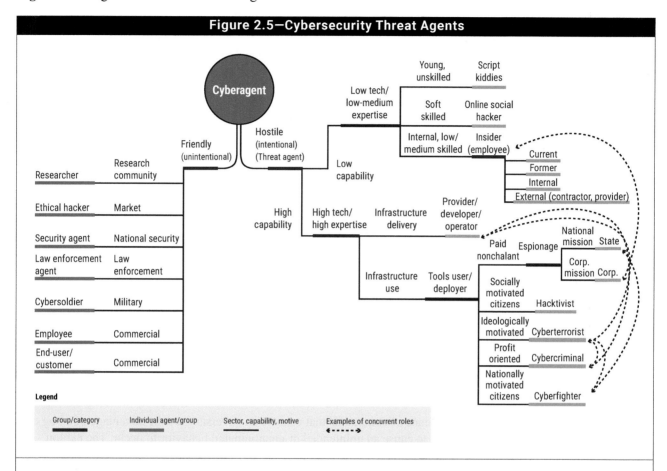

Figure 2.5—Cybersecurity Threat Agents

Source: European Union Agency For Network And Information Security (ENISA), *ENISA Threat Landscape 2015*, January 2016, Greece, www.enisa.europa.eu/publications/etl2015/at_download/fullReport

Common threat agents include the following:

- **Corporations**—Corporations have been known to breach security boundaries and perform malicious acts to gain a competitive advantage.

- **Cybercriminals**—Motivated by the desire for profit, these individuals are involved in fraudulent financial transactions.

- **Cyberterrorists**—Characterized by their willingness to use violence to achieve their goals, cyberterrorists frequently target critical infrastructures and government groups.

- **Cyberwarriors**—Often likened to hacktivists, cyberwarriors, also referred to as cyberfighters, are nationally motivated citizens who may act on behalf of a political party or against another political party that threatens them.

- **Employees**—Although they typically have fairly low-tech methods and tools, dissatisfied current or former employees represent a clear cybersecurity risk. Employers are wise to identify employees in research and development areas as well as others outside the IT or security groups with above average knowledge and skills.

- **Hacktivists**—Although they often act independently, politically motivated hackers may target specific individuals or organizations to achieve various ideological ends.

- **Nation states**—Nation states often target government and private entities with a high level of sophistication to obtain intelligence or carry out other destructive activities.

- **Online social hackers**—Skilled in social engineering, these attackers are frequently involved in cyberbullying, identity theft and collection of other confidential information or credentials.

- **Script kiddies**—Script kiddies are individuals who are learning to hack; they may work alone or with others and are primarily involved in code injections and Denial of Service (DoS) and distributed denial-of-service (DDoS) attacks.

2.6 Attack Attributes

Although risk is measured by potential activity, an attack is the actual occurrence of a threat. More specifically, an attack is an activity by a threat agent (or adversary) against an asset. From an attacker's point of view, the asset is a target, and the path or route used to gain access to the target (asset) is known as an attack vector.

There are two types of attack vectors: ingress and egress (also known as data exfiltration). While most attack analysis concentrates on ingress, or intrusion, hacking into systems, some attacks are designed to remove data (e.g., employees that steal data) from systems and networks. Therefore, it is important to consider both types of attack vectors.

The attacker must defeat any controls in place and/or use an exploit to take advantage of a vulnerability. Another attribute of an attack is the attack mechanism, or the method used to deliver the exploit. Unless the attacker is personally performing the attack, the attack mechanism may involve an exploit that delivers the payload to the target. An example can be a crafted malicious PDF, crafted by the attacker and delivered by email.

Attack vectors are the pathways that an adversary uses. Common attack vectors include email attachments, instant messages, web pages and pop-ups.

An exploit is software, data, or some sequence of commands that enables an adversary to take advantage of a bug or vulnerability in an application or a system to cause an unintended or unanticipated behavior to occur. The exploit carries and thus delivers the payload. A vulnerability is a weakness in the design, implementation, operation, or internal control of a process.

Payload is the malicious executable code that does harm. Payload is not always immediately triggered as it may lie dormant for some amount of time. Conversely, payload may quietly run, as is the case with cryptocurrency mining.

A target is some asset that an adversary is targeting. While they are often IT assets, there are many notable instances whereby OT was on the receiving end of a cyberattack.

The attributes of an attack are illustrated in **figure 2.6**.

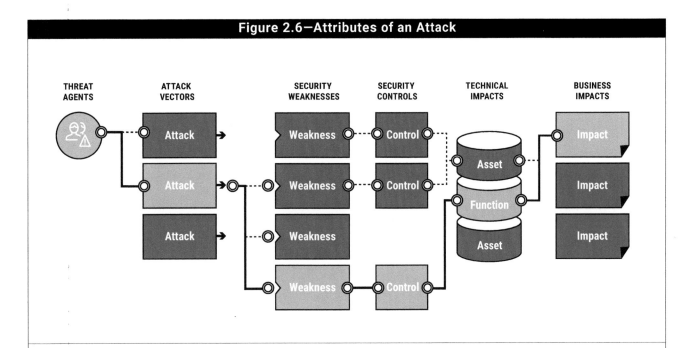

Figure 2.6—Attributes of an Attack

Source: Open Web Application Security Project® (OWASP), OWASP® Top Ten, https://owasp.org/www-project-top-ten/assets/images/Risks-2017.png. Creative Commons License 2.5, https://creativecommons.org/licenses/by-sa/2.5/deed.en_CA. No changes were made.

Detailed analysis of cyberattacks requires significant technical and subject-matter expertise, and it is an important part of cybersecurity. Each of the attack attributes (attack vector, exploit, payload, vulnerability, target) provides unique points where controls to prevent or detect the attack can be placed. It is also essential to understand each of these attributes when analyzing and investigating an actual attack. For example, the exploit used to deliver the payload often leaves artifacts or evidence that can be used by technical analysts and investigators to understand the attack and potentially identify the perpetrators. Analysis of the data exfiltration path may identify additional opportunities to prevent or detect the removal of data or obtain evidence, even if the attack was able to gain access to the target.

Attacks can be analyzed and categorized based on their type and patterns of use. From these characteristics, it is possible to make generalizations that facilitate better design and controls.

2.7 Attack Process

There are few absolutes in the cybersecurity domain. This subsection discusses generally accepted components of a cyberattack; however, it is not unusual to find variations among sources.[51, 52, 53]

Industry is still laden with illustrations that depict the cyberattack life cycle as linear. The ability for attackers to move sideways often results in additional entry points and implicit damage once inside the target network. For this reason, ISACA favors the FireEye® Mandiant® illustration of an attack life cycle (**figure 2.7**) as it appropriately calls out the iterative nature of the life cycle associating with lateral movement—often referred to as pivoting.

---

[51] Deloitte Touche Tohmatsu Limited, "Cyber 101: 7 Stages of Cyber Kill Chain Supplemental Reading," 2017, www2.deloitte.com/content/dam/Deloitte/sg/Documents/risk/sea-risk-cyber-101-july2017.pdf
[52] Rapid7, "Common Types of Cybersecurity Attacks," www.rapid7.com/fundamentals/types-of-attacks/
[53] International Association of Chiefs of Police, "Cyber Attack Lifecycle," Law Enforcement Cyber Center, www.iacpcybercenter.org/resource-center/what-is-cyber-crime/cyber-attack-lifecycle/

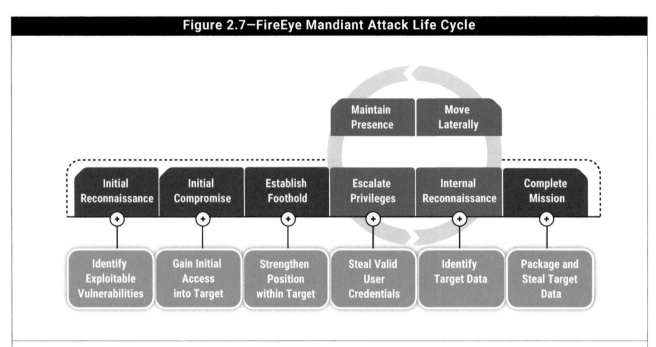

Figure 2.7—FireEye Mandiant Attack Life Cycle

Source: Mandiant Attack Life Cycle, Reprinted from Red Team Operations (RTO) Data Sheet, by Mandiant. Copyright 2019 by Mandiant, a FireEye company. Reprinted with permission.

1. **Reconnaissance**—Often shorted to recon, the adversary gathers information using a variety of techniques, passive or active, which may include:

   a. Passive:

      i. Sniffing network traffic

      ii. Using open source discovery of organizational information (news groups; company postings on IT design and IT architecture)

      iii. Google hacking

   b. Active:

      i. Scanning the network perimeter

      ii. Social engineering (fake phone calls, low-level phishing)

2. **Initial compromise**—The adversary procures or crafts the mechanisms to successfully execute malicious code on systems. Common pathways include:

   a. Social engineering (e.g., spear phishing)

   b. Directly exploiting a known device or system vulnerability

   c. Leveraging supply chain weaknesses

3. **Establish foothold**—Footholds enable attackers a means of persistent access using backdoors or other malware.

4. **Escalate privileges**[54]—During this phase, an adversary seeks greater access by escalating their privileges. Privilege escalation consists of techniques that adversaries use to gain higher-level permissions on a system or network. Examples of elevated access include:

   a. System/root level

   b. Local administrator

   c. User account with admin-like access

   d. User accounts with access to specific system or perform specific function

---

[54] MITRE ATT&CK, "Tactics: Privilege Escalation," TA0004, 19 July 2019, https://attack.mitre.org/tactics/TA0004/

5. **Internal recon**—The adversary is gaining situational awareness of the environment to include the types and location of data of possible interest. MITRE ATT&CK® framework refers to this as *discovery,* which entails using techniques that enable adversaries to explore and re-orient as necessary to fulfill their objectives.[55] Example discovery techniques include:

   a. Account discovery

   b. Cloud service discovery

   c. Domain trust discovery

   d. Remote system discovery

6. **Move laterally**[56]—Often referred to as *pivoting,* an adversary uses their access to traverse the compromised environment. Here, adversaries may leverage any gained legitimate credentials or install their own remote access tools in their quest to gather and steal information. Common lateral movement techniques include:

   a. Internal spearphishing[57]

   b. Pass the Hash (PtH)[58]

   c. Pass the Ticket (PtT)[59]

   d. SSH hijacking

7. **Maintain presence**—The adversary maintains continued access to the compromised environment through some sort of backdoor that allows the adversary to return at a later time. When communication is established, it is referred to as command and control (C2) which enables data exfiltration, network disruption, or denial of service.

8. **Complete mission**—When an adversary completes their objective, they typically try to cover their tracks and transfer the data away to some server in such a way as to avoid detection. Data may be exfiltrated using any number of techniques[60] that include compression or encryption of data and transmitted over alternate protocols or networks.

Some have chosen to simplify the stages or phases of cyberattacks as follows:

- The US Naval Academy[61] defined cyberattacks as occurring in three phases—reconnaissance, infiltration and maneuver, and exfiltrate and maintaining access.

- Australian Edith Cowan University[62] recognizes five phases—reconnaissance, access, exploration, increase privileges and cyberattack.

Conversely, many others have chosen to adopt the Cyber Kill Chain®, which is sometimes abbreviated to CKC.[63] Developed by Lockheed Martin, the seven steps include: reconnaissance, weaponization, delivery, exploitation, installation, command and control (C2), and actions on objectives, as illustrated in **figure 2.8**. A notable use of the Lockheed Martin model (then called *Intrusion Kill Chain)* was by the US Senate[64] during its investigation of the 2013 Target Corporation data breach, which included analysis based on CKC that highlighted several stages where

---

[55] The MITRE Corporation, "Getting Started," MITRE ATT&CK®, https://attack.mitre.org/resources/getting-started/
[56] MITRE ATT&CK, "Tactics: Lateral Movement," TA0008, 19 July 2019, https://attack.mitre.org/tactics/TA0008/
[57] MITRE ATT&CK, "Techniques: Internal Spearphishing," T1534, 22 October 2019, https://attack.mitre.org/techniques/T1534
[58] MITRE ATT&CK, "Techniques: Pass the Hash," TA1075, 18 July 2019, https://attack.mitre.org/techniques/T1075
[59] MITRE ATT&CK, "Techniques: Pass the Ticket," TA1097, 18 July 2019, https://attack.mitre.org/techniques/T1097
[60] MITRE ATT&CK, "Tactics: Exfiltration," TA0010, 19 July 2019, https://attack.mitre.org/tactics/TA0010/
[61] *Op cit* United States Naval Academy, *SY110*
[62] Edith Cowan University, "How to control the five phases of a cyber attack," ECU Blog, 23 July 2019, https://studyonline.ecu.edu.au/blog/five-phases-of-a-cyber-attack
[63] Lockheed Martin, "The Cyber Kill Chain," www.lockheedmartin.com/en-us/capabilities/cyber/cyber-kill-chain.html
[64] US Senate, "A 'Kill Chain' Analysis of the 2013 Target Data Breach," Committee on Commerce, Science, and Transportation, 26 March 2014, www.commerce.senate.gov/services/files/24d3c229-4f2f-405d-b8db-a3a67f183883

controls did not prevent or detect progression of the attack. There are, however, some in the industry who believe CKC is somewhat limited,[65, 66, 67] which resulted in proposed improvements and amendments since its release.

Notable alternative models include those of Bryant, Laliberte, Nachreiner and Malone,[68] as shown in **figures 2.9** to **2.13**, respectively. As written by Pols, a Unified Kill Chain (UKC) arose from thorough literature study and case studies. UKC is portrayed as a "significant improvement over the scope limitations of the CKC and the time-agnostic nature of the ATT&CK™ model."[69]

Figure 2.8—Lockheed Martin's Cyber Kill Chain® (CKC)

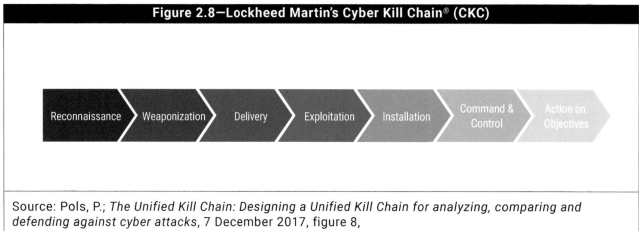

Source: Pols, P.; *The Unified Kill Chain: Designing a Unified Kill Chain for analyzing, comparing and defending against cyber attacks*, 7 December 2017, figure 8, www.csacademy.nl/images/scripties/2018/Paul_Pols_-_The_Unified_Kill_Chain_1.pdf

Figure 2.9—Laliberte's Kill Chain

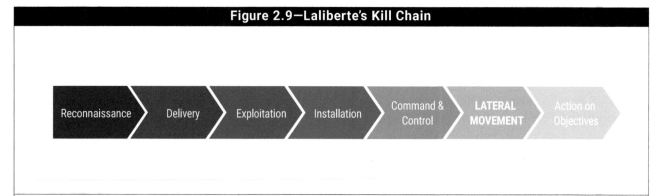

Source: Pols, P.; *The Unified Kill Chain: Designing a Unified Kill Chain for analyzing, comparing and defending against cyber attacks*, 7 December 2017, figure 5, www.csacademy.nl/images/scripties/2018/Paul_Pols_-_The_Unified_Kill_Chain_1.pdf. See also Laliberte, M.; "A Twist On The Cyber Kill Chain: Defending Against A JavaScript Malware Attack," Dark Reading, www.darkreading.com/attacks-breaches/a-twist-onthe-cyber-kill-chain-defending-against-a-javascript-malware-attack/a/d-id/1326952.

[65] Pols, P.; *The Unified Kill Chain: Designing a Unified Kill Chain for analyzing, comparing and defending against cyber attacks*, 7 December 2017, www.csacademy.nl/images/scripties/2018/Paul_Pols_-_The_Unified_Kill_Chain_1.pdf

[66] Laliberte, M.; "A Twist On The Cyber Kill Chain: Defending Against A JavaScript Malware Attack," Information Week IT Network, 21 September 2016, www.darkreading.com/attacks-breaches/a-twist-onthe-cyber-kill-chain-defending-against-a-javascript-malware-attack/a/d-id/1326952

[67] Tan, A.; "Cyber kill chain is outdated, says Carbon Black," ComputerWeekly.com, 29 July 2019, www.computerweekly.com/news/252467482/Cyber-kill-chain-is-outdated-says-Carbon-Black

[68] *Op cit* Pols

[69] *Ibid.*

Figure 2.10—Bryant's Kill Chain

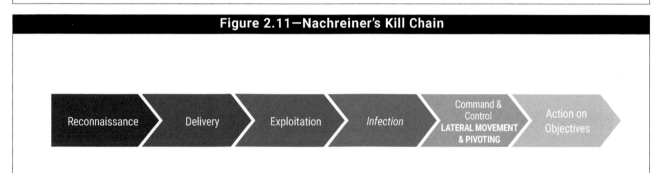

Source: Pols, P.; *The Unified Kill Chain: Designing a Unified Kill Chain for analyzing, comparing and defending against cyber attacks*, 7 December 2017, figure 7, www.csacademy.nl/images/scripties/2018/Paul_Pols_-_The_Unified_Kill_Chain_1.pdf. See also Bryant, B.D.; H. Saiedian; "A novel kill-chain framework for remote security log analysis with SIEM software," *Computers & Security*, vol. 67, pp. 198–210, June 2017.

Figure 2.11—Nachreiner's Kill Chain

Source: Pols, P.; *The Unified Kill Chain: Designing a Unified Kill Chain for analyzing, comparing and defending against cyber attacks*, 7 December 2017, figure 6, www.csacademy.nl/images/scripties/2018/Paul_Pols_-_The_Unified_Kill_Chain_1.pdf. See also Nachreiner, C.; "Kill Chain 3.0: Update the cyber kill chain for better defense," Help Net Security, 10 February 2015, https://www.helpnetsecurity.com/2015/02/10/kill-chain-30-update-the-cyber-kill-chain-for-better-defense/

Figure 2.12—Malone's Internal Kill Chain

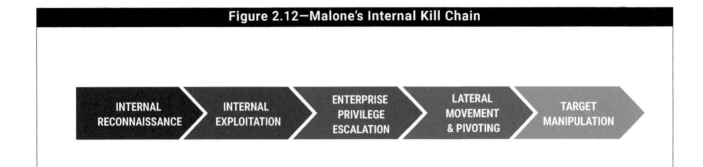

Source: Pols, P.; *The Unified Kill Chain: Designing a Unified Kill Chain for analyzing, comparing and defending against cyber attacks*, 7 December 2017, figure 9, www.csacademy.nl/images/scripties/2018/Paul_Pols_-_The_Unified_Kill_Chain_1.pdf. See also Malone, S.; "Using an expanded cyber kill chain model to increase attack resiliency," BlackHat USA, 2016, www.blackhat.com/docs/us-16/materials/us-16-Malone-Using-An-Expanded-Cyber-Kill-Chain-Model-To-Increase-Attack-Resiliency.pdf

Figure 2.13—Malone's Target Manipulation Kill Chain

Source: Pols, P.; *The Unified Kill Chain: Designing a Unified Kill Chain for analyzing, comparing and defending against cyber attacks*, 7 December 2017, figure 10, www.csacademy.nl/images/scripties/2018/Paul_Pols_-_The_Unified_Kill_Chain_1.pdf. See also Malone, S.; "Using an expanded cyber kill chain model to increase attack resiliency," BlackHat USA, 2016, www.blackhat.com/docs/us-16/materials/us-16-Malone-Using-An-Expanded-Cyber-Kill-Chain-Model-To-Increase-Attack-Resiliency.pdf

The comprehensive 18-phase UKC is illustrated in **figure 2.14**.

Figure 2.14—Unified Kill Chain

# Unified Kill Chain			
1	Reconnaissance	10	Discovery
2	Weaponization	11	Privilege escalation
3	Delivery	12	Execution
4	Social engineering	13	Credential access
5	Exploitation	14	Lateral movement
6	Persistence	15	Collection
7	Defense evasion	16	Exfiltration
8	Command & control	17	Target manipulation
9	Pivoting	18	Objectives

Source: Pols, P.; *The Unified Kill Chain: Designing a Unified Kill Chain for analyzing, comparing and defending against cyber attacks*, 7 December 2017, Table 1, www.csacademy.nl/images/scripties/2018/Paul_Pols_-_The_Unified_Kill_Chain_1.pdf

Cybersecurity professionals working for the US Government may use either the National Security Agency/Central Security Service (NSA/CSS) Technical Cyber Threat Framework v2 (NTCTF v2) or the Office of the Director of Naval Intelligence (ODNI) Cyber Threat Framework.[70] NTCTF v2 was developed as an extension of the Director of National Intelligence Cyber Threat Framework to standardize how the National Security Agency characterizes and categorizes adversary activity that is operating system independent and closely aligned with industry definitions.[71]

Another solid source of information is ENISA, which provides kill chain positioning for each of the 15 top cyberthreats outlined in its ENISA *Threat Landscape Report 2018*.[72]

Cybersecurity professionals may also encounter Red Team attack frameworks.

The kill chain models discussed in this section may change over time or be adapted to new ones. The use of one kill chain over another is not as important as the activity itself, because kill chain models help enterprises understand the totality of a cyberattack, which, in turn, informs about the types and sources of preventative and detective measures.

---

[70] Office of the Director of National Intelligence, "Building Blocks of Cyber Intelligence," www.dni.gov/index.php/cyber-threat-framework
[71] US National Security Agency, *Cybersecurity Report: NSA/CSS Technical Cyber Threat Framework v2*, 13 November 2018, www.nsa.gov/Portals/70/documents/what-we-do/cybersecurity/professional-resources/ctr-nsa-css-technical-cyber-threat-framework.pdf
[72] European Union Agency for Cybersecurity, *ENISA Threat Landscape Report 2018*, January 2019, www.enisa.europa.eu/topics/threat-risk-management/threats-and-trends/enisa-threat-landscape

2.8 Malware and Attacks

Malware[73], also called malicious code, is a broad term for software designed to gain access to targeted computer systems, steal information, or disrupt computer operations. The damage caused by malware varies largely, based on type and intended purpose; however, following are some symptoms of malware:

- Increased CPU usage
- Slow computer
- Higher than normal network traffic
- Pop-ups
- Freezing or crashing
- Browser homepage changes
- Security software such as anti-virus is turned off
- Unwanted ads

There are several types of malware, the most important being computer viruses, network worms, and Trojan horses, which are differentiated by the way in which they operate or spread.

2.8.1 Common Types of Malware

Following are well-known types of malware:[74]

- **Viruses**—A computer virus is a piece of code that can replicate itself and spread from one computer to another. It requires intervention or execution to replicate and/or cause damage.
- **Worms**—A variant of the computer virus, which is essentially a piece of self-replicating code designed to spread itself across computer networks. It does not require intervention or execution to replicate.
- **Keyloggers**—A class of malware that secretly records user keystrokes and, in some cases, screen content.
- **Rootkit**—A class of malware that hides the existence of other malware by modifying the underlying operating system.
- **Trojan horses**—Often referred to just as a trojan, it is a piece of malicious code or software that gains access to a targeted system by hiding within a genuine application. Trojan horses are often broken down into categories reflecting their purposes. Because trojans can be used as standalone malware, a tool for future payloads, future communication, or simply an access point to a system, they have many uses in hacking.[75]
- **Fileless malware**—Fileless malware infects computers using legitimate programs, allowed applications and protocols, which make it difficult to detect because it is written to RAM and not disk.[76]
- **Botnets**—Derived from robot network, a botnet (or bot) is a large, automated and distributed network of previously compromised computers that can be simultaneously controlled to launch large-scale attacks such as denial of service.
- **Ransomware**—Also called hostage code, a class of extortive malware that either locks or encrypts data or functions and demands a payment to unlock them. Two main types include crypto ransomware and locker ransomware.
- **Spyware**—A class of malware that gathers information about a person or organization without the knowledge of that person or organization.

---

[73] ISACA, *Advanced Persistent Threats: How to Manage the Risk to Your Business*, USA, 2013, www.isaca.org/bookstore/cybersecurity-resources/apt

[74] CrowdStrike, "The 11 Most Common Types of Malware," 15 October 2019, www.crowdstrike.com/epp-101/types-of-malware/

[75] Malwarebyte, "Trojan," www.malwarebytes.com/trojan

[76] Morley, E.; "What is a Non-Malware (or Fileless) Attack?," VMware Carbon Black, https://www.carbonblack.com/blog/non-malware-fileless-attack/

- **Adware**—Designed to present advertisements (generally unwanted) to users.
- **Mobile malware**—Category of malware that specifically targets mobile devices.

Another category of malicious software that requires explanation is potentially unwanted programs (PUP)[77]—also called bundleware, junkware or potentially unwanted applications (PUA). PUPs may be confused with trojans due to similar delivery vehicles; however, PUP makers argue that they are not malicious because they include consent information in download agreements, which resulted in their less malicious sounding name. PUPs add toolbars, collect private information, display advertisements and consume system resources.

2.8.2 Attacks

In addition to malware and ransomware, there are many other types of attacks. Some of the most common attack patterns are as follows:

- **Advanced persistent threats (APTs)**—APTs are complex, coordinated attacks directed at a specific entity or enterprise that require a substantial amount of research and time—typically years—using multiple attack vectors. APT has received a lot of industry coverage over the years but there is no single test to quickly ascertain whether an attack is an APT or not. Rather, an attack cannot be classified as an APT until the attack is discovered, the level of complexity is determined and the amount of time and resources spent on the attack is investigated. APTs are discussed in greater detail below.

- **Backdoor**—A means of regaining access to a compromised system by installing software or configuring existing software to enable remote access under attacker-defined conditions. Note that backdoors may also be manufacturer-enabled as is often the case with IoT devices.

- **Brute force attack**—An attack made by trying all possible combinations of passwords or encryption keys until the correct one is found.

- **Buffer overflow**—Occurs when a program or process tries to store more data in a buffer (temporary data storage area) than it was intended to hold. Since buffers are created to contain a finite amount of data, the extra information—which has to go somewhere—can overflow into adjacent buffers, corrupting or overwriting the valid data held in them. Although it may occur accidentally through programming error, buffer overflow is an increasingly common type of security attack on data integrity. In buffer overflow attacks, the extra data may contain codes type of security attack on data integrity.

- **Covert channel**—Means of illicitly transferring information between systems using existing infrastructure. Covert channels are simple, stealthy attacks that often go undetected.

- **Cross-site scripting (XSS)**—A type of injection in which malicious scripts are injected into otherwise benign and trusted websites. XSS attacks occur when an attacker uses a web application to send malicious code, generally in the form of a browser side script, to a different end user. Flaws that allow these attacks to succeed are quite widespread and occur anywhere a web application uses input from a user within the output it generates without validating or encoding it.

- **DoS attack**—An assault on a service from a single source that floods it with so many requests that it becomes overwhelmed and is either stopped completely or operates at a significantly reduced rate.

- **Man-in-the-middle attack**—An attack strategy in which the attacker intercepts the communication stream between two parts of the victim system and then replaces the traffic between the two components with the intruder's own, eventually assuming control of the communication.

- **Social engineering**—An attack based on deceiving users or administrators at the target site into revealing confidential or sensitive information. When successful, social engineering can permit unauthorized access to systems. It involves a con game that tricks others into divulging information or opening malicious software or programs.

---

[77] Zamora, W.; "How to avoid potentially unwanted programs," 16 August 2018, https://blog.malwarebytes.com/101/2016/02/how-to-avoid-potentially-unwanted-programs/

- **Phishing**—A type of email attack that attempts to convince a user that the originator is genuine, but with the intention of obtaining information for use in social engineering.

- **Race condition**—According to Rouse, "an undesirable situation that occurs when a device or system attempts to perform two or more operations at the same time, but because of the nature of the device or system, the operations must be done in the proper sequence in order to be done correctly."[78] Race conditions vary; however, these vulnerabilities all afford opportunities for unauthorized network access.

- **Return-oriented programming attack**—Frequently used technique to exploit memory corruption vulnerabilities. Simply stated, is an exploit technique in which the attacker uses control of the call stack to indirectly execute cherry-picked machine instructions immediately prior to the return instruction in subroutines within the existing program code. In other words, it allows an attacker to execute code despite the technological advances such as nonexecutable stacks and nonexecutable heaps. Memory corruption vulnerabilities occur "when a privileged program is coerced into corrupting its own memory space, such that the memory areas corrupted have an impact on the secure functioning of the program."[79]

- **Side-channel attack**—An attack enabled by leakage of information from a physical cryptosystem. Characteristics that could be exploited in a side-channel attack include timing, power consumption and electromagnetic and acoustic emissions.[80]

- **Spearphishing**—A phishing attack designed to entice specific individuals or groups in order to obtain important information.[81]

- **Spoofing**—Faking the sending address of a transmission in order to gain illegal entry into a secure system.

- **Steganography**—A form of covert channel, it is the art or practice of concealing a message, image or file within another message, image or file. Media files are ideal because of their large size.

- **Structure Query Language (SQL) injection**—According to OWASP,[82] "A SQL injection attack consists of insertion or 'injection' of a SQL query via the input data from the client to the application. A successful SQL injection exploit can read sensitive data from the database, modify database data (Insert/Update/Delete), execute administration operations on the database (such as shutdown the DBMS), recover the content of a given file present on the DBMS file system and in some cases issue commands to the operating system. SQL injection attacks are a type of injection attack, in which SQL commands are injected into data-plane input in order to effect the execution of predefined SQL commands."

- **Whaling**—A variation of phishing attacks that targets high profile individuals or others with access to valuable information, systems, or programs.

- **Zero-day exploit**—A vulnerability that is exploited before the software creator/vendor is aware of its existence. Zero-day may also refer to known flaws which do not have a patch available.

2.8.3 Advanced Persistent Threats

Advanced persistent threats (APTs) have received a great deal of coverage over the years despite a traditionally lower probability of attack for most enterprises. Most enterprises have at some point encountered one or more opportunistic attacks from small-time criminals, hackers, or other mischief makers, but most APT attacks originate from more sinister sources. They are often the work of professional teams employed by organized crime groups, determined activists or governments. This means they are likely to be well-planned, sophisticated, well-resourced and potentially more damaging.

[78] Rouse, M., "Race Condition," September 2005, http://searchstorage.techtarget.com/definition/race-condition
[79] Herath, N.; "The State of Return Oriented Programming in Contemporary Exploits," Security Intelligence, 3 March 2014, http://securityintelligence.com/return-oriented-programming-rop-contemporary-exploits/#.VFkNEBa9bD0
[80] *Op cit* National Institute of Standards and Technology, "Glossary"
[81] Swinhoe, D.; "What is spear phishing? Why targeted email attacks are so difficult to stop," CSO, 21 January 2019, www.csoonline.com/article/3334617/what-is-spear-phishing-why-targeted-email-attacks-are-so-difficult-to-stop.html
[82] OWASP, "SQL Injection," www.owasp.org/index.php/SQL_Injection

Although the motives behind them are not entirely new, the degree of planning, resources employed and techniques used in APT attacks are unprecedented. As such, APT groups typically target high value targets of national or economic importance and each have different targets and weapons of choice.[83] These threats demand a degree of vigilance and a set of countermeasures that are above and beyond those routinely used to counter everyday security threats from computer hackers, viruses, or spammers.[84]

It should be noted that not everyone agrees on precisely what constitutes an APT. Many experts regard it as nothing new. Some view them as the latest evolution in attack techniques that have been developing over many years. Others claim the term is misleading, pointing out that many attacks classed as APTs are not especially clever or novel. APTs were once believed to be the only sophisticated attack but that is no longer case. Many cyberattacks offer high reward when compared to level of effort.

The truth is that *all* cyberattacks are increasingly sophisticated. Cyberattacks can be compared to speed enforcement. Using this example, law enforcement continues to roll out advanced technology to detect speeding drivers, which drives the market for avoidance technologies (i.e., radar detectors, jammers) trying to keep pace. In this sense, as cyberthreat detection solutions get better so too must attackers and vice versa.

As written in *Cyber Warfare—Truth, Tactics, and Strategies,*[85] Dr. Chase Cunningham writes of a few general criteria accepted by *some* cross-industry analysts when determining whether to classify the attack as an APT or not:

- **Demonstrated advanced tradecraft**—Characterized by full-spectrum, intelligence-gathering techniques and robust tactics, techniques and procedures
- **Persistence**—Methodical, long-term operations that are often low and slow
- **Threat**—Characterized by both capability and intent, using highly-skilled operators who are organized and well-funded

Even though no two APT attacks are exactly alike, they often follow the attack life cycle, shown in **figure 2.7**. APT groups start with intelligence gathering, which includes selecting and researching their target, planning the attack and collecting and analyzing data from an initial penetration which often stems from phishing emails. The attacker then establishes command and control, collecting targeted information, which is then exfiltrated to the attacker's location to be disseminated or exploited. Due to the length of time APT groups often occupy exploited networks, "threat actors must be adept at handling attempts to remove their access."[86]

APTs target companies of all sizes across all sectors of industry and all geographic regions that contain high-value assets. Staff of all levels of seniority, ranging from administrative assistants to chief executives, can be selected as a target for a spear phishing attack. Small companies and contractors might be penetrated because they are a supplier of services to a targeted victim. Individuals might be selected if they are perceived to be a potential stepping stone to help gain access to the ultimate target.

No industry with valuable secrets or other sources of commercial advantage that can be copied or undermined through espionage is safe from an APT attack. No enterprise that controls money transfers, processes credit card data, or stores personally identifiable data on individuals can be sheltered from criminal attacks. Likewise, no industry that supplies or supports critical national infrastructure is immune from an intrusion by cyberwarriors.

APT attacks often encompass third-party organizations delivering services to targeted enterprises. Third-party suppliers can be perceived by an attacker as the weakest link of large companies and government departments because they are generally less protected. No matter how effective a company's external perimeter security might be, it can be of limited value unless it is extended across its supply chain.

[83] Sobers, R.; "9 Infamous APT Groups: Fast Fact Trading Cards," 29 March 2020, www.varonis.com/blog/apt-groups/
[84] *Op cit* ISACA, *Advanced Persistent Threats: How to Manage the Risk to Your Business*
[85] Cunningham, C.; *Cyber Warfare – Truth, Tactics, and Strategies: Strategic concepts and truths to help you and your organization survive on the battleground of cyber warfare,* Packt Publishing, Kindle Edition
[86] FireEye Mandiant, *M-Trends Report 2020,* 2020, https://content.fireeye.com/m-trends/rpt-m-trends-2020

Figure 2.15 lists the primary actors behind APT threats. It sets out their overall goals as well as the potential business impact of their attacks.

Figure 2.15—APT Types and Impacts		
Threat	**What They Seek**	**Business Impact**
Intelligence agencies	Political, defense or commercial trade secrets	Loss of trade secrets or commercial, competitive advantage
Criminal groups	Money transfers, extortion opportunities, personal identity information or any secrets for potential onward sale	Financial loss, large-scale customer data breach or loss of trade secrets
Terrorist groups	Production of widespread terror through death, destruction and disruption	Loss of production and services, stock market irregularities and potential risk to human life
Activist groups	Confidential information or disruption of services	Major data breach or loss of service
Armed forces	Intelligence or positioning to support future attacks on critical national infrastructure	Serious damage to facilities in the event of a military conflict

2.8.4 Ransomware

As its name implies, ransomware[87] is a mode of digital extortion that prevents access to systems and sensitive information in exchange for a ransom payment.

Ransomware first originated in 1989—Joseph L. Popp created the first ransomware virus called the AIDS Trojan. Popp sent 20,000 infected diskettes labeled "AIDS Information—Introductory Diskettes" to attendees of the World Health Organization's international AIDS conference in Stockholm, which contained malicious code that hid file directories, locked file names and demanded victims send $189 to a PO Box in Panama. This early ransomware used symmetric cryptography which was easily decrypted and later deemed a nonserious threat.[88]

In 1996, researchers warned that a new ransomware would eventually appear using asymmetric cryptography; however, it did not appear until 2005. Bitcoin came on scene in 2008, which resulted in larger ransoms. The year 2011 realized the first large-scale ransomware attack—a ransomware worm that imitated the Windows product activation. Anonymous payment services also appeared in 2011. New and variant ransomware strains continue to gain widespread notoriety, from the havoc attacks are wreaking on businesses, industries, government agencies and public education.[89]

Ransomware is often delivered via malicious spam (malspam) or malicious advertising (malvertising). Malspam involves social engineering techniques, such as phishing, whereas malvertising either uses infected online ads or redirects to fraudulent websites. Although malspam or malvertising may be the initial attack vector, operating system vulnerabilities have played a large part in the scope and magnitude of attacks. Ransomware is not subtle as it offers sizeable return on investment and near real-time return on an attacker's investment.

In their annual *Internet Organized Crime Threat Assessment (IOCTA)*, the European Union Agency for Law Enforcement Cooperation (Europol) reported ransomware as "the most prominent threat in terms of prevalence and financial damage."[90] Ransomware predictions are disturbing in that the number of ransomware families are leveling

---

87 Malwarebytes, "Ransomware," https://www.malwarebytes.com/ransomware/
88 KnowBe4, Inc., "Ransomware," https://www.knowbe4.com/ransomware
89 Digital Guardian, "A History of Ransomware Attacks: The Biggest and Worst Ransomware Attacks of All Time," Data Insider, https://digitalguardian.com/blog/history-ransomware-attacks-biggest-and-worst-ransomware-attacks-all-time
90 Malwarebytes Labs, "Europol: Ransomware remains top threat in IOCTA report," 14 October 2019, https://blog.malwarebytes.com/awareness/2019/10/europol-ransomware-remains-top-threat-in-iocta-report/

off; however, ransomware is becoming more sophisticated and thus more lethal. McAfee® Advanced Threat Research (ATR) predicts 2020 will bring about two-stage extortion attacks, whereby the first stage extorts per usual but involves a second-stage attack in which attacks strike again, threatening to disclose sensitive data that was stolen the first time.[91]

Three notable ransomware attacks in recent history include:

- **WannaCry**—In early 2017, a global ransomware attack that affected more than 200,000 computers running Microsoft® Windows operating systems in more than 100 countries[92]. WannaCry was a worm that quickly spread and affects many computers in mere days. WannaCry was severe enough to prompt Microsoft to issue patches for older unsupported versions of its Windows software.[93]

- **Petya**—Originally discovered in 2016, a new strain of Petya was found to be spreading quickly mid-2017, using the Windows Server Message Block (SMB) vulnerability previously patched during the WannaCry outbreak. However, this variant possessed the additional functionality of encrypting the master boot record (MBR) and master file table (MFT), which made recovery extremely difficult to recover, if at all. Unlike most other ransomware, Petya did not allow infected users to use the infected machine to pay the ransom forcing users to use a different computer to make the payment and receive a decryption key.[94]

- **Travelex**—Global currency exchange giant, Travelex, experienced a ransomware attack on December 31, 2019, forcing the company to shut down websites in 30 countries. The group claiming responsibility advised media outlet BBC the ransom demand is $6M USD,[95] but allegedly settled for a $2.3M USD payout.[96]

The Great Ruse

The most devastating cyberattack in modern history was cloaked to resemble ransomware. Dubbed NotPetya, this virus targeted Ukraine but spread further.[97] Caught in the crossfire was global shipping giant Maersk who experienced 50,000 infected endpoints across 130 countries.[98]

NotPetya included a ransom screen with payment directions however the ransomware feature was worthless as it resulted in randomly generated string. Unable to reverse file corruption, many began categorizing the virus as a wiper. Unlike the original Petya which required admin privileges, NotPetya spreads on its own using several methods. Worse yet, NotPetya encrypted everything resulting in mass destruction. Of note, the key vulnerability patch to prevent infection was available since WannaCry thus highlighting poor patching practices.[99]

Global issue—International response

Law enforcement and IT security companies have joined forces to disrupt cybercriminal businesses with ransomware connections. Founded in 2016, the "No More Ransom" website[100] is an initiative by the National High Tech Crime Unit of the Netherland police, Europol European Cybercrime Centre, Kaspersky and McAfee with a stated goal to

---

[91] Samani, R.; "5 Threat Predictions for 2020: Are You Prepared?" CISOMAG, 13 January 2020, https://cisomag.eccouncil.org/threat-predictions-for-2020/

[92] National Audit Office, Department of Health, *Investigation: WannaCry cyber attack and the NHS*, HC 414 Session 2017–2019, 25 April 2018, www.nao.org.uk/wp-content/uploads/2017/10/Investigation-WannaCry-cyber-attack-and-the-NHS.pdf

[93] Krebs on Security, "Microsoft Issues WanaCrypt Patch for Windows 8, XP," 13 May 2017, https://krebsonsecurity.com/tag/wanna-cry-ransomware/

[94] Alvarez, R.; "Ransomware and the Boot Process," Fortinet, 1 February 2017, www.fortinet.com/blog/threat-research/ransomware-and-the-boot-process.html

[95] Tidy, J.; "Travelex being held to ransom by hackers," BBC News, 7 January 2020, www.bbc.com/news/business-51017852

[96] Asokan, A.; "Travelex Paid $2.3 Million to Ransomware Gang: Report," BankInfoSecurity, 10 April 2020, www.bankinfosecurity.com/travelex-paid-23-million-to-ransomware-attackers-report-a-14094

[97] Palmer, D.; "Ransomware: The key lesson Maersk learned from battling the NotPetya attack," ZDNet, 29 April 2019, www.zdnet.com/article/ransomware-the-key-lesson-maersk-learned-from-battling-the-notpetya-attack/

[98] *Ibid.*

[99] Fruhlinger, J.; "Petya ransomware and NotPetya malware: What you need to know now," CSO, 17 October 2017, www.csoonline.com/article/3233210/petya-ransomware-and-notpetya-malware-what-you-need-to-know-now.html

[100] NoMoreRansom, "No More Ransom!," www.nomoreransom.org/en/index.html

help victims of ransomware retrieve their encrypted data without having to pay the criminals. Its secondary goal is to educate users. The project is open to other public and private parties and, on its third anniversary, reportedly deterred more than US $108 million in ransom payments.[101]

2.8.5 Mobile Attacks

Mobile devices continue to be a threat for enterprises and it no longer matters whether they are company issued or employee owned. Today's threat landscape includes a growing number of employees using smartphones to access enterprise data—likely fueled by cloud-based productivity software. Mobile devices are vulnerable to application, network and operating system threats.[102]

Of the three, mobile apps are the top attack vector for mobile devices, which means bad actors are still publishing malicious apps in stores, despite the existence of app store review processes. Mobile apps are notorious for requiring more permissions than are required and leaking data, such as contact information and call logs. Network threats include unsafe wireless access, which increases the likelihood of man-in-the-middle attacks—or an intercept of communication. Enterprises routinely review and patch mobile device operating systems; however, those updates are not always initiated on the device. Outdated software and applications are recipes for malicious software and data loss.

Beyond mobile devices, there are other attack vectors of which to be aware. Social engineering has expanded to mobile devices thanks to SMiShing (for SMS Phishing). SMiShing uses short message service (SMS) to send fraudulent text messages or links. Like phishing, SMiShing may result in users downloading malware that infects the device.

Mobile device short-range communications, such as Bluetooth® and Near Field Communication (NFC), are also exploitable. One harmless Bluetooth technique called Bluejacking is primarily used for pranking, whereas Bluesnarfing uses a similar method to steal data from the target device. Security concerns regarding NFC technology include eavesdropping, data corruption and manipulation, interception attacks, and device theft. As with any technology, security professionals are encouraged to remain abreast of security issues, educate employees and provide guidance on device settings to minimize risk.

2.9 Risk Assessment

Chapter 1 defined risk management as the coordination of activities that direct and control an enterprise with regard to risk and further stated that risk management requires the development and implementation of internal controls to manage and mitigate risk. While it is true that senior level individuals are often responsible for guiding governance and risk-related activities, everyone working in IT and OT must have a fundamental understanding of the sometimes delicate compromise that must occur to manage risk.

2.9.1 Approaches to Risk

A number of methodologies are available to measure risk. Different industries and professions have adopted various tactics based on the following criteria:

- Risk tolerance
- Size and scope of the environment in question
- Amount of data available

---

[101] Cimpanu, C.; "No More Ransom project has prevented ransomware profits of at least $108 million," ZDNet, 26 July 2019, www.zdnet.com/article/no-more-ransom-project-has-prevented-ransomware-profits-of-at-least-108-million/

[102] Pradeo, *Enterprise Mobile Threat Landscape*, 2020, www.pradeo.com/media/enterprise-mobility-security-report.pdf

It is particularly important to understand the risk tolerance of an enterprise when considering how to measure and report risk. There are few absolutes with regard to managing risk, because every industry has unique attributes and variables. For example, a general approach to measuring risk is typically sufficient for risk-tolerant enterprises, such as academic institutions or small businesses. However, more rigorous and in-depth risk assessment is required for entities with a low tolerance for risk or those subject to robust legal and regulatory requirements (e.g., financial institutions or airlines).

2.9.2 Approaches to Cybersecurity Risk

Cybersecurity risk is synonymous with cyberrisk. There are three different approaches to implementing cybersecurity. Each approach is described briefly below:

- **Ad hoc**—An ad hoc approach simply implements security with no particular rationale or criteria. Ad hoc implementations may be driven by vendor marketing, or they may reflect insufficient subject matter expertise, knowledge, or training when designing and implementing safeguards.

- **Compliance based**—Also known as standards-based security, this approach relies on regulations or standards to determine security implementations. Controls are implemented regardless of their applicability or necessity, which often leads to a checklist attitude toward security.

- **Risk based**—Risk-based security relies on identifying the unique risk a particular enterprise faces and designing and implementing security controls to address that risk above and beyond the entity's risk tolerance and business needs. The risk-based approach is usually scenario-based.

In reality, most enterprises with mature security programs use a combination of risk-based and compliance-based approaches. In fact, most standards or regulations such as ISO 27001, the Payment Card Industry Data Security Standard (PCI DSS), Sarbanes–Oxley Act (SOX), or the US Health Insurance Portability and Accountability Act (HIPAA) require risk assessments to drive the particular implementation of the required controls.

2.9.3 Third-party Risk

Cybersecurity can be more difficult to control when third parties are involved (e.g., supply chain vendors), especially when different entities have different security cultures and risk tolerances. No enterprise exists in a vacuum, and information must be shared with other individuals or enterprises, often referred to as third parties. It is important to understand third-party risk, such as information sharing and network access, as it relates to cybersecurity.

Outsourcing is common, both onshore and offshore, as enterprises focus on core competencies and ways to cut costs. However, an outsourced/offshored function usually ends up costing more given the significant amount of re-work often required—not to mention the difference in context from the home enterprise to the environment of the offshored entity.

From an information security point of view, these arrangements can present risk that may be difficult to quantify and potentially difficult to mitigate. Typically, the enterprise does not have visibility to the outsourced functions, which itself presents risk to the enterprise. Providers may operate on different standards and can be difficult to control. The security strategy of an enterprise should consider outsourced security services carefully to ensure that they either are not a critical single point of failure or that there is a viable backup plan in the event of service provider failure.[103]

Risk posed by outsourcing can also materialize as the result of mergers and acquisitions. Typically, significant differences in culture, systems, technology and operations between the parties present a host of security challenges that must be identified and addressed. Often, in these situations, security is an afterthought, and the security manager must strive to gain a presence in these activities and assess the risk for management consideration.[104]

---

[103] ISACA, CISM Review Manual 15th Edition, USA, 2016, https://www.isaca.org/bookstore/cism-exam-resources/cm15ed
[104] Ibid.

2.10 Supply Chain Considerations

According to NIST, "the information and communications technology (ICT) relies on a complex, globally distributed and interconnected ecosystem that is long, has geographically diverse routes, and consists of multiple tiers of outsourcing. This ecosystem is interdependent on public and private entities for development, integration and delivery of ICT products and services."[105]

The complexity of supply chains and impact requires persistent awareness of risk and consideration. Significant factors contributing to the fragility of supply chains are economic, environmental, geopolitical, technological and security.

Whether it is the rapid adoption of open-source software, tampering of physical hardware or natural disasters taking down data centers, supply chains require risk management. An example of this was described in an article in Forbes: Flooding in Thailand created significant shortages in the hard disk drive market, which cost well-known electronics manufacturers millions of dollars in losses.[106]

Products or services manufactured anywhere may contain vulnerabilities that can present opportunities for ICT supply chain-related compromises. It is especially important to consider supply chain risk from system development, to include research and development (R&D) through useful life and ultimately retirement/disposal of products.

2.11 Risk Management Life Cycle

IT risk management is a cyclical process,[107] as illustrated in **figure 2.16**. The first step in the IT risk management process is the identification of IT risk, which includes determining the risk context and risk framework, and the process of identifying and documenting risk. The risk identification effort should result in the listing and documentation of risk, which serves as the input for the next phase of the process, IT risk assessment.

The effort to assess and prioritize risk provides management with the data needed for risk responses. Risk response—the third phase of the cycle—seeks and implements cost-effective ways to address the risk that has been identified and assessed. The final phase is risk and control monitoring and reporting, in which the effectiveness of the risk responses and the current risk state are monitored, and the results are reported back to senior management. The process repeats as the risk environment changes, which may occur as a result of internal or external factors.

[105] Boyens, J.; C. Paulsen.; R. Moorthy; N. Bartol; *NIST SP 800-161, Supply Chain Risk Management Practices for Federal Information Systems and Organization*, NIST, USA, 2015

[106] Culp, S.; "Supply Chain Risk a Hidden Liability for Many Companies," Forbes, 8 October 2012, www.forbes.com/sites/steveculp/2012/10/08/supply-chain-risk-a-hidden-liability-for-many-companies

[107] *Op cit* ISACA, *CRISC Review Manual 6th Edition*

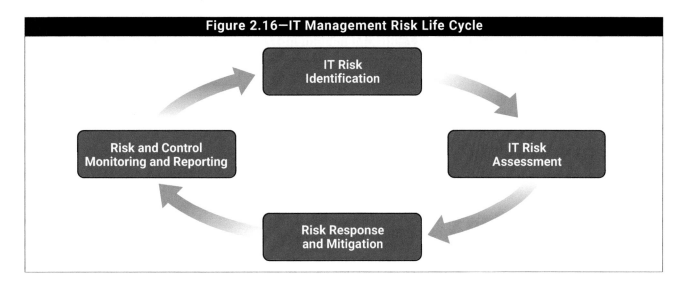

Figure 2.16—IT Management Risk Life Cycle

2.11.1 IT Risk Identification (Risk Scenarios)

There is a fundamental tension (**figure 2.17**) between the services an information system provides (functionality) and security. A building with no doors or windows is quite secure but is very limited in its utility. Similarly, an information system with no way for data to flow in or out is very secure, but it is unable to provide a service. The more services an enterprise provides/allows, the more ways in and out of their system that need securing. Thus, for each service one needs to weigh the value of the service against the security implications of providing/allowing it.[108] Two commonly used equations are *Risk = Likelihood x Impact* and *Risk = Threat x Vulnerability*.

Risk can be discussed in quantitative or qualitative terms, and the specific definitions of risk vary from source to source. However, the fundamental nature of risk management is that it addresses the odds that some event will happen (probability or likelihood) and what it would mean for the enterprise if that event did happen (consequences). Early attempts to define risk observed that the probability of something happening was a combination of two things: whether something was attempted (threat) and whether the target of the attempt was susceptible to what was tried (vulnerability).

As the study of risk matured, risk practitioners began to distinguish between delineation of the impact and the extent to which those impacts affected the value-creation activities of the enterprise (impact). It is now common to distinguish between different types of threats, to evaluate them on the basis of specific organizational assets against which they may be directed and to assess those assets in terms of their individual weaknesses(vulnerabilities) that might be exploited to create consequences for the assets. When viewed from the perspective of how these assets are used within the organization, it becomes possible to quantify impact in terms of lost productivity and other specific measures of value, which is useful for two reasons:

1. It is easier for managers to set a dollar value of total losses that they are willing to incur (risk appetite) than it is to define what consequences are or are not acceptable in a dozen or more different areas of operations.

2. Knowing the potential losses associated with risk provides a basis for deciding how to respond to risk that is beyond acceptable levels because it does not make sense to spend more to respond to a risk than the risk itself presents in terms of the cost of impact.

Risk is a critical part of business and businesses must be willing to take calculated risk. However, taking too much risk may lead to increased likelihood of failure of the business and loss of investment. Senior management is responsible for setting the risk appetite for the organization—a clear statement of how much risk to take and what opportunities to forego.

---

[108] ISACA, *COBIT 5 for Risk*, USA, 2013, www.isaca.org/bookstore/cobit-5/wcb5rk

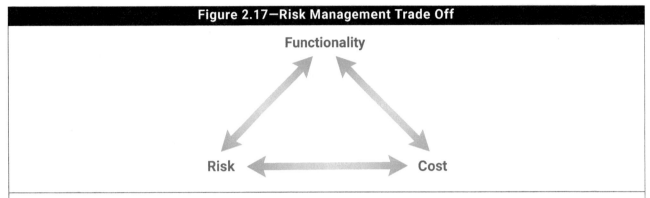

Figure 2.17—Risk Management Trade Off

Source: ISACA, CRISC Review Manual 6th Edition, 2015, https://www.isaca.org/bookstore/crisc-exam-resources/crr6ed

A risk scenario is a description of a possible event whose occurrence will have an uncertain impact on the achievement of the enterprise's objectives, which may be positive or negative. The development of risk scenarios provides a way of conceptualizing risk that can aid in the process of risk identification. Scenarios are also used to document risk in relation to business objectives or operations impacted by events, making them useful as the basis for quantitative risk assessment. Each identified risk should be included in one or more scenarios, and each scenario should be based on an identified risk.

The development of risk scenarios is based on describing a potential risk event and documenting the factors and areas that may be affected by the risk event. Each scenario should be related to a business objective or impact. Risk events may include system failure, loss of key personnel, theft, network outages, power failures, or any other situation that could affect business operations and mission. The key to developing effective scenarios is to focus on real and relevant potential risk events.

The development of risk scenarios purely from imagination is an art that often requires creativity, thought, consultation and questioning. Incidents that have occurred previously may be used as the basis of risk scenarios with far less effort put into their development. Risk scenarios based on past events should be fully explored to ensure that similar situations do not recur in ways that might have been avoided. Risk scenarios can be developed from a top-down perspective driven by business goals or from a bottom-up perspective originating from several inputs, as shown in **figure 2.18.**

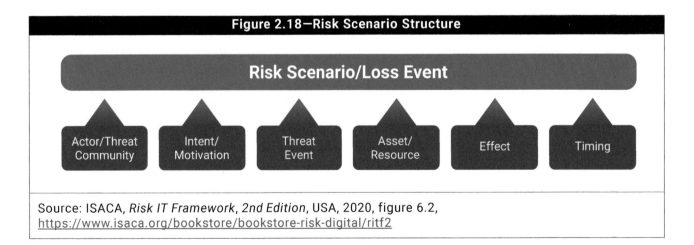

Figure 2.18—Risk Scenario Structure

Source: ISACA, *Risk IT Framework, 2nd Edition*, USA, 2020, figure 6.2, https://www.isaca.org/bookstore/bookstore-risk-digital/ritf2

Top-down Approach

A top-down approach to scenario development is based on understanding business goals and how a risk event could affect the achievement of those goals. Under this model, the security practitioner looks for the outcome of events that may hamper business goals identified by senior management. Various scenarios are developed that allow the organization to examine the relationship between the risk event and the business goals, so that the impact of the risk event can be measured. By directly relating a risk scenario to the business, senior managers can be educated and involved in how to understand and measure risk.

The top-down approach is suited to general risk management of the company because it looks at both IT- and non-IT-related events. A benefit of this approach is that because it is more general, it is easier to achieve management buy-in even if management usually is not interested in IT. The top-down approach also deals with the goals that senior managers have already identified as important to the enterprise.

Bottom-up Approach

The bottom-up approach to developing risk scenarios is based on describing risk events that are specific to cybersecurity-related situations, typically hypothetical situations envisioned by the people performing the job functions in specific processes. The cybersecurity professional and assessment team start with one or more generic risk scenarios, then refine them to meet their individual organizational needs, including building complex scenarios to account for coinciding events.

Bottom-up scenario development can be a good way to identify scenarios that are highly dependent on the specific technical workings of a process or system, which may not be apparent to anyone who is not intimately involved with that work but could have substantial consequences for the organization. One downside of bottom-up scenario development is that it may be more difficult to maintain management interest in highly specialized technical scenarios.

2.11.2 IT Risk Assessment

During risk identification, risk scenarios are developed and used to identify and describe potential risk events.[109] These scenarios are useful to communicate with the business and gather input data required to understand the potential or probable impact of the risk event if it were to occur.

The impact of a risk event is hard to calculate with any degree of accuracy because there are many factors that affect the outcome of an event. If the event is detected quickly and appropriate measures are taken to contain the incident, then the impact may be minimized, and the recovery process may be fairly rapid. However, if the enterprise is unable to detect the incident promptly, the same incident could cause severe damage and result in much higher recovery costs. Some factors that can affect the calculation of risk assessment are discussed in the following sections.

Risk analysis (**figure 2.19**) is a complex and important process that is often needed to provide the data necessary for effective risk response. Risk may be analyzed on either a quantitative or qualitative basis or in a way that reflects some combination of the two (semiquantitative).

---

[109] *Op cit* ISACA, *CRISC Review Manual* 6th Edition

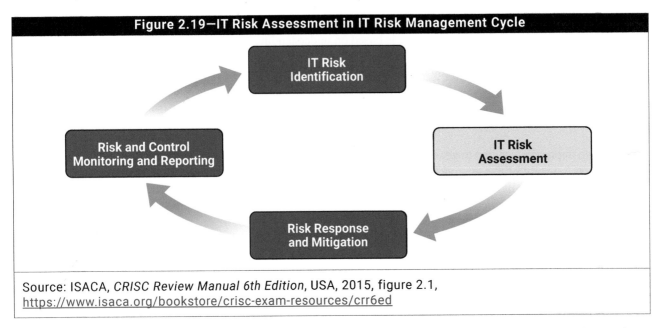

Figure 2.19—IT Risk Assessment in IT Risk Management Cycle

Source: ISACA, *CRISC Review Manual 6th Edition*, USA, 2015, figure 2.1,
https://www.isaca.org/bookstore/crisc-exam-resources/crr6ed

Technical and nontechnical professionals interested in learning more about analyzing risk are encouraged to explore the ISACA Certified in Risk and Information Systems Control (CRISC) certification program.

2.11.3 Risk Response and Mitigation

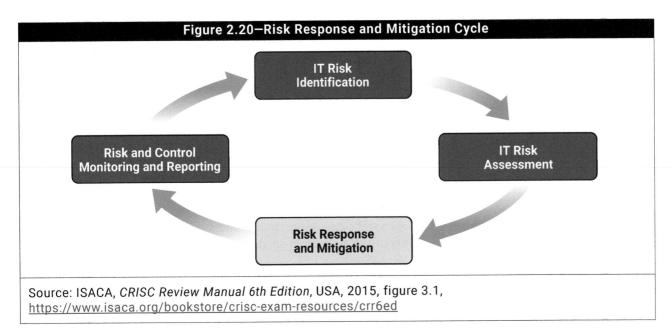

Figure 2.20—Risk Response and Mitigation Cycle

Source: ISACA, *CRISC Review Manual 6th Edition*, USA, 2015, figure 3.1,
https://www.isaca.org/bookstore/crisc-exam-resources/crr6ed

The risk assessment report and risk register document the risk identified during the identification and assessment phases (**figure 2.20**) of the risk management process. Both the report and the register should indicate the assessed level or priority of each risk. The recommendations for remediation in the report are guidelines, and several recommendations may be provided.

Management is responsible for evaluating and responding to the recommendations included in the report, first by determining the best response and then developing an action plan and implementation strategy that addresses the risk in a manner consistent with the risk appetite and risk tolerance of the enterprise.

Management must always be aware of the drivers for risk management, such as compliance with regulations and the need to support and align the risk response with business priorities and objectives. A risk response that would negatively impact the ability of the organization to meet its mission must be considered very carefully.

Evaluation of an appropriate risk response is part of the risk management process cycle, not a one-time effort. There are four commonly accepted options for risk response:

- Risk acceptance
- Risk mitigation
- Risk sharing (transfer)
- Risk avoidance

Risk acceptance refers to a conscious decision made by senior management to recognize the existence of risk and knowingly decide to allow (assume) the risk to remain without (further) mitigation. Management is responsible for the impact of a risk event should it occur, so the decision to accept a risk is made according to the risk appetite and risk tolerance set by senior management.

Risk mitigation refers to actions that the enterprise takes to reduce a risk. Mitigation is typically achieved through security controls, which affect the frequency and/or impact of the risk.

Risk transfer is a decision to reduce loss by having another enterprise incur the cost. The most common example of risk transfer is the purchasing of insurance, which provides a guarantee of compensation or replacement should a loss occur. Cyberinsurance is discussed further in Chapter 3.

Risk avoidance means exiting the activities or conditions that give rise to risk. Risk avoidance is not a decision to make lightly, but it may be the best choice in some instances. Risk avoidance is the choice that remains when no other response is adequate, meaning the following are true:

- The exposure level is deemed unacceptable by management.
- The risk cannot be transferred.
- Mitigation that would bring the risk in line with acceptable levels is either impossible or would cost more than the benefits that the organization derives from the activities.

Examples of risk avoidance include:

- Relocating a data center away from a region with significant natural hazards
- Declining a project whose business case shows a substantial likelihood of failure
- Deciding not to use proprietary technology or software from a vendor because it has only recently begun operations or is undergoing bankruptcy

2.11.4 Risk and Control Monitoring and Reporting

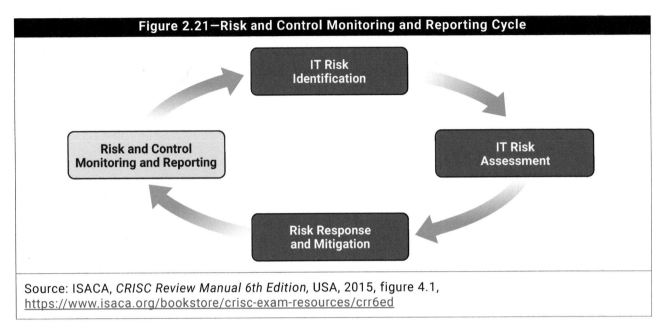

Figure 2.21—Risk and Control Monitoring and Reporting Cycle

Source: ISACA, *CRISC Review Manual 6th Edition*, USA, 2015, figure 4.1, https://www.isaca.org/bookstore/crisc-exam-resources/crr6ed

The enterprise relies on its monitoring and reporting functions (**figure 2.21**) to identify risk for assessment and mitigation. The risk practitioner is able to best manage risk when monitoring is broad enough to provide a reasonable view of the risk environment, but not so broad that the results are lost in a flood of data. Indicators for both performance and risk should be carefully considered and deliberately chosen based on their alignment with organizational goals. Identification and use of key risk indicators (KRIs) and key performance indicators (KPIs) can greatly improve the process of continuous monitoring. In addition, periodic assessments and testing may also be necessary as a means of identifying new and emerging risk. Because of the changing nature of risk and associated controls, ongoing monitoring is an essential step of the risk management life cycle.

A KRI is a subset of risk indicators that are highly relevant and possess a high probability of predicting or indicating important risk. Examples of KRIs include:

- Quantity of unauthorized equipment or software detected in scans
- Average time to deploy new security patches to servers
- Number of desktops/laptops that do not have current antivirus signatures or have not run a full scan within scheduled periods

A KPI is a measure that determines how well the process is performing in enabling the goal to be reached.

Monitoring is essential, but its effectiveness depends in large part on its successful integration with reporting. Consistent, repeatable methods of reporting provide management with a means of assessing the efficacy of the risk response and mitigation activities and justify the expenses of supporting security controls. Reports also assist management in exercising due care and due diligence in protecting the assets of the enterprise and meeting regulatory requirements.

Security practitioners should always consider how their individual actions affect changes in risk over time and the impact of changes in the risk environment.

2.12 Managing Risk

For risk that has inadequate or no controls, there are many options to address each risk, as shown in **figure 2.22**.

Figure 2.22—Risk Response Strategy	
Risk Response	**Description**
Risk reduction	The implementation of controls or countermeasures to reduce the likelihood or impact of a risk to a level within the enterprise risk tolerance.
Risk avoidance	Risk can be avoided by not participating in an act or business.
Risk transfer or sharing	Risk can be transferred to a third party (e.g., insurance) or shared with a third party via contractual agreement.
Risk acceptance	If the risk is within the enterprise risk tolerance or if the cost of otherwise mitigating the risk is higher than the potential loss, then an enterprise can assume the risk and absorb any losses.
Source: ISACA, *CRISC Review Manual 6th Edition*, USA, 2015, figure 4.4, https://www.isaca.org/bookstore/crisc-exam-resources/crr6ed	

The strategy an enterprise chooses depends on many things, such as regulatory requirements, culture, mission, ability to mitigate risk and risk tolerance.

2.13 Using the Results of Risk Assessments

Risk assessment results are used for a variety of security management functions. These results need to be evaluated in terms of the enterprise mission, risk tolerance, budgets and other resources, and cost of mitigation. Based on this evaluation, a mitigation strategy can be chosen for each risk and appropriate controls and countermeasures can be designed and implemented.

Risk assessment results can also be used to communicate the risk decisions and expectations of management throughout the enterprise through policies and procedures.

Page intentionally left blank

2.14 Chapter 2 Knowledge Check

REVIEW QUESTIONS

1. Which three elements of the current threat landscape have provided increased levels of access and connectivity, and, therefore, increased opportunities for cybercrime?

   A. Text messaging, Bluetooth® technology and SIM cards
   B. Web applications, botnets and primary malware
   C. Cloud computing, social media and mobile computing

2. Which of the following statements about advanced persistent threats (APTs) are true? (Select all that apply.)

   A. APTs typically originate from sources such as organized crime groups, activists or governments.
   B. APTs use obfuscation techniques that help them remain undiscovered for months or even years.
   C. APTs are often long-term, multiphase projects with a focus on reconnaissance.
   D. The APT attack cycle begins with target penetration and collection of sensitive information.

3. The core duty of cybersecurity is to:

   A. Manage risk
   B. Secure endpoints
   C. Protect enterprise infrastructure

4. Which of the following is NOT true of likelihood?

   A. Measures frequency of an event occurring
   B. Is often a component of external factors
   C. Does not take into account current controls and countermeasures

5. Match the following terms to their definitions.

A. Asset	1. An adverse effect that results from an event occurring
B. Capability	2. The combination of the likelihood of an event and its impact.
C. Impact	3. The probability of something happening
D. Intent	4. The knowledge and skill set required by a threat to carry out an event
E. Likelihood	5. Something of either tangible or intangible value that is worth protecting, including people, information, infrastructure, finances and reputation
F. Opportunity	6. An actor or event with the potential to adversely impact an information system
G. Risk	7. Anything that is capable of acting against an asset in a manner that can result in harm
H. Threat	8. A weakness in the design, implementation, operation or internal control of a process that could expose the system to adverse threats from threat events
I. Vulnerability	9. The resources and positioning required by a threat to carry out an action

Answers on page 82

Chapter 2 ANSWER KEY

Review Questions

1. A. Text messaging, Bluetooth® technology and SIM cards
    B. Web applications, botnets and primary malware
    C. Cloud computing, social media and mobile computing. Refer to page 53.

2. **A. APTs typically originate from sources such as organized crime groups, activists or governments.**
    B. APTs use obfuscation techniques that help them remain undiscovered for months or even years.
    C. APTs are often long-term, multiphase projects with a focus on reconnaissance. Refer to pages 66-68.
    D. The APT attack cycle begins with target penetration and collection of sensitive information.

3. **A. Manage risk. Refer to page 44.**
    B. Secure endpoints
    C. Protect enterprise infrastructure

4. A. Measures frequency of an event occurring
    B. Is often a component of external factors
    C. Does not take into account current controls and countermeasures. Refer to pages 47-48.

5. Match the following terms to their definitions.

A. Asset	5. Something of either tangible or intangible value that is worth protecting, including people, information, infrastructure, finances and reputation
B. Capability	4. The knowledge and skill set required by a threat to carry out an event
C. Impact	1. An adverse effect that results from an event occurring
D. Intent	6. An actor or event with the potential to adversely impact an information system
E. Likelihood	3. The probability of something happening
F. Opportunity	9. The resources and positioning required by a threat to carry out an action
G. Risk	2. The combination of the likelihood of an event and its impact.
H. Threat	7. Anything that is capable of acting against an asset in a manner that can result in harm
I. Vulnerability	8. A weakness in the design, implementation, operation or internal control of a process that could expose the system to adverse threats from threat events

Securing Assets

Securing Assets

Securing Assets

3.1 Learning Objectives

After completing this chapter, learners will be able to:

1. Distinguish categories of resources used to identify and classify risk.
2. Identify components of a security architecture.
3. Compare security models.
4. Explain defense in depth.
5. Compare traditional security and assume-breach philosophies.
6. Identify three main types of security controls.
7. Distinguish types of logical access controls.
8. Identify and explain types of administrative controls.
9. Explain each component of authentication, authorization and accounting (AAA).
10. Explain methods to achieve isolation and segmentation.
11. Identify network security hardware.
12. Distinguish types of firewalls.
13. Explain system hardening.
14. Recognize system life cycle management principles, including software security and usability.
15. Identify and analyze cloud service models.
16. Discuss risk associated with cloud computing.
17. Summarize data protection means and methods.
18. Identify elements of cryptographic systems.
19. Identify and discuss key systems.

3.2 Risk Identification, Standards, Frameworks and Industry Guidance

Chapter 2 concluded with an understanding of risk and the risk management life cycle. To effectively secure anything, one must first understand the risk associated with the particular environment. Fortunately, there are many resources available to assist enterprises to not only identify and measure risk but also support secure design, development and implementation.

Two major categories of resources are available to information security professionals to help identify and classify risk[110]—standards and frameworks. A standard is a mandatory requirement, code of practice, or specification approved by a recognized external standards organization.[111] A framework is a system of rules, ideas, or beliefs used to plan or decide something.[112] Put another way, frameworks are conceptual models that help attain business objectives.

---

[110] *Ibid.*
[111] *Op cit* ISACA, "Glossary"
[112] *Op cit* Cambridge University Press

3.2.1 Standards

Three major global organizations develop international standards—the International Electrotechnical Commission (IEC), the International Organization for Standardization (ISO) and the International Telecommunication Union (ITU). Founded in 1906, the IEC publishes international standards for all electrical, electronic and related technologies.[113] ISO, formally created in 1947, is an independent, non-governmental international organization comprised of national standards bodies that develops and publishes international standards.[114] A current list of national standards bodies is available at www.iso.org/members.html. Originally founded in 1865 to promote cooperation among international telegraphy networks, ITU is the United Nations specialized agency for information and communication technologies (ICT). ITU is credited with first standardizing the use of Morse code and world's first radio communication and fixed telecommunication networks.[115] On occasion, these bodies may publish joint standards, which is evident in the information technology realm.

The use of a recognized standard may provide credibility and completeness for the risk assessment and management program of the organization and help ensure that the risk management program is comprehensive and thorough. Many countries and industries specify which standards to follow. In absence of official guidance, the following are commonly referenced standards suitable for an enterprise. Many international standards must be purchased from the standard setting body.

- **ISO/IEC 27000:2018** *Information technology – Security techniques – Information security management systems – Overview and vocabulary*—This joint standard is publicly available free of charge to aid industry alignment and provides an overview of the ISMS family of standards, introduction to information security management system, and terms and definitions used throughout the ISO 27000 series.

- **ISO/IEC 27001:2013** *Information technology – Security techniques – Information security management systems – Requirements*—The joint standard provides normative requirements for the development and operation of an ISMS and provides a set of controls to mitigate enterprise risk.

- **ISO/IEC 27002: 2013** *Information technology – Security techniques – Code of practice for information security controls*—This document provides common control objectives and best practices when selecting and implementing information security controls.

- **ISO/IEC 27005: 2018** *Information technology – Security techniques – Information security risk management*—This joint standard provides guidelines for information security risk management and is intended to assist in fulfilling requirements specified in ISO/IEC 27001.

- **ISO/IEC 27032:2012** *Information technology – Security techniques – Guidelines for cybersecurity*—This joint standard provides guidance for improving cybersecurity and addresses dependencies on other security domains.

- **ISO/IEC 31000: 2018** *Risk Management – Risk management guidelines*—This joint standard provides non-industry specific advice for managing any type of risk.

- **ISO/IEC 31010: 2019** *Risk Management – Risk assessment techniques*—This joint standard provides guidance on the selection and application of techniques for assessing risk in diverse situations and has been updated to include greater detail on planning, implementation and validation of techniques.

- **Federal Information Processing Standards (FIPS)**—NIST develops FIPS publications as required by statute or to fulfill US government cybersecurity requirements.[116]

---

[113] International Electrotechnical Commission, "About the IEC," www.iec.ch/about/?ref=menu
[114] International Organization for Standardization, "About Us," ISO, www.iso.org/about-us.html
[115] International Telecommunication Union, "About International Telecommunication Union (ITU)," ITU, www.itu.int/en/about/Pages/default.aspx
[116] NIST Information Technology Laboratory, "Federal Information Processing Standards Publications (FIPS PUBS)," www.nist.gov/itl/publications-0/federal-information-processing-standards-fips

3.2.2 Frameworks

Like standards, there are multiple frameworks from which to choose. For information security, there are two prominent issuers – National Institute for Standards and Technology (NIST) and ISACA. Founded in 1901, NIST is part of the US Department of Commerce whose primary contributions in the information security space is to foster collaboration between industry and the United States government as well as enable innovation through various frameworks. Although their primary consumer may be the US government, NIST products are increasingly collaborative and either adopted or adapted by a growing number of entities across the globe as is the case with the NIST Cybersecurity Framework (CSF).

- **NIST Cybersecurity Framework (CSF)**—NIST continues to make substantial progress with regard to cybersecurity. Their increasingly popular Cybersecurity Framework is organized in three parts. The *Core* documents five broad security functions—Identify, Protect, Detect, Respond, Recover. These functions enable the industry to conceptualize and organize the continuous nature of security work. The continued use of CSF and feedback have undoubted increased its international popularity.[117, 118, 119]

- **COBIT®[120]**—COBIT is a framework for the governance and management of enterprise information and technology. Governance frameworks are built on three principles—based on a conceptual model, open and flexible, and aligned to major standards. COBIT is not an (IT-)technical framework to manage all technology nor does it prescribe any IT-related decisions. Rather, COBIT defines all the components that describe which decisions should be taken, and how and by whom they should be taken.

As was the case with the NIST in the United States, the European Union also strengthened the role of ENISA in 2019. The EU Cybersecurity Act bolstered the role of ENISA to include the creation and maintenance of the European cybersecurity certification framework for digital products, services and processes.[121] The EU cybersecurity certification framework is intended to provide EU-wide certification schemes as a comprehensive set of rules, technical requirements, standards and procedures to minimize fragmentation across Europe.[122]

3.2.3 Best Practices

Beyond standards and frameworks are many best practices aimed at minimizing both technical and nontechnical risk. It is not practical to attempt to list them all but below are some sources of information for cybersecurity professionals.

- **Center for Internet Security® (CIS®)**—CIS offers best practice in several ways—CIS Controls™, CIS Benchmarks™, hardened images, and build kits. These are available at www.cisecurity.org/cybersecurity-best-practices/.

- **NIST Special Publications**—NIST has a wide range of special publications available at https://csrc.nist.gov. Certain Special Publications in later sections.

- **Open Web Application Security Project (OWASP)**—OWASP is a nonprofit foundation whose work is to improve software security. They are widely known for the OWASP Top 10 Web Application Security Risks, often referred to as OWASP Top 10.[123] Other notable resources include the Mobile Security Testing Guide[124] and Web Security Testing Guide.[125]

[117] National Institute of Standards and Technology, "NIST Marks Fifth Anniversary of Popular Cybersecurity Framework," 12 February 2019, NIST, www.nist.gov/news-events/news/2019/02/nist-marks-fifth-anniversary-popular-cybersecurity-framework

[118] Brumfield, C.; "Why NIST is so popular in Japan," Cyberscoop, 8 November 2018, www.cyberscoop.com/nist-japan-workforce/

[119] Sussman, B.; "5 Things to Know as NIST Cybersecurity Framework Turns 5," SecureWorld, 13 February 2019, www.secureworldexpo.com/industry-news/nist-cybersecurity-framework-facts

[120] ISACA, *COBIT 2019 Framework: Introduction & Methodology*, 2018, USA, www.isaca.org/bookstore/bookstore-cobit_19-print/cb19fim

[121] European Union Agency for Cybersecurity, "The EU Cybersecurity Act," ENISA, https://ec.europa.eu/digital-single-market/en/eu-cybersecurity-act

[122] European Union Agency for Cybersecurity, "The EU cybersecurity certification framework," ENISA, https://ec.europa.eu/digital-single-market/en/eu-cybersecurity-certification-framework

[123] Open Web Application Security Project, "OWASP Top Ten," OWASP, https://owasp.org/www-project-top-ten/

[124] Open Web Application Security Project, "OWASP Mobile Security Testing Guide," OWASP, https://owasp.org/www-project-mobile-security-testing-guide/

[125] Open Web Application Security Project, "OWASP Web Security Testing Guide," OWASP, https://owasp.org/www-project-web-security-testing-guide/

- **Security Technical Implementation Guides (STIGs)**[126]—The Defense Information Systems Agency (DISA) is mandated to support and sustain the Department of Defense (DoD) Cyber Exchange, formally called the Information Assurance Support Exchange (IASE). Within the portal is content available by user category. The public version is https://public.cyber.mil.

- **Australian Essential Eight**[127]—The Australian Government's Signals Directorate and the Australian Cyber Security Centre regularly publishes IT Essential Eight which has become a *de facto* standard for Australian Security Professionals.

- **European Union Agency for Network and Information Security (ENISA) Publications**—ENISA actively contributes to European cybersecurity policy and collaborates with Member States to deliver a wide range of publications available at www.enisa.europa.eu/publications.

- **King IV Report on Corporate Governance™**—is a nonlegislative governance code for South Africa based on principles and practices. King Reports and other resources are available at www.iodsa.co.za/page/governance_main.

3.2.4 Compliance Sources

In a global landscape, different laws, regulations, and starts may apply to each industry or jurisdiction. The practitioner should identify specific compliance regulations applicable to their business. The following are a sample of the most common:

- **Health Insurance Portability and Accountability Act of 1996 (HIPAA)**—modernized transmission of information but more importantly addresses technical and nontechnical safeguards that organizations must put in place to secure individuals' "electronic protected health information" (e-PHI).[128]

- **Payment Card Industry (PCI)**—The Payment Card Industry council (founded in 2006 by American Express, Discover, JCB International, Mastercard and Visa) equally share governance and Council work. PCI security standards help merchants protect their payment systems.

- **EU Payment Services Directive 2 (PSD2)**[129]—Improves on the initial version of PSD adopted in 2007, which applied to digital payments. PSD2 enhances security and protection of consumer data[130] through strong customer authentication (SCA) and common and secure communications (CSC standards). PSD2 also opened the EU payments market to third-party payment service providers by forcing financial institutions grant access to consumer bank account access with account holder consent.[131]

- **General Data Protection Regulation (GDPR)**[132]—This European regulation applies to any business in any nation that does business with European citizens—regardless of location. GDPR is the toughest privacy and security law in the world and levies harsh fines for violating privacy and security standards. A GDPR fine tracker is available at www.privacyaffairs.com/gdpr-fines/.

- **Australian Prudential Regulation Authority (APRA) Prudential Guides**[133]—ARPA is an independent statutory authority accountable to the Australian Parliament that provides a comprehensive framework of reporting standards and guides.

---

[126] Defense Information Systems Agency (DISA), DoD Cyber Exchange, https://public.cyber.mil/

[127] Australian Government, "Essential Eight Explained," Australian Cyber Security Centre (ACSC), https://www.cyber.gov.au/acsc/view-all-content/publications/essential-eight-explained

[128] US Department of Health & Human Services, "Summary of the HIPAA Security Rule," HHS.gov, www.hhs.gov/hipaa/for-professionals/security/laws-regulations/index.html

[129] EUROPA, "Document 02015L2366-20151223," EUR-Lex, https://eur-lex.europa.eu/eli/dir/2015/2366/2015-12-23

[130] European Central Bank, "The revised Payment Services Directive (PSD2) and the transition to stronger payments security," March 2018, www.ecb.europa.eu/paym/intro/mip-online/2018/html/1803_revisedpsd.en.html

[131] Constantin, L.; "What is PSD2? And how it will impact the payments processing industry," CSO, 13 September 2019, www.csoonline.com/article/3390538/what-is-psd2-and-how-it-will-impact-the-payments-processing-industry.html

[132] Wolford, B.; "What is GDPR, the EU's new data protection law?," GDPR.EU, https://gdpr.eu/what-is-gdpr/

[133] Australian Prudential Regulation Authority, "APRA Regulated Industries," www.apra.gov.au/industries

---

- **Federal Information Security Management Act (FISMA)**[134]—Originally passed in 2002 to require federal agencies to implement an information security and protection program, it was amended in 2014 to codify authorities to authorize Department of Homeland Security additional authorities.

- **California Consumer Privacy Law (CCPA)**[135]—Enacted in 2018, CCPA creates new consumer rights with respect to personal information collected during business activities and was the first law of its kind in the United States. Unfortunately, if falls far short of GDPR in that it only applies to businesses that meet at least one of the following criteria:

    a. Has gross annual revenues in excess of US $25 million

    b. Buys, receives, or sells the personal information of 50,000 or more consumers, households, or devices

    c. Derives 50 percent or more of annual revenues from selling consumers' personal information

3.3 Architecture, Models and Frameworks

Technological changes continue to shape how we work and communicate at a rapid pace. In short, the business that fails to adapt to changing conditions will either struggle or worse, fail altogether. In other instances, businesses may find themselves in an iterative cycle of change that results in many anxious employees and a poor security climate. Recognizing that rapid change occurs both locally and globally, your security structure must be flexible enough to account for not just today's threats but also future threats.

An enterprise's security structure is better known as security architecture. ISO/IEC/IEEE 42010:2011 defines architecture as "the fundamental concepts or properties of a system in its environment embodied in its elements, relationships, and in the principles of its design and evolution."[136] For the purpose of this guide, security architecture refers to a unified security design that describes the structure, components, connections and layout of security controls within an enterprise IT infrastructure.

Just as no two enterprises are alike, no two security architectures are identical. There remain security professionals with a traditional mind-set who view security architecture as nothing more than having security policies, controls, tools, and monitoring in place.[137] As previously stated, rapid change is constant and trends such as cloud usage and an increasingly mobile workforce results in a fragmented approach ripe for cyberattacks.

To illustrate, an analogy of building architecture is used to describe security architecture. Architects are building designers who often project manage and oversee creation of buildings (InfoSec Goals). As such, they are knowledgeable in codes and ordinances (laws, regulations, best practice, etc.) that account for local conditions (IT environment and threat landscape). He or she will then collect requirements and any nice to have features from customers (enterprise stakeholders i.e. Board of Directors, senior management, business owners, security professionals). In turn, the architect begins designing a house in an iterative fashion, beginning with exterior shell (security framework or model) involving formal reviews, whereby the homeowners (stakeholders) review the design form and function (security components are complimentary, appropriate and responsive to business needs).

The pieces described previously largely influence an enterprise approach to defense in depth, or the practice of layering defenses to provide added protection. Security architecture informs layered defenses and relationships between each layer. Security architecture is essential to designing and implementing security controls in any complex environment.

Each component of a given system poses its own security risk. Because the topology of security architecture varies from one organization to another, a number of different variables and risk should be considered when addressing the

---

[134] Department of Homeland Security, "Federal Information Security Modernization Act," www.cisa.gov/federal-information-security-modernization-act

[135] State of California Department of Justice Office of the Attorney General, "California Consumer Privacy Act (CCPA)," https://oag.ca.gov/privacy/ccpa

[136] The Open Group, "2. Core Concepts," https://pubs.opengroup.org/architecture/togaf9-doc/arch/chap02.html

[137] Ghaznavi-Zadeh, R.; "Enterprise Security Architecture—A Top-down Approach," *ISACA Journal*, 28 July 2017, www.isaca.org/resources/isaca-journal/issues/2017/volume-4/enterprise-security-architecturea-top-down-approach

topology of a particular organization. This section discusses those variables individually, along with best practices for successfully managing their related risk.

3.3.1 The Perimeter

Many current security controls and architectures were developed with the concept of a perimeter—a well-defined (if mostly virtual) boundary between the enterprise and the outside world. In these models of cybersecurity, the focus is network- or system-centric. In the system-centric model, the emphasis is on placing controls at the network and system levels to protect the information stored within. An alternative model is data-centric, which emphasizes the protection of data regardless of its location.

With the advent of the Internet, outsourcing, mobile devices, cloud and other hosted services, the perimeter has expanded considerably. Consequently, there are significant new risk and vulnerabilities to confront in this hyper-connected and extended environment. The perimeter, then, is an important line of defense that protects the enterprise against external threats, and its design should reflect a proactive stance toward preventing potential risk.

A key component of the security perimeter is the Internet perimeter. This perimeter ensures secure access to the Internet for enterprise employees and guest users residing at all locations, including those involved in telecommuting or remote work. To provide security of email, front-end mobile and web apps, domain name system (DNS), etc., the Internet perimeter should:

- Route traffic between the enterprise and the Internet
- Prevent executable files from being transferred through email attachments or web browsing
- Monitor internal and external network ports for rogue activity
- Detect and block traffic from infected internal end point
- Control user traffic bound toward the Internet
- Identify and block anomalous traffic and malicious packets recognized as potential attacks
- Eliminate threats such as email spam, viruses and worms
- Enforce filtering policies to block access to websites containing malware or questionable content

The perimeter should also provide protection for virtual private networks (VPNs), wide area networks (WANs) and wireless local area networks (WLANs).

For VPNs, this protection should be threefold:

1. Terminate encrypted VPN traffic initiated by remote users.
2. Provide a hub for terminating encrypted VPN traffic from remote sites and organizations.
3. Provide a hub for terminating traditional dial-in users.

3.3.2 Interdependencies

As previously discussed, modern IT architectures are increasingly decentralized and therefore lack a solid perimeter. This includes a growing number of cloud-based platforms and services, and a shift in computing power and utilization patterns toward intelligent mobile devices, such as tablets or smartphones. Therefore, both the number of potential attack targets outside the organizational boundary and the number of attack vectors have grown. Conversely, the degree of control over perimeter-less environments is significantly lower—especially in enterprises permitting partial or full integration of user-owned mobile devices (i.e., BYOD). These changes have important ramifications for security architecture.

In distributed and decentralized IT architectures, the third-party risk is likely to increase, often as a function of moving critical applications, platforms and infrastructure elements into the cloud. For platforms, storage infrastructure and cloud-based data repositories, the focus of cybersecurity is shifting toward contracts and service level agreements (SLAs). Simultaneously, third-party cloud providers are facing an increased risk of attacks and breaches due to the agglomeration and clustering of sensitive data and information. In addition to concerns about third-party services, there is significant legal risk. Enterprises experiencing a loss of sensitive data may not be able to bring an action against the perpetrators because the cloud provider often must initiate legal action.

Regardless of the generic information security arrangements made by an enterprise, there are often exposed areas within IT architectures. Cybercrime and cyberwarfare perpetrators continue to aim at weak spots in architectural elements and systems. In contrast to indiscriminate and opportunistic attacks, APTs and cybercrime always rely on preparatory research and insight into the target enterprise. This, in turn, raises the level of exposure for weak or unsecured parts of the overall architecture. These vulnerable spots include legacy systems, unpatched parts of the architecture, shared use of mobile devices and many others.

3.3.3 Architectural Aids

A considerable number of architectural approaches currently exist, and many of them have evolved from the development of enterprise architecture. Although their specific details may differ, they all generally aim to articulate what processes a business performs and how those processes are executed and secured. They articulate the organization, roles, entities and relationships that exist or should exist to perform a set of business processes.

Similarly, models of security architecture typically fall into two categories: process models and framework models. By design, frameworks allow a great deal of flexibility in how each element of the architecture is developed. The essence of a framework is to describe the elements of architecture and how they relate to one another, while a process model is more directive in its approach to the processes used for the various elements. A recent example of a process model is a web server building block where it is exactly specified how a web server should be deployed and what processing is and is not allowed within that block.

3.3.4 Security Architecture Frameworks

As discussed previously, a framework is a system of rules, ideas, or beliefs used to plan or decide something[138] that helps attain business objectives. A security architecture framework helps enterprises take a system of systems approach tailored to their unique features and threats.

Architecture management allows enterprises a means of identifying present (as-is) and future (to-be) states and determine the set of actions and timeline to achieve it (evolution) while monitoring and reporting the achievement of architectural objectives. Just as there are many unique business enterprises, there are multiple approaches to security architecture.

---

[138] *Op cit* Cambridge University Press

Zachman Framework

According to Zachman International, Inc.:[139]

The Zachman Framework™ is a schema—the intersection between two historical classifications that have been in use for literally thousands of years. The first is the fundamentals of communication found in the primitive interrogatives: What, How, When, Who, Where, and Why. It is the integration of answers to these questions that enables the comprehensive, composite description of complex ideas. The second is derived from reification, the transformation of an abstract idea into an instantiation that was initially postulated by ancient Greek philosophers and is labeled in the Zachman Framework™: Identification, Definition, Representation, Specification, Configuration and Instantiation.

The Zachman Framework™ typically is depicted as a bounded 6x6 "matrix" with the Communication Interrogatives as Columns and the Reification Transformations as Rows. The Framework classifications are represented by the Cells, that is, the intersection between the Interrogatives and the Transformations. This matrix would necessarily constitute the total set of descriptive representations that are relevant for describing something... anything: in particular an enterprise.

The Zachman Framework™ is an ontology—a theory of the existence of a structured set of essential components of an object for which explicit expressions is necessary and perhaps even mandatory for creating, operating, and changing the object (the object being an Enterprise, a department, a value chain, a "sliver," a solution, a project, an airplane, a building, a product, a profession or whatever or whatever).

The Zachman Framework™ IS NOT a methodology for creating the implementation (an instantiation) of the object. The Framework IS the ontology for describing the Enterprise. The Framework (ontology) is a STRUCTURE whereas a methodology is a PROCESS. A Structure is NOT a Process. A Structure establishes definition whereas a Process provides Transformation.

The *Zachman Framework™* is represented as a matrix (**figure 3.1**) of columns and rows. Columns show aspects of the enterprise that can be described or modeled, while the rows represent various viewpoints from which those aspects can be considered. This approach provides a logical structure for classifying and organizing design elements, which improves the completeness of security architecture.

---

[139] Zachman, J.A.; "The Concise Definition of the Zachman Framework," 2008, www.zachman.com/about-the-zachman-framework

---

Figure 3.1—The Zachman Framework for Enterprise Architecture™

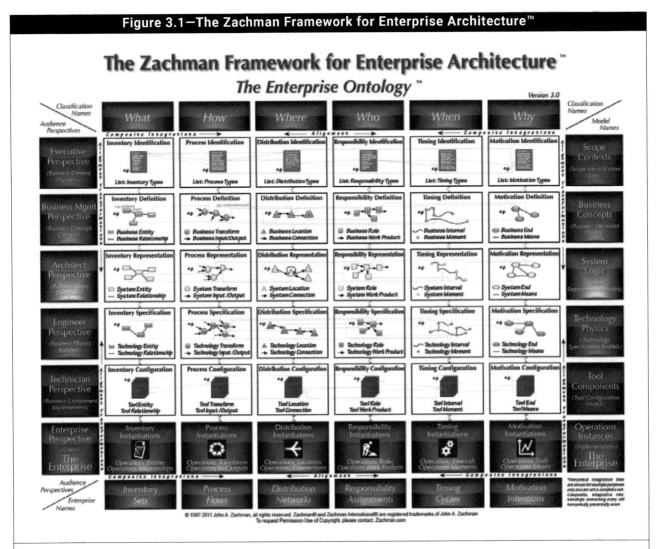

Source: Zachman, J.A.; "The Concise Definition of the Zachman Framework," 2008, www.zachman.com/about-the-zachman-framework. Published with the permission of John A. Zachman and *Zachman International*®, *Inc.*, www.zachman.com.

SABSA Framework

According to the SABSA Institute, the Sherwood Applied Business Security Architecture (SABSA) comprises integrated frameworks, models, methods and processes, used independently or as a holistic integrated enterprise solution.[140] SABSA offers seven primary features and benefits which are customizable by audience (i.e., board of directors, CEO, CISO, security architects)

- Business-driven
- Risk and opportunity balanced
- Comprehensive
- Modular
- Open source

[140] SABSA, Executive Summary, https://sabsa.org/sabsa-executive-summary/

- Auditable

- Transparent

SABSA is intended to be a life-cycle approach—that is, from requirements gathering through delivery and management of the security architecture. The SABSA Model comprises six layers that allow for different focus and deliverables. **Figure 3.2** illustrates the six perspectives alongside their associated functions and key activities.

Figure 3.2— SABSA Life Cycle Approach		
Perspective	**Function**	**Key Activity**
The Business View	Contextual Security Architecture	Understanding the business requirements
The Architect's View	Conceptual Architecture	Overall concept that defines principles and fundamental concepts that guide selection and organization of logical and physical elements
The Designer's View	Logical Security Architecture	Systems engineering activities based on outputs from above layers
The Builder's View	Physical Security Architecture	Logical specifications are turned into a physical security architecture model that specifies the detailed design of the various system components.
The Trademan's View	Component Security Architecture	Systems installation and integration
The Service Manger's View	Security Service Management Architecture	Ongoing operations and service

Source: Adapted from the SABSA Institute, "SABSA Enterprise Security Architecture Whitepaper," Table 1: Layered Architecture Views, page 9 or 25, https://sabsa.org/sabsa-white-paper-download-request

The Open Group Architecture Framework (TOGAF)

Another architecture framework is The Open Group TOGAF®Framework.[141] Developed by The Open Group in the 1990s, this high-level and holistic approach addresses security as an essential component of the overall enterprise design. The TOGAF Standard was revised in 2018 to version 9.2, which introduced structural changes, fixed errors, and removed obsolete content that enhanced usability and maintenance of the standard.

TOGAF documents consist of the TOGAF standard, TOGAF library, and TOGAF Series guides, which together support business, data, application, and technology architectures. The TOGAF standard comprised six parts, whereas the TOGAF library has four parts. At the time of this writing, TOGAF documentation includes 14 series guides. A current list is available at: www.opengroup.org/togaf-library. **(figure 3.3).**

Figure 3.3—The Open Group TOGAF® Framework				
TOGAF Standard		**TOGAF Library**		
Part 1: Introduction	• Provides a high-level introduction to the key concepts of enterprise architecture (EA), the TOGAF approach and glossary	Section 1 : Foundation Documents	• Broadly applicable information regarding the TOGAF framework	TOGAF Series Guides
Part II: Architecture Development Method	• Framework core which describes the TOGAF architecture development method (ADM)—a step-by-step approach to developing enterprise architecture	Section 2: Generic Guidelines and Techniques	• Describes architecture styles and adaptation of the TOGAF framework	

---

[141] The Open Group, "The TOGAF® Standard - Version 9.2," www.opengroup.org/togaf

Figure 3.3—The Open Group TOGAF® Framework *(cont.)*				
TOGAF Standard		**TOGAF Library**		
Part III: ADM Guidelines and Techniques	• Collection of guidelines and techniques to apply the TOGAF approach and the TOGAF ADM • Additional guidelines and techniques are also in the TOGAF library	Section 3: Industry-Specific Guidance and Techniques	• Describes architecture styles and adaptation of the TOGAF framework	TOGAF Series Guides
Part IV: Architecture Content Framework	• Describes the TOGAF content framework and provides an overview of typical architecture deliverables			
Part V: Enterprise Continuum and Tools	• Discusses taxonomies and tools to categorize and store architectural outputs	Section 4: Organization-Specific Guidance and Techniques	• Describes how the TOGAF framework and EA have been applied to specific enterprises	
Part VI: Architecture Capability Framework	• Discusses the organization, processes, skills, roles, and responsibilities required to establish and operate and enterprise architecture practice			

Source: Adapted from Andrew Josey, "Introduction to the TOGAF Standard, Version 9.2," The Open Group, April 2018, Tables 1 and 2, https://publications.opengroup.org/c182

3.3.5 Security Models

Security models are engineering models informed by policies that specify how a system will enforce security.[142],[143],[144] In this regard, an engineer decides what the system should do and then constructs the system to fulfill that need. These models differ from physical science, whereby models are used to make predictions about associated events and measures.

Two terms requiring explanation for this section include subjects and objects. Subjects are active and typically refer to either users or programs. Objects on the other hand are passive and typically refer to files and folders.

This section explores four security models: Bell-LaPadula, Biba, Clark-Wilson, and Brewer-Nash. These largely serve as a basis for access controls which are discussed later in this chapter.

Bell-LaPadula Confidentiality Model

The Bell-LaPadula (BLP) Model is a state machine[145] confidentiality model that protects hierarchies of classified data. BLP uses mandatory access controls (MACs), data classification, and security clearances. The BLP model

[142] Millen, J.K.; C.M. Cerniglia; "Computer Security Models," The MITRE Corporation, September 1984, https://apps.dtic.mil/dtic/tr/fulltext/u2/a166920.pdf

[143] Gregg, M.; *CISSP Exam Cram: Security Architecture and Models*, Pearson IT Certification, 4 February 2013, https://www.pearsonitcertification.com/articles/article.aspx?p=1998558&seqNum=4

[144] Miller, L.C.; Gregory, P.H.; *Common Access Control Models You Should Know for the CISSP Exam*, John Wiley & Sons, Inc., www.dummies.com/programming/certification/common-access-control-models-know-cissp-exam/

[145] A state machine is any device storing the status of something at a given time. Techopedia, "State Machine," 17 November 2015, www.techopedia.com/definition/16447/state-machine

allows subjects to read down and objects can write or append up. BLP has two access modes: simple security property and star (*) property.

- **Simple security (SS) property**—Subjects with lower clearance cannot read up but subjects with higher clearance can read down

- **Star (*) property**—Information from higher clearance cannot be written to lower levels (i.e., top secret to secret)

BLP was originally developed for the US Department of Defense and, because of its age (designed during the mainframe era), it is flawed by not addressing covert channels.

Biba Integrity Model

The Biba model is an integrity model that ensures objects or subjects cannot have less integrity through information processing. This model assigns integrity levels to subjects and objects using two properties:

- **Simple integrity (read)**—Allows subject to have read access to object only if subject possesses a security level equal to or lower than the object

- **Integrity * (write)**—Allows subject to have write access to object only if subject possesses a security level equal to or higher than the object

This model prevents contaminating data of higher integrity with data of lower integrity and is the go-to model when data integrity is paramount.

Clark & Wilson Integrity Model

The Clark & Wilson Integrity Model is built for commercial data, e.g., financial sector. It is based on change control principles and a concept of a well-formed transaction. Well-formed transactions ensure consistency and decrease the likelihood of unauthorized changes. Change control principles address three goals of integrity:

- No changes by unauthorized subjects

- No unauthorized changes by authorized subjects

- Maintains internal and external consistency

The Clark & Wilson model establishes a system of subject-program-object relationships that prevent direct access between subject and object. Instead, subjects must access objects using a program. This model provides an environment for separation of duty.

Brewer-Nash Model

This model is similar to BLP and was developed to prevent conflicts of interest whereby users who are permitted to view one set of data are prohibited from accessing the conflicting data. Also referred to as the Chinese Wall model, it is commonly used by accounting and consulting firms.

3.3.6 Layered Security

Because no single control or countermeasure can eliminate risk, it is often important to use several controls to protect an asset. This process of layering defenses is known as defense in depth, but it may also be called protection in depth or security in depth. It forces an adversary to defeat or avoid more than one control to gain access to an asset.

Defense in depth is an important concept in designing an effective information security strategy or architecture. When designed and implemented correctly, multiple control layers provide multiple opportunities for monitoring to detect the attack. Adding additional controls to overcome also creates a delay so that the attack may be interrupted and prevented.

The number and types of layers needed are a function of asset value, criticality, the reliability of each control and the degree of exposure. Excessive reliance on a single control is likely to create a false sense of confidence. For example, an enterprise that depends solely on a firewall can still be subject to numerous attack methodologies. A further defense may be to use education and awareness to create a human firewall, which can constitute a critical layer of defense. Segmenting the network can constitute yet another defensive layer.

Using a defense-in-depth strategy for implementing controls has several advantages, including increasing the effort required for a successful attack and creating additional opportunities to detect or delay an attacker. There are several ways defense in depth can be implemented, as shown in **figure 3.4**.

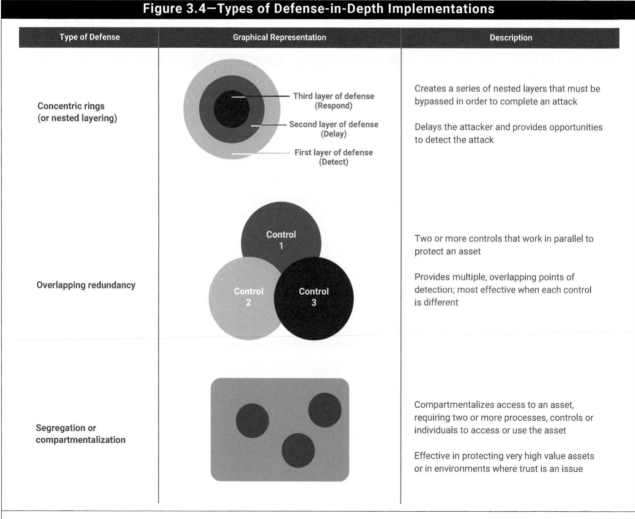

Figure 3.4—Types of Defense-in-Depth Implementations

Type of Defense	Graphical Representation	Description
Concentric rings (or nested layering)	Third layer of defense (Respond); Second layer of defense (Delay); First layer of defense (Detect)	Creates a series of nested layers that must be bypassed in order to complete an attack Delays the attacker and provides opportunities to detect the attack
Overlapping redundancy	Control 1; Control 2; Control 3	Two or more controls that work in parallel to protect an asset Provides multiple, overlapping points of detection; most effective when each control is different
Segregation or compartmentalization		Compartmentalizes access to an asset, requiring two or more processes, controls or individuals to access or use the asset Effective in protecting very high value assets or in environments where trust is an issue

Source: Anderson, K.; "Security Controls: Introduction and Theory," Encurve, LLC Training PowerPoint Presentation, 2020

Another way to think about defense in depth is from an architectural perspective:

- **Horizontal defense in depth**—Controls are placed in various places in the path of access for an asset, which is functionally equivalent to concentric ring model shown in **figure 3.5**

- **Vertical defense in depth**—Controls are placed at different system layers—hardware, operating system, application, database, or user levels

Using defense-in-depth techniques requires effective planning and understanding of each type's strengths and weaknesses as well as how the controls interact. It is easy to create an overly complex system of controls, and too many layers can be as bad as too few. When developing defense-in-depth implementations, consider the following questions:

- What vulnerabilities are addressed by each layer or control?

- How does the layer mitigate the vulnerability?

- How does each control interact with or depend on the other controls?

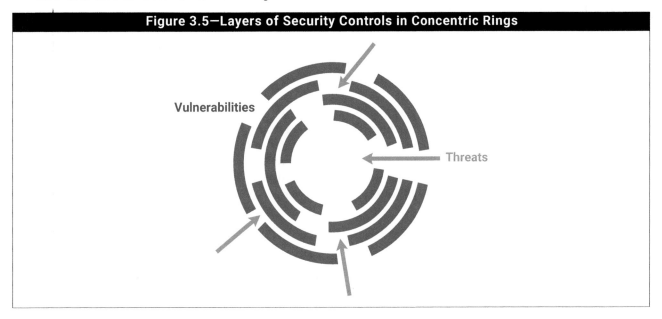

Figure 3.5—Layers of Security Controls in Concentric Rings

3.3.7 Zero Trust

Network perimeters are no longer well-defined and security professionals face the daunting task of protecting increasingly decentralized corporate assets. Traditional security philosophy entailed a "castle and mote" model whereby enterprises believed that shoring up defenses at the outermost perimeter would thwart all attacks. They further believed that a layered or tiered approach would catch anyone who successfully penetrated the castle. Ultimately discredited by countless breach reports, this philosophy is obviously flawed.

Zero Trust is not new—it originated in 2009 by then Forrester® researcher and analyst John Kindervag, who is widely referenced as the "Godfather of Zero Trust Networking."[146] Zero Trust continues to gain popularity and advance the assume-breach mindset. Assume breach philosophy teaches that:

- Networks are generally not secure.

- Networks likely have already breached.

- Breaches have just not yet been discovered.

---

[146] For more information regarding Zero Trust, see ShortestPathFirst blog, "Interview with John Kindervag, the Godfather of Zero Trust Networking," 30 April 2019, https://youtu.be/yo6Z7fIJ11A. See also Cunningham, C.; J. Pollard; S. Balaouras; "The Tao Of Zero Trust," Forrester, 25 March 2019, https://go.forrester.com/blogs/the-tao-of-zero-trust/; and Cunningham, C.; "Zero Trust in Action," Forrester, 8 August 2019, https://go.forrester.com/blogs/zero-trust-in-practice/.

Forrester continues to drive the industry towards widespread Zero Trust adoption with a wealth of research that includes periodic vendor reviews and their Zero Trust eXtended (ZTX) framework.

So why Zero Trust? The reason is simple—trust relationships have failed miserably (and repeatedly). Further, trying to fix security woes from the outside in is a losing proposition.

The premise behind Zero Trust is to "never trust, always verify."[147] Traditional network security devices (i.e., firewalls, IDS, IPS) primarily exist to govern data in and out of an enterprise's entry point—sometimes referred to as north-south traffic.[148] Enterprises should focus on restricting lateral movement (or east-west traffic) within the environment and enhancing identity-based decisions within the environment. Material covered in the Network Security section later in this chapter is foundational and important as ever. However, just as the threat landscape matures, so too must our defenses.

Today, authentication, key infrastructures, microsegmentation and virtualization are important components towards achieving a Zero Trust environment. New methods and technologies will undoubtedly appear in the future but should only enhance the ability of an enterprise to inspect and verify identity and health of users, endpoints, services and applications.

Admittedly, most enterprises may be unwilling to scrap their enterprise IT ecosystem and rebuild it. A mistake made by many enterprises is to tackle the totality of the problem—which results in various mediocre outcomes.

The major thing to consider when embarking on a Zero Trust journey is to start small. Pick one thing and fix that before moving on. Use a building block approach, rather than trying to win the war immediately.

Since at least 2019, there has been a resurgence of interest in Zero Trust, and vendors are responding, flooding the market with purported Zero Trust solutions. Note, however, that Kindervag states there are no Zero Trust products—there are only products that help enterprises make Zero Trust networks.

3.4 Security Controls

Security controls are actions, devices, procedures, techniques, or other measures that reduce the vulnerability of an information system.[149] Controls differ by category and purpose. The remainder of this chapter serves to provide foundational understanding of the many countermeasures available to enterprises to defend their networks, intellectual property and resources. Control selection is a deliberate activity that requires the outputs from risk assessments. Risk assessments craft statements that identify end goals, which then inform control selection, as illustrated in **figure 3.6**. Security controls are categorized by type and function. There are two key aspects that controls should address—what should be achieved and what should be avoided.[150]

---

[147] Bonderud, D.; "Verify to Simplify: Demystifying Zero Trust," *Security Intelligence*, 28 January 2020, https://securityintelligence.com/media/verify-to-simplify-demystifying-zero-trust/
[148] Bendnarz, A.; "What is microsegmentation? How getting granular improves network security," NetworkWorld, 30 January 2020, https://www.networkworld.com/article/3247672/what-is-microsegmentation-how-getting-granular-improves-network-security.html
[149] National Institute of Standards and Technology, *FIPS 200: Minimum Security Requirements for Federal Information and Information Systems*, March 2006, https://csrc.nist.gov/publications/detail/fips/200/final
[150] ISACA, *CISA Review Manual 27th Edition*, USA, www.isaca.org/bookstore/cisa-exam-resources/crm27ed

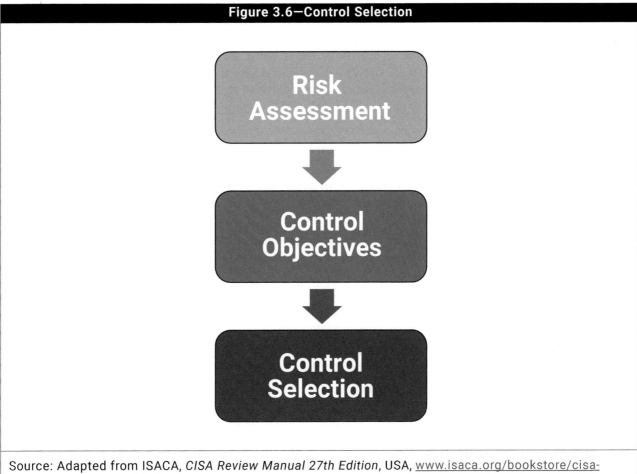

Figure 3.6—Control Selection

Source: Adapted from ISACA, *CISA Review Manual 27th Edition*, USA, www.isaca.org/bookstore/cisa-exam-resources/crm27ed

3.4.1 Types of Controls

There are three main types of security controls—physical, technical and administrative. It is not unusual to also see these referred to as *categories* of controls.

Physical Controls

Chapter 1 defined physical security as the part of security concerned with physical measures designed to safeguard personnel; to prevent unauthorized access to equipment, installations, material and documents; and to safeguard against espionage, sabotage, damage and theft.[151] Therefore, physical controls are security measures meant to deter or prevent access to sensitive equipment and information processing. Examples of physical security controls include:

- Alarm systems
- Badges
- Locks
- Security guards
- Video surveillance systems

[151] Department of the Army, *Physical Security*, "Chapter 1," Field Manual 3-19.30, 8 January 2001, www.globalsecurity.org/military/library/policy/army/fm/3-19-30/index.html

Physical Security Components

It is common to narrowly limit our understanding of physical security mechanisms to the examples above. As illustrated in **figure 1.7**, the modern physical security landscape is robust and often encompasses environmental controls. It is possible that many security professionals will never deal with all the following physical security components; however they are all important considerations for the overall security posture and risk profile of an enterprise:

- **Emergency power**—Improper equipment shutdowns and power surges damage sensitive electronic equipment. Backup power sources are sized for intended system load which requires an understanding of your core systems and service needs during power outages.

- **Electromagnetic interference (EMI) shielding**—EMI shielding prevents data leakage and interference. Additionally, modern electrical code typically addresses this by specifying how to run network communications cables in buildings.

- **Fire suppression**—Modern building codes require fire suppression systems for life safety. Types and locations of fire suppression systems should be considered during business continuity planning.

- **Infrastructure**—Server rooms and datacenters are typically occupied which minimizes the likelihood of unauthorized access and any damage should be easily observable by employees in rooms. However, distributed networking equipment (i.e., wireless access points) and cabling runs require periodic checks. Business continuity plans must also account for underground distribution interruptions (i.e., fiber) due to construction.

- **Locks**—Locks may be traditional types or electronic (e.g., PIN codes and proximity) or biometric. The type and style of lock is influenced by the sensitivity of the information processing facility.

- **Airlock (also known as a mantrap)**—An airlock is an access control mechanism used for accessing sensitive areas. Mantraps have locked doors on both sides with a lock mechanism closest to the sensitive space. Failure to successfully enter a personal access code (e.g., keycode, proximity reader and biometrics) locks the person in the room pending a human response.

- **Proximity readers**—These are access cards that are read for a short distance away via electromagnetic waves.

- **Temperature and humidity controls**—Environmental controls are increasingly connected to IT networks. The Target Breach[152] is a popular reminder of the threat that external access allows.

The physical security profession has a proud, longstanding history and, although physical security continues to converge with IT-related security, the two worlds remain very much distinct today. Cybersecurity professionals working in either IT or OT, who may have greater involvement with physical security, are encouraged to check out the Security Industry Alliance, which offers many resources for standards and security-specific project management.[153]

Technical Controls

Technical controls are IT specific software, tools and technologies that help minimize cyberrisk. Cybersecurity is a dynamic and ever-changing environment and requires continuous monitoring, updating, testing, patching and changing as technology and business evolve. These controls are critical to maintaining security within any enterprise IT infrastructure. Failure to address these processes is one of the top causes of security breaches in enterprises. Examples include:

- Antivirus software

- Data loss prevention (DLP) solutions

- Encryption

- Firewalls

---

[152] *Op cit* US Senate
[153] Security Industry Association, 2020, www.securityindustry.org/

Mandatory and Discretionary Access Controls

Mandatory access controls (MACs) are logical access control filters used to validate access credentials that cannot be controlled or modified by normal users or data owners; they act by default. Controls that may be configured or modified by the users or data owners are called discretionary access controls (DACs)[154].

MACs are a good choice to enforce a ground level of critical security without possible exception, if this is required by enterprise security policies or other security rules. A MAC can be carried out by comparing the sensitivity of the information resources, such as files, data or storage devices, which is kept on a user-unmodifiable tag that is attached to the security object, with the security clearance of the accessing entity, such as a user or an application. With MACs, only administrators may make decisions that are derived from policy. Only an administrator may change the category of a resource, and no one may grant a right of access that is explicitly forbidden in the access control policy. MACs are prohibitive; anything that is not expressly permitted is forbidden.

DACs are a protection that may be activated or modified at the discretion of the data owner. This would be the case of data owner-defined sharing of information resources, where the data owner selects who is enabled to access his/her resource and the security level of this access. DACs cannot override MACs; DACs act as an additional filter, prohibiting still more access with the same exclusionary principle.

When information systems enforce MAC policies, the systems must distinguish between MAC and the discretionary policies that offer more flexibility. This distinction must be ensured during object creation, classification downgrading and labeling.

Administrative Controls

Administrative controls address the human element and therefore are occasionally called management controls. Administrative controls include:

- Policies
- Procedures
- Guidance
- Security Awareness Training

Purpose of Policies

Information security policies are a primary element of security and overall security governance. They specify requirements and define the roles and responsibilities of everyone in the enterprise, along with expected behaviors in various situations. Therefore, they must be properly created, accepted and validated by the board and senior management before being disseminated throughout the enterprise. During this process, there may be occasions where other documents must be created to address unique situations separate from the bulk of the enterprise. This may be necessary when part of the enterprise has a specific regulatory requirement to protect certain types of information. Policies will often cascade down to procedures and guidelines.

---

[154] *Op cit* ISACA, *CISA Review Manual 27th Edition*

Policy Life Cycle

In addition to a policy framework, another important aspect of information security policies is their life cycle of development, maintenance, approval and exception.

Every compliance document should have a formal process of being created, reviewed, updated and approved at least once a year. Additionally, there may be legitimate need for an exception to a policy; therefore, a clear process of how an exception is approved by senior management and monitored during the life cycle is necessary.

Guidelines

There are several attributes of good policies that should be considered:

- Security policies should be an articulation of a well-defined information security strategy that captures the intent, expectations and direction of management.
- Policies must be clear and easily understood by all affected parties.
- Policies should be short and concise, written in plain language.

Most enterprises should create security policies prior to developing a security strategy. Although many enterprises tend to follow an ad hoc approach to developing security strategy, there are also instances, especially in smaller enterprises, where effective practices have been developed that may not be reflected in written policies. Existing practices that adequately address security requirements may usefully serve as the basis for policy and standards development. This approach minimizes organizational disruptions, communications of new policies, and resistance to new or unfamiliar constraints.

3.4.2 Compliance Documents and Policy Frameworks

Compliance documents, such as policies, standards and procedures, outline the actions that are required or prohibited. Violations may be subject to disciplinary actions.

Some common compliance document types are shown in **figure 3.7**.

Figure 3.7—Compliance Document Types	
Type	**Description**
Policies	Communicate required and prohibited activities and behaviors
Standards	Interpret policies in specific situations
Procedures	Provide details on how to comply with policies and standards
Guidelines	Provide general guidance on issues such as "what to do in particular circumstances." These are not requirements to be met but are strongly recommended.

Some enterprises may not implement all of these types of documents. For example, smaller enterprises may simply have policies and procedures; others may have policies, standards and procedures, but not guidelines.

Policy Frameworks

The way that compliance documents relate to and support each other is called a policy framework. A framework defines different types of documents and what is contained in each. Enterprises may have simple or relatively complex policy frameworks depending on their unique needs. Enterprises may define a separate cybersecurity policy, but this should always be part of the overarching information security policy framework.

The number and type of policies that an enterprise chooses to implement varies based on the enterprise size, culture, risk, regulatory requirements and complexity of operations. However, following are some common examples and the type of information they might contain.[155]

Types of Policies

General Information Security Policy

Most enterprises have a general, high-level information security policy that may stand alone as a single policy or serve as a foundation for other compliance documents.

A comprehensive security policy should include statements that clearly document information security processes and procedures and drive compliance. Comprehensive policy would cover items including:

- Application security
- Architecture
- Cloud security
- Controls
- Encryption
- Endpoint security
- Engineering
- Information asset management
- Information classification
- Information security management (ISM)
- Mobile security
- Network and Internet security
- Patch management
- Program management
- Risk management
- Secure development
- Security assurance
- Security awareness and training
- Security configuration
- Security monitoring
- Security operations center (SOC)
- Security reporting
- Security testing
- Strategy
- Systems security
- Third-party risk
- Vulnerability management

---

[155] ISACA, *COBIT® 5 for Information Security*, USA, 2012, www.isaca.org/bookstore/cobit-5/wcb5is

For larger enterprises, it is common practice to subdivide policies by topic to address all of the information security. An example of such a subdivision is shown in **figure 3.8**.

Figure 3.8—COBIT 5 Information Security Policy Set

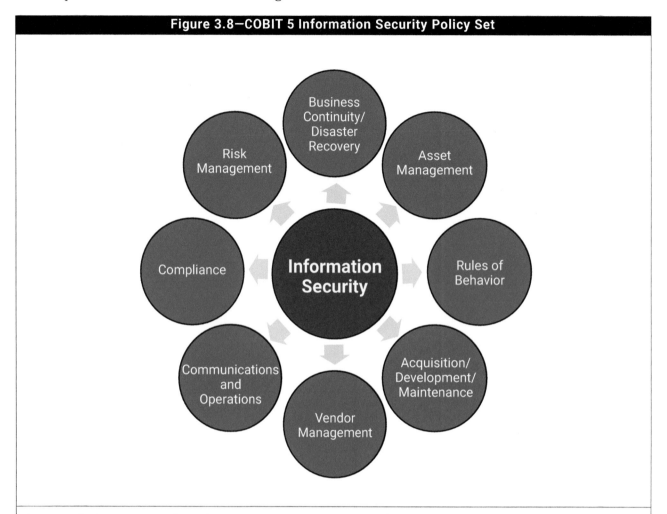

Source: ISACA, *COBIT® 5 for Information Security*, USA, 2012, figure 23, www.isaca.org/bookstore/cobit-5/wcb5is; see Section 3.7.2 of ISACA, *COBIT Focus Area: Information Security*, USA, 2020, https://www.isaca.org/bookstore/bookstore-cobit_19-print/cb19is, for the latest guidance.

Each of these policies requires the input of information security. Examples for a possible relevant scope for information security are as follows:[156]

- Business continuity and disaster recovery:
  - Business impact analysis (BIA)
  - Business contingency plans with trusted recovery
  - Recovery requirements for critical systems
  - Defined thresholds and triggers for contingencies and escalation
- Disaster recovery plan (DRP)
  - Training and Testing
- Asset management:
  - Data classification and ownership

---

[156] *Ibid.*

- ■ System classification and ownership
- ■ Resource utilization and prioritization
- ■ Asset life cycle management
- ■ Asset protection
- Rules of behavior:
  - ■ At-work acceptable use and behavior, including privacy, Internet/email, mobile devices, BYOD, etc.
  - ■ Offsite acceptable use and behavior, including social media, blogs
- Acquisition/development/maintenance:
  - ■ Information security within the life cycle, requirements definition and procurement/acquisition processes
  - ■ Secure coding practices
  - ■ Integration of information security with change and configuration management
- Supply chain management:
  - ■ Contract management
  - ■ Communication and operations:
  - ■ IT information security architecture and application design
  - ■ Service level agreements
- Compliance:
  - ■ IT information security compliance assessment process
  - ■ Development of metrics
  - ■ Assessment repositories
- Risk management:
  - ■ Organizational risk management plan
  - ■ Information risk profile

The appearance and length of an information security policy varies greatly among enterprises. Some enterprises consider a one-page overview to be a sufficient information security policy. In these cases, the policy could be considered a directive or a policy statement, and it should clearly describe links to other specific policies. In other enterprises, the information security policy is fully developed, containing nearly all the detailed guidance needed to put the principles into practice. It is important to understand what the information stakeholders expect in terms of coverage and to adapt to this expectation.

Regardless of its size or degree of detail, the information security policy needs a clearly defined scope. This involves:

- The enterprise definition of information security
- The responsibilities associated with information security
- The vision for information security, accompanied by appropriate goals, metrics, and rationale of how the vision is supported by the information security culture and awareness
- Explanation of how the information security policy aligns with other high-level organizational policies
- Elaboration on specific information security topics, such as data management, information risk assessment and compliance with legal, regulatory and contractual obligations

In addition to the elements discussed above, a policy may potentially affect the security life cycle budget and cost management. Information security strategic plans and portfolio management can be added as well. The information security strategy ideally aligns with the technology strategy and cascades from the overall corporate vision.

The policy should be actively communicated to the entire enterprise and distributed to all employees, contractors, temporary employees, and third-party vendors. Stakeholders need to know the information principles, high-level requirements, and roles and responsibilities for information security. The responsibility for updating and revalidating the information security policy lies with the cybersecurity function.

Other possible security policies or procedures include access control, personnel information, and security incidents.

Access Control Policy

An access control policy provides proper access to internal and external stakeholders to accomplish business goals. This can be measured by metrics such as, but not limited to, the:

- Number of access violations that exceed the amount allowed
- Amount of work disruption due to insufficient access rights
- Number of segregation of duties incidents or audit findings

Additionally, the access control policy should ensure that emergency access is appropriately permitted and revoked in a timely manner. Metrics related to this goal include the number of emergency access requests and the number of active emergency accounts in excess of approved time limits.

The access control policy should cover the following topics, among others:

- Physical and logical access provisioning life cycle
- Least privilege/need to know
- Segregation of duties
- Emergency access

This policy is meant for all corresponding business units, vendors and third parties. Updates and revalidation should involve Human Resources, data and system owners, information security, and senior management. A new or updated policy should be distributed to all corresponding business units, vendors and third parties.

Personnel Information Security Policy

The personnel information security policy objective includes, but is not limited to, the following goals:

- Identify key personnel.
- Execute background checks of all employees and people in key positions. This goal can be measured by counting the number of completed background checks for key personnel. This should be a standard part of onboarding that ideally eliminates any omissions. Some jurisdictions and enterprises require periodic renewals which may identify issues if employees did not self-report.
- Acquire information about key personnel in information security positions.
- Develop a succession plan for all key information security positions. A starting point is to list all the critical information security positions that lack backup personnel.
- Define and implement appropriate procedures for termination. This should include details about revoking account privileges and access.

This policy is meant for all corresponding business units, vendors, and third parties. Updates and revalidation should involve Human Resources, the privacy officer, the legal department, information security, and facility security. A new or updated policy needs to be distributed to employees, contract personnel, vendors under contract and temporary employees.

Security Incident Response Policy

This policy addresses the need to respond to (security) incidents in a timely manner in order to recover business activities. This policy is meant for all corresponding business units and key employees. Updates and revalidation should involve the information security function. A new or updated policy should be distributed to key employees.

A Security Incident Response Policy should include:

- A definition of an information security incident
- A statement of how incidents will be handled
- Requirements for the establishment of the incident response team, with organizational roles and responsibilities
- Requirements for the creation of a tested incident response plan, which will provide documented procedures and guidelines for:
    - Criticality of incidents
    - Reporting and escalation processes
    - Recovery (including):
        - **Recovery point objectives (RPOs)**—The RPO is determined based on the acceptable data loss in case of disruption of operations. It indicates the most recent point in time to which it is acceptable to recover the data, which generally is the latest backup. RPO effectively quantifies the permissible amount of data loss in case of interruption. Depending on the volume of data, it may be advisable to reduce the time between backups to prevent a situation where recovery becomes impossible because of the volume of data to be restored. It may also be the case that the time required to restore a large volume of data makes it impossible to achieve the RTO.[157]
        - **Recovery time objectives (RTOs)** for return to the trusted state, including:
            - Investigation and preservation of process
            - Testing and training
            - Post incident meetings to document root cause analysis and enhancements of information security practices that prevent similar future events
            - Incident documentation and closing

Security Incident Response Policies should align with applicable laws and regulations for the enterprise industry and jurisdiction.

3.4.3 Control Functions

Next, security controls are divided into three functions[158] or classes—preventative, detective and corrective—illustrated in **figure 3.9**:

- As the name implies, preventative controls are used to prevent errors, omissions, or malicious acts. These controls monitor conditions to detect problems early and may be predictive in nature allowing for adjustments to thwart big problems.
- Detective controls detect and report the occurrence of an error, omission, or malicious act.
- Corrective controls remedy problems discovered by detective controls to minimize the impact of a threat. They further serve to minimize future occurrences of the problem.

---

[157] ISACA, *CISM Review Manual 15th Edition*, USA, 2016, www.isaca.org/bookstore/cism-exam-resources/cm15ed
[158] *Op cit* ISACA, CISA Review Manual 27th Edition

Figure 3.9—Security Controls and Functions			
		CONTROL TYPES	
	Physical	Technical	Administrative
Preventative	Locks, barriers (e.g., fences, gates), air lock	Surveillance cameras	Maintenance of preventative controls, verification of authorized access
Detective	Firewall, endpoint protections	Intrusion detection systems, honeypots	System patching and maintenance, virus quarantine
Corrective	HR policies (e.g., new hire and termination), segregation of duties, principle of least privilege	Identity and access management, audit findings	BCP and IRP implementation

(CONTROL FUNCTIONS shown along left vertical axis)

3.4.4 Control Resources

An excellent resource for gaining more in-depth knowledge on cybersecurity controls is the Center for Internet Security (CIS) Critical Security Controls.[159] It provides actionable guidance to stop the most pervasive and dangerous attacks in the current environment. The CIS Critical Security Controls are derived from common attack patterns as provided by leading threat reports from a wide community of industry practitioners. They provide an organized means for cybersecurity professionals to address these common threats and attacks.

3.4.5 Evaluating Security Controls

After risk is identified and prioritized, existing controls should be analyzed to determine their effectiveness in mitigating the risk. This analysis will result in a final risk ranking based on adequate controls, inadequate controls or no controls being in place.

A very important criterion in control selection and evaluation is that the cost of the control (including its operation) should not exceed value of the asset or data it is protecting.

3.4.6 Identity and Access Management

Identity and access management encapsulates people, processes and products to identify and manage the data used in an information system to authenticate users and grant or deny access rights to data and system resources. The goal of identity and access management (IAM) is to provide appropriate access to enterprise resources.[160] IAM relies on access control to carry out who can do what on information systems. Access control consists of identification, authentication and authorization. Another key aspect of access control is accounting. An industry framework to control access is often referred to as AAA—authentication, authorization and accounting.

Identification

Cybersecurity relies upon the establishment and maintenance of user profiles that define the authentication, authorization and access controls for each user. Today, enterprises have a variety of ad hoc processes and tools to manage and provision user identity information. Identity management focuses on streamlining various business processes needed to manage all forms of identities in an organization—from enrollment to retirement. Usernames remain the prominent method of user identification.

---

[159] Center for Internet Security®, "CIS Controls®," www.cisecurity.org/controls/
[160] *Op cit* ISACA, "Glossary"

The ability to integrate business processes and technology is critically important in the emerging model because it links people to systems and services. A key objective of identity management is to centralize and standardize this process so that it becomes a consistent and common service across the enterprise.

Identity management comprises many components that provide a collective and common infrastructure, including directory services, authentication services (validating who the user is) and authorization services (ensuring the user has appropriate privileges to access systems based on a personalized profile). It also includes user-management capabilities, such as user provisioning and deprovisioning, and can include the utilization of federated identity management (FIM).

FIM allows a user from one business entity to seamlessly access resources of another business entity in a secure and trustworthy manner. Federated single sign-on (SSO) between the issuing domain (identity provider) and a relying domain (service provider) facilitates the secure and trusted transfer of user identifiers and other attributes. FIM also supports standards-based trust and security for applications exposed as web services.

Authentication

Authentication is the process of proving that people are who they say they are. This procedure is at the core of every security system in use today. These systems have layers of protection to keep people who are not meant to be there, or to have access, out of the network and away from data.[161] These processes cover the back doors and prevent the infiltration of malware. Authentication is the process of allowing permitted access through the front door of a network.

Types (or factors)

Generations of security professionals have been taught three foundational factors of authentication:[162]

- **Something you know**—passwords, PINs, challenge-response answers
- **Something you have**—ID cards, smart cards
- **Something you are**—biometrics (i.e., fingerprints, retinal scanners)

Over time, these have expanded to five types of authorization to account for technological advances:[163],[164]

- **Type 1**—Something you know
- **Type 2**—Something you have
- **Type 3**—Something you are
- **Type 4**—Somewhere you are; options include geofencing or MAC address
- **Type 5**—Something you do; generally, pattern-based options (i.e., drawing patterns or pictures) that take advantage of touch screen technology; commonly known as behavioral biometrics

We strengthen authentication using multifactor authentication (MFA). Every authentication system can be compromised and should not, particularly those with high-value assets (e.g., banks, power plants), rely on a single form of authentication. "The goal of MFA is to create a layered defense and make it more difficult for an unauthorized person to access a computer system or network."[165]

[161] Hale, C.; "Security in Depth," *ISACA Journal*, vol 3, 2018, www.isaca.org/resources/isaca-journal/issues/2018/volume-3/security-in-depth

[162] Gibson, D.; "Understanding the Three Factors of Authentication," Pearson IT Certification, 6 June 2011, www.pearsonitcertification.com/articles/article.aspx?p=1718488

[163] Dias, R.; "The 5 Factors of Authentication," Medium, 8 December 2017, https://medium.com/@renansdias/the-5-factors-of-authentication-bcb79d354c13

[164] Pederson, T.; "CISSP – IAAA (Identification and Authentication, Authorization and Accountability)," 13 April 2019, https://thorteaches.com/cissp-iaaa/

[165] Mohamed, T.S.; "Security of Multifactor Authentication Model to Improve Authentication Systems," *Information and Knowledge Management*, vol. 4, issue 6, 2014, www.iiste.org/Journals/index.php/IKM/article/viewFile/13871/13939

Designers can use several options to achieve MFA. Security designers combine two or more of the three categories to create MFA. Two-factor authorization (2FA) always uses two factors whereas MFA could involve two or more. The procedure is effective only when two or more passwords are required. For example, a person accessing a financial database may be required to enter a password (something he/she knows), then enter the code from a smart card (something he/she has), and may still be required to scan a fingerprint or iris for access. Following this process allows for layered security during authentication. 2FA or MFA are absolute musts for a Zero Trust approach.

Behavioral Biometrics[166]

Behavioral biometrics is the measurement and recording of human behavioral patterns and their use to verify and authenticate an individual computer user, either in real time or retrospectively. Rather than focusing on the outcome of an activity, behavioral biometrics focuses on how a user conducts the specified activity, such as how quickly a user is typing or identifying abnormal use or activities.

Behavioral biometrics technology is commonly deployed four ways—continuous authentication, risk-based authentication, insider threat detection and fraud detection and prevention.

Multifactor Pitfalls

Just because an enterprise uses two factors of authentication does not make it multifactor. True multifactor authentication requires users to provide the multiple factors *before* authentication occurs. If the second factor is only requested after the first is successful, this is "multi-step" authentication. As written by Dias, "this approach is not ideal because if the username and password are correct, the process then becomes single-factor authentication."[167]

Multistep Authentication ≠ Multifactor Authentication

Authorization

The authorization process used for access control requires that the system be able to identify and differentiate among users.[168] Access rules (authorizations) specify who can access what. For example, access control is often based on least privilege, which means granting users only those accesses required to perform their duties. Access should be on a documented need-to-know and need-to-do basis by type.

Computer access can be set for various levels (e.g., files, tables, and data items). When information systems auditors review computer accessibility, they need to know what can be done with the access and what is restricted. For example, access restrictions at the file level generally include the following:

- Read only
- Write, create, update only
- Delete only
- Execute only
- A combination of the above

The least dangerous type of access is read-only, so long as the information being accessed is not sensitive or confidential. This is because the user cannot alter or use the computerized file beyond basic viewing or printing.

---

[166] International Biometrics+Identity Association, "Behavioral Biometrics," www.ibia.org/download/datasets/3839/Behavioral%20Biometrics%20white%20paper.pdf
[167] *Op cit* Dias, Renan
[168] *Op cit* ISACA, *CISA Review Manual 27th Edition*

Accountability

Accountability is the ability to map a given activity or event back to the responsible party.[169] This aspect reinforces nonrepudiation—which denies that the event or transaction occurred.

Provisioning and Deprovisioning

User provisioning is part of the enterprise hiring process where user accounts are created. Passwords and access control rights are generally assigned based on the job duties of the users. This can be a complicated process, because users may need access to many resources, such as systems, databases, email, applications and remote services, each of which has its own access control, passwords, encryption keys, or other authorization and authentication requirements. Additionally, access control rights often change based on shifting job requirements, so it is frequently necessary to update access controls and remove access that is no longer needed. Likewise, when a user leaves an enterprise, their accounts need to be deprovisioned—meaning that all accounts and accesses must be suspended or deleted in a timely manner.

Privileged User Management

Privileged access permits administrators to maintain and protect systems and networks. Privileged users can often access any information stored within a system, which means they can modify or circumvent existing safeguards such as access controls and logging. Privileged user typically refers to the administrators of systems, networks, servers or workstations.

Because of this elevated access, enterprises need to think carefully about privileged users and accounts and apply additional controls to them. Common controls include:

- Limiting privileged access to only those who require it to perform their job functions
- Performing background checks on individuals with elevated access
- Implementing additional logging of activity associated with privileged accounts
- Maintaining accountability by never sharing privileged accounts
- Using stronger passwords or other authentication controls to protect privileged accounts from unauthorized access
- Reviewing accounts regularly for privileges and removing those no longer required
- Requiring privileged users to maintain two accounts (elevated and nonelevated) and mandate the use of nonelevated access accounts to general duties, such as email, documenting, and accessing the Internet

3.4.7 Network Security

As discussed in Chapter 1, network security is a subset of cybersecurity and by extension—information security. National Institute of Standards and Technology (NIST) defines network security very rigidly for its publications.[170] Very similar to the NIST definition is the ISO/IEC 27033-1:2015 definition which states, "network security applies to the security of devices, security of management activities related to the devices, applications/services and end users, in addition to security of the information being transferred across the communication links."[171] Various aspects of security are interrelated and nowhere is that more prevalent than in network security. Network security is more

---

[169] *Op cit* ISACA, "Glossary"
[170] *Op cit* National Institute of Standards and Technology, "Glossary"
[171] International Organization for Standardization, ISO/IEC 27033-1:2015 *Information technology — Security techniques — Network security — Part 1: Overview and concepts*, www.iso.org/standard/63461.html

than securing network traffic (logical connections)—it has become a complex aspect that includes protecting physical networking equipment, such as routers and access points and a growing number of cloud services.

Isolation and Segmentation

Network segmentation and systems isolation has always been an important strategy however the convergence of vulnerable OT systems has amplified this. Security professionals must be business partners in the sense that they understand the business owner's needs and concerns and work with them to implement security strategies that appropriately mitigate risk.

Security professionals will find systems in service that are no longer supported (e.g., Windows XP), OT systems that cannot be taken offline, and a plethora of IoT devices with vulnerabilities. Oftentimes, isolating them from core IT business services is best. Although still vulnerable, treating them in isolation minimizes the likelihood of lateral movement if an attack occurs. Further, it enables individualizing protection and monitoring.

The Zero Trust approach heavily leverages virtualization and entails very granular segmentations to minimize the damage when attacks occur—because they will.

Security and Demilitarized Zones

By creating separate zones, controls can be applied at a more granular level based on the systems, information, and applications in each area. Separate zones can create defense in depth where additional layers of authentication, access control, and monitoring can take place. Isolation and segmentation are shown in **figure 3.10**.

Most enterprises separate their internal systems from the Internet using a firewall. However, some systems and services, such as web servers, need to be available outside the internal network. This can be accomplished with a network segment called a demilitarized zone (DMZ), which places limited systems, applications and data in a public-facing segment. Servers located in a DMZ minimize the exposure to attacks.

The DMZ functions as a small, isolated network for enterprise public servers, virtual private network (VPN) termination, and modem pools. Typically, DMZs are configured to limit access from the Internet and the enterprise private network. Incoming traffic access is restricted into the DMZ network by the outside router and firewall, protecting the enterprise against certain attacks by limiting the services available for use. Consequently, external systems can access only the systems in the DMZ.

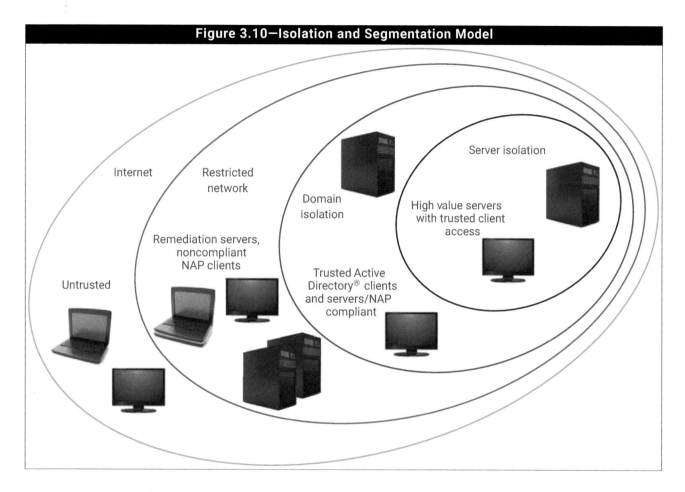

Figure 3.10—Isolation and Segmentation Model

Virtual Local Area Networks

A common technique for implementing network security is to segment an enterprise network so that each segment can be separately controlled, monitored, and protected. Virtual local area networks (VLANs) are groups of devices on one or more logically segmented LAN, usually without additional encryption used.

A VLAN is set up by configuring ports on a switch, so devices attached to these ports may communicate as if they were attached to the same physical network segment, although the devices are actually located on different LAN segments. Segmenting network traffic in this way enables an enterprise to keep different types of data separate from one another.

A VLAN is based on logical rather than physical connections, and thus, it allows great flexibility. This flexibility enables administrators to segment network resources for optimal performance by restricting users' access of network resources to the necessary individuals only. In Layer 4 switching (transport layer), some application information is taken into account along with Layer 3 addresses. For IP, this information includes the port numbers from protocols such as UDP and TCP. These devices, unlike Layer 3 switches, are more resource intensive because they have to store application-based protocol information. Only address information is stored at the Layer 2 and Layer 3 levels.

Firewalls

The openness of the Internet makes every enterprise network connected to it vulnerable to attack. Hackers on the Internet could break into an enterprise network and do harm in a number of ways—by stealing or damaging

important data, by damaging individual computers or the entire network, by using the enterprise computer resources or by using the enterprise network and resources to pose as an enterprise employee. Firewalls remain a primary means of perimeter security for these networks.

A firewall is a protective layer and defined as a system or combination of systems that enforces a boundary between two or more networks, typically forming a barrier between a secure and an open environment, such as the Internet. It applies rules to control the type of network traffic flowing in and out. Most commercial firewalls are built to handle commonly used Internet protocols. Firewalls may be hardware, software or virtual.

Software Firewalls

Software firewalls are software programs installed on computing devices that run at the application layer. Many providers of antivirus software now offer robust security suites making them popular in the consumer market.

Hardware Firewalls

Hardware firewalls are typically used in enterprise networks. Effective firewalls should allow individuals on the enterprise network to access the Internet and simultaneously prevent others on the Internet from gaining access to the enterprise network to cause damage. Most enterprises follow a deny-all philosophy, which means that access to a given resource will be denied unless a user can provide a specific business reason or need for access to the information resource. The converse of this access philosophy—which is not widely accepted—is the accept-all philosophy, under which everyone is allowed access unless someone can provide areas for denying access.

Implementing hardware will provide performance with minimal system overhead. Although hardware-based firewall platforms are faster, they are not as flexible or scalable as software-based firewalls. Software-based firewalls are generally slower with significant systems overhead. However, they are flexible with additional services; for example, they may include content and virus checking before traffic is passed to users.

It is generally better to use appliances, rather than normal servers, for the firewall. An appliance is a device with all software and configurations set up on a physical server that is plugged in between two networks. Appliances are normally installed with hardened operating systems. When server-based firewalls are used, operating systems in servers are often vulnerable to attacks. When attacks on operating systems succeed, the firewall can be compromised. In general, appliance-type firewalls are significantly faster to set up and recover.

Firewall General Features

Firewalls separate networks from one another and screen the traffic between them. See **figure 3.11.**

Along with other types of security (e.g., intrusion detection systems [IDS]/intrusion prevention systems [IPS]), firewalls control the most vulnerable point between an enterprise network and the Internet, and they can be as simple or complex as the enterprise information security policy demands.

There are many types of firewalls, but most of them enable enterprises to:

- Block access to particular sites on the Internet
- Limit traffic on an enterprise public services segment to relevant addresses and ports
- Prevent certain users from accessing certain servers or services
- Monitor and record communications between an internal and an external network in order to investigate network penetrations or detect internal subversion

Encrypt packets that are sent between different physical locations within an enterprise by creating a VPN over the Internet (e.g., IP security [IPSec], secure VPN tunnels). The capabilities of some firewalls can be extended, so they can also provide for protection against viruses and attacks directed to exploit known operating system vulnerabilities.

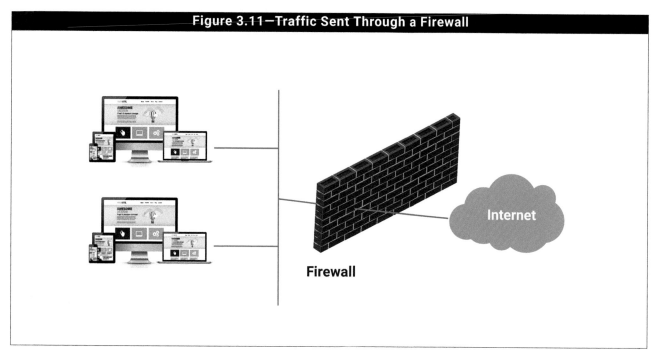

Figure 3.11—Traffic Sent Through a Firewall

Access Lists

Access lists filter traffic at network interfaces based on specified criteria, thus affording basic network security. Without access lists, network devices pass all packets. Conversely, after an access list is created and applied to an interface, it then only passes traffic permitted by rules due to an implied deny-all statement automatically appended to the list. Understanding the placement and impact of an access list is essential because errors can halt network traffic entirely.[172, 173]

Hardware Firewall Types

Generally, the types of network firewalls available today fall into the following categories:

- Packet filtering
- Application firewall systems
- Stateful inspection
- Next generation firewall (NGFW)

Each type of hardware firewall is discussed in the following sections.

Packet Filtering Firewalls

First generation firewalls were packet filtering-based firewalls deployed between the private network and the Internet. In packet filtering, a screening router examines the header of every packet of data traveling between the

[172] Wilson, T.; "Securing Networks: Access Control List (ACL) Concepts," 16 May 2012, http://blog.pluralsight.com/access-control-list-concepts
[173] Cisco Systems, Inc., *Security Configuration Guide: Access Control Lists, Cisco IOS Release 12.4T*, 18 January 2012, www.cisco.com/c/en/us/td/docs/ios-xml/ios/sec_data_acl/configuration/12-4t/sec-data-acl-12-4t-book/sec-acl-ov-gdl.html

Internet and the enterprise network. Packet headers contain information, including the IP address of the sender and receiver, along with the port numbers (application or service) authorized to use the information transmitted. Based on that information, the router knows what kind of Internet service (e.g., web-based service or File Transfer Protocol [FTP]) is being used to send the data and the identities of the sender and receiver of the data. Then, the router can prevent certain packets from being sent between the Internet and the enterprise network. For example, the router could block any traffic to and from suspicious destinations. See **figure 3.12**.

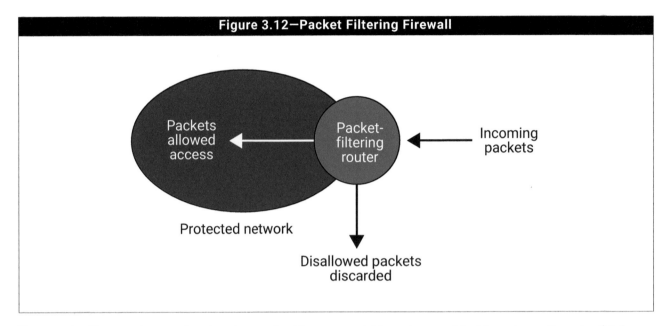

Figure 3.12—Packet Filtering Firewall

Because the direct exchange of packets is permitted between outside systems and inside systems, the potential for an attack is determined by the total number of hosts and services to which the packet filtering router permits traffic. Packet filtering firewalls are, therefore, best suited for smaller networks. Enterprises with many routers may face difficulties in designing, coding and maintaining the rule base.

Because their filtering rules are performed at the network layer, packet filtering firewalls are generally stable and simple. This simplicity has both advantages and disadvantages, as shown in **figure 3.13**.

Figure 3.13—Packet Filtering Firewalls	
Advantages	**Disadvantages**
Simplicity of one network choke point	Vulnerable to attacks from improperly configures filters
Minimal impact on network performance	Vulnerable to attacks tunneled over permitted services
Inexpensive or free	All private network systems vulnerable when a single packet filtering router is compromised

In light of these advantages and disadvantages, packet filtering is most effective when implemented with basic security and monitoring in mind. Some of the more common attacks against packet filtering firewalls are:

- **IP spoofing**—In this type of attack, the attacker fakes the IP address of either an internal network host or a trusted network host. This enables the packet being sent to pass the rule base of the firewall and penetrate the system perimeter. If the spoofing uses an internal IP address, the firewall can be configured to drop the packet on the basis of packet flow direction analysis. However, attackers with access to a secure or trusted external IP address can spoof on that address, leaving the firewall architecture defenseless.

- **Source routing specification**—This type of attack centers around the routing that an IP packet must take when it traverses the Internet from the source host to the destination host. In this process, it is possible to define the route so that it bypasses the firewall. However, the attacker must know the IP address, subnet mask, and default gateway settings to accomplish this. A clear defense against this attack is to examine each packet and drop packets that have source routing specification enabled. Note that this countermeasure will not be effective if the topology permits a route that skips the choke point.

- **Miniature fragment attack**—Using this method, an attacker fragments the IP packet into smaller ones and pushes it through the firewall. This is done with the hope that only the first sequence of fragmented packets will be examined, allowing the others to pass without review. This is possible only if the default setting is to pass residual packets. Miniature fragment attacks can be countered by configuring the firewall to drop all packets where IP fragmentation is enabled.

Application Firewall Systems

Packet filtering routers allow the direct flow of packets between internal and external systems. The primary risk of allowing packet exchange between internal and external systems is that the host applications residing on the protected network's systems must be secure against any threat posed by the allowed packets.

In contrast to packet filtering routers, application- and circuit-level gateways allow information to flow between systems but do not allow the direct exchange of packets. Therefore, application firewall systems provide greater protection capabilities than packet filtering routers.

The two types of application firewall systems sit atop hardened (i.e., tightly secured) operating systems, such as Windows® and UNIX®. They work at the application level of the OSI model.

The two types of application firewall systems are:

- **Application-level gateways**—Application-level gateways are systems that analyze packets through a set of proxies—one for each service (e.g., Hypertext Transmission Protocol [HTTP] proxy for web traffic, FTP proxy). The implementation of multiple proxies, however, impacts network performance. When network performance is a concern, a circuit-level gateway may be a better choice.

- **Circuit-level gateways**—Commercially, circuit-level gateways are quite rare. Because they use one proxy server for all services, they are more efficient and operate at the application level. There, TCP and UDP sessions are validated, typically through a single, general-purpose proxy before opening a connection. This differs from application-level gateways, which require a special proxy for each application-level service.

Both application firewall systems employ the concept of bastion hosting in that they handle all incoming requests from the Internet to the enterprise network, such as FTP or web requests. Bastion hosts are heavily fortified against attack. When there is only one host handling incoming requests, it is easier to maintain security and track attacks. In the event of a break-in, only the firewall system is compromised, not the entire network.

This way, none of the computers or hosts on the enterprise network can be contacted directly for requests from the Internet, providing an effective level or layer of security.

Additionally, application-based firewall systems are set up as proxy servers to act on behalf of someone inside an enterprise private network. Rather than relying on a generic packet-filtering tool to manage the flow of Internet services through the firewall, a special-purpose code called a proxy server is incorporated into the firewall system.

For example, when someone inside the enterprise network wants to access a server on the Internet, a request from the computer is sent to the proxy server. The proxy server contacts the Internet server, and the proxy server then sends the information from the Internet server to the computer inside the enterprise network. By acting as a go-between, proxy servers can maintain security by examining the program code of a given service (e.g., FTP, Telnet). It then

modifies and secures it to eliminate known vulnerabilities. The proxy server can also log all traffic between the Internet and the network.

One feature available on both types of firewall systems is the network address translation (NAT) capability. This capability takes private internal network addresses, which are unusable on the Internet, and maps them to a table of public IP addresses assigned to the enterprise, which can be used across the Internet.

Application firewalls have advantages and disadvantages, as shown in **figure 3.14**.

Figure 3.14—Application Firewalls	
Advantages	**Disadvantages**
Provide security for commonly used protocols	Reduced performance and scalability as Internet usage grows
Generally hide the network from outside untrusted networks	
Ability to protect the entire network by limiting break-ins to the firewall itself	
Ability to examine and secure program code	

Stateful Inspection Firewalls

A stateful inspection firewall, also referred to as dynamic packet filtering, tracks the destination IP address of each packet that leaves the enterprise internal network. Whenever a response to a packet is received, its record is referenced to ascertain whether the incoming message was made in response to a request that the enterprise sent out. This is done by mapping the source IP address of an incoming packet with the list of destination IP addresses that is maintained and updated. This approach prevents any attack initiated and originated by an outsider.

In contrast to application firewalls, stateful inspection firewalls provide control over the flow of IP traffic. They do this by matching information contained in the headers of connection-oriented or connectionless IP packets at the transport layer against a set of rules authorized by the enterprise. Consequently, they have advantages and disadvantages, as shown in **figure 3.15**.

Figure 3.15—Stateful Inspection Firewalls	
Advantages	**Disadvantages**
Provide greater control over the flow of IP traffic	Complex to administer
Greater efficiency in comparison to CPU-intensive, full-time application firewall systems	

Stateless vs. Stateful

Stateless filtering does not keep the state of ongoing TCP connection sessions. In other words, it has no memory of what source port numbers the sessions' client selected. Stateful firewalls keep track of TCP connections. The firewall keeps an entry in a cache for each open TCP connection. Stateless firewalls perform more quickly than stateful firewalls, but they are not as sophisticated.

Because UDP traffic is stateless, applications that require UDP to operate from the Internet into an enterprise network should be used sparingly and/or alternate controls implemented (e.g., network segregation or use of application-aware firewalls, NGFWs, and application-aware IDS/IPS).

Examples of Firewall Implementations

Firewall implementations can take advantage of the functionality available in a variety of firewall designs to provide a robust layered approach in protecting enterprise information assets. Commonly used implementations available today include:

- **Screened-host firewall**—Using a packet filtering router and a bastion host, this approach implements basic network layer security (packet filtering) and application server security (proxy services). An intruder in this configuration must penetrate two separate systems before the security of the private network can be compromised. This firewall system is configured with the bastion host connected to the private network with a packet filtering router between the Internet and the bastion host. Router filtering rules allow inbound traffic to access only the bastion host, which blocks access to internal systems. Because the inside hosts reside on the same network as the bastion host, the security policy of the enterprise determines whether inside systems are permitted direct access to the Internet, or whether they are required to use the proxy services on the bastion host.

- **Dual-homed firewall**—This is a firewall system that has two or more network interfaces, each of which is connected to a different network. A dual-homed firewall usually acts to block or filter some or all of the traffic trying to pass between the networks. A dual-homed firewall system is a more restrictive form of a screened-host firewall system in which a dual-homed bastion host is configured with one interface established for information servers and another for private network host computers.

- **Demilitarized zone (DMZ) or screened-subnet firewall**—As shown in **figure 3.16**, this is a small, isolated network for enterprise public servers, bastion host information servers and modem pools. The DMZ connects the untrusted network to the trusted network, but it exists in its own independent space to limit access and availability of resources. As a result, external systems can access only the bastion host and possibly information servers in the DMZ. The inside router manages access to the private network, accepting only traffic originating from the bastion host. The filtering rules on the outside router require the use of proxy services by accepting only outbound traffic on the bastion host. Key benefits of this system are that an intruder must penetrate three separate devices, private network addresses are not disclosed to the Internet, and internal systems do not have direct access to the Internet.

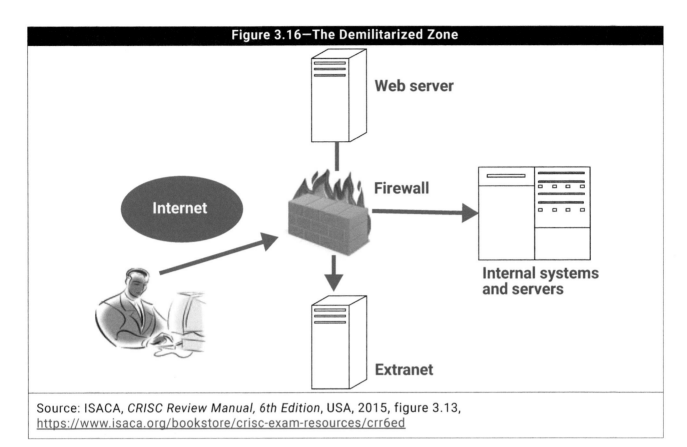

Figure 3.16—The Demilitarized Zone

Source: ISACA, *CRISC Review Manual, 6th Edition*, USA, 2015, figure 3.13,
https://www.isaca.org/bookstore/crisc-exam-resources/crr6ed

Next Generation Firewall (NGFWs)

Next Generation Firewalls (NGFWs) are firewalls aimed at addressing two key limitations of earlier variants: the inability to inspect packet payload and the inability to distinguish between types of web traffic. An NGFW is an adaptive network security system capable of detecting and blocking sophisticated attacks. NGFWs typically perform traditional functions such as packet filtering, stateful inspection and network address translation (NAT), but introduce application awareness, incorporate deep packet inspection (DPI) technology, and offer varying degrees of integrated threat protection, such as data loss prevention (DLP), intrusion prevention system (IPS), secure sockets layer (SSL)/secure shell (SSH) inspection, and web filtering.[174, 175, 176]

Application awareness is "the capacity of a system to maintain information about connected applications to optimize their operation and that of any subsystems that they run or control."[177] This is important because discriminating between legitimate and malicious traffic has become increasingly difficult amid the upsurge in web-based services. The ability of an NGFW to differentiate between types of web traffic such as an authorized business web application and a streaming media site aids enforcement of enterprise policies—regardless of port or protocol—and similarly offers insight to user activities and behavior.

DPI allows for payload interrogation against signatures for known exploits, malware, etc. DPI affords a great deal of information about the traffic, which aids in determination of normal traffic making anomaly detection more effective, especially in more complex networks.

---

[174] Ohlhorst, F.; "Next-Generation Firewalls 101," *Network Computing*, 1 March 2013, https://www.networkcomputing.com/careers-and-certifications/next-generation-firewalls-101

[175] Miller, L.C.; *Next-Generation Firewalls for Dummies*, Wiley Publishing, Inc., USA, 2011

[176] Wigmore, Ivy; "Application Awareness," January 2013, TechTarget, https://whatis.techtarget.com/definition/application-awareness

[177] *Op cit* Wigmore

Depending on the enterprise, the security professional may be asked to review, recommend, or specify vendor solutions. Bear in mind that while many next-generation solutions advertise similar functions, how they do so is often decided by their interpretation of concepts and implementation of proprietary technology. As sophisticated as NGFWs may be today, it should not be the only line of defense.

Web Application Firewalls

A web application firewall (WAF) is a server plug-in, appliance, or additional filter that can be used to apply rules to a specific web application (usually to an HTTP conversation). It operates at the higher levels of the OSI model, generally level 7, while network firewalls operate at level 3 and/or level 4. It can be customized to identify and block many types of attacks, such as cross-site scripting (XSS) and Structured Query Language (SQL) injection. Customization of the WAF rules requires a lot of work and effort. When changes to the application are made, the WAF rules need to be changed as well.[178]

Rare Firewalls

There is another category of firewalls called signaling firewalls typically reserved for telephony providers.[179] [180] They include:

- Session Initiation Protocol (SIP) firewalls protect VoIP telephone systems.

- Short message service (SMS) firewalls protect SMS traffic at mobile network operators (MNO) which most know as their wireless service providers.

- Signaling System 7 (SS7) firewalls protect MNOs from SS7 attacks.[181] Early 2G and 3G networks rely on SS7, which remains a prominent protocol in telecommunications today. Unfortunately, SS7 has a longstanding vulnerability that allows interception of calls and text messages, fraud and data leakage.[182]

- Diameter firewalls protect against attacks Long Term Evolution (LTE) networks. Diameter is an improvement upon SS7 but subject to SS7 vulnerabilities and man-in-the-middle attacks.

This category of firewalls is certain to evolve as 5G technology expands.

Intrusion Detection Systems (IDS)

Another element to securing networks that complements firewall implementation is an IDS.[183] An IDS works in conjunction with routers and firewalls by monitoring network usage anomalies. It protects enterprise IS resources from external as well as internal misuse. An IDS operates continuously on the system, running in the background and notifying administrators when it detects a perceived threat. Broad categories of IDSs include:

- **Network-based IDSs**—These identify attacks within the monitored network and issue a warning to the operator. If a network-based IDS is placed between the Internet and the firewall, it will detect all the attack attempts, regardless of whether they enter the firewall. If the IDS is placed between a firewall and the enterprise network, it will detect those attacks that enter the firewall (i.e., it will detect intruders). The IDS is not a substitute for a firewall, but rather it complements the function of a firewall.

- **Host-based IDSs**—These are configured for a specific environment and monitor various internal resources of the operating system to warn of a possible attack. They can detect the modification or execution of files and issue a warning when an attempt is made to run a privileged command.

---

[178] Open Web Application Security Project (OWASP), "Web Application Firewall," https://owasp.org/www-community/Web_Application_Firewall
[179] BroadForward BV, "Diameter Firewall (DFW)," 2020, www.broadforward.com/diameter-firewall-dfw/
[180] Cellusys, "Diameter Firewall," 2020, www.cellusys.com/products/cellusys-protect/diameter-firewall/
[181] Infradata Inc, "What is the SS7 Firewall?," 2020, www.infradata.com/resources/what-is-the-ss7-firewall/
[182] Positive Technologies, "SS7 Vulnerabilities in the Spotlight," 5 March 2018, https://positive-tech.com/research/ss7-vulnerability-2018/
[183] *Op cit* ISACA, *CISA Review Manual 27th Edition*

Components of an IDS include:

- Sensors responsible for collecting data in the form of network packets, log files, system call traces, etc.
- Analyzers that receive input from sensors and determine intrusive activity
- Administration console

Types of IDSs include:

- **Signature-based**—These IDS systems protect against detected intrusion patterns. The intrusive patterns they can identify are stored in the form of signatures.
- **Statistical-based**—These systems need a comprehensive definition of the known and expected behavior of systems.
- **Neural networks**—An IDS with this feature monitors the general patterns of activity and traffic on the network and creates a database. It is similar to the statistical model but with added self-learning capability.

Signature-based IDSs are not able to detect all types of intrusions due to the limitations of their detection rules. On the other hand, statistical-based systems may report many events outside of the defined normal activity that are still normal activities on the network. A combination of signature- and statistical-based models provides better protection.

IDS Features

The features available in an IDS include:

- Intrusion detection
- Ability to gather evidence on intrusive activity
- Automated response (e.g., termination of connection, alarm messaging)
- Security policy
- Interface with system tools
- Security policy management

IDS Limitations

An IDS cannot help with the following weaknesses:

- Weaknesses in the policy definition (see Policy section)
- Application-level (programming) vulnerabilities
- Back doors into applications
- Weaknesses in identification and authentication schemes

IDS Policy

An IDS policy should establish the action to be taken by security personnel if an intruder is detected. Actions include:

- **Terminate the access**—If there is a significant risk to the enterprise data or systems, immediate termination is the usual procedure.
- **Trace the access**—If the risk to the data is low, the activity is not immediately threatening, or analysis of the entry point and attack method is desirable, the IDS can be used to trace the origin of the intrusion. This can be used to determine and correct any system weaknesses and to collect evidence of the attack that may be used in a subsequent court action.

In either case, the action required should be determined by management in advance and incorporated into a procedure. This will save time when an intrusion is detected, which may impact the possible data loss.

Intrusion Prevention Systems (IPS)

An IPS is a system designed to not only detect attacks, but also to prevent the intended victim hosts from being affected by the attacks. It complements firewall, antivirus and antispyware tools to provide a more complete protection from emerging threats.

IPS technology is commonly placed at the perimeter of the enterprise network—at all ingress/egress points—to examine network traffic flows and prevent zero-day attacks, such as worms or viruses. The detection methods used by an IPS are anomaly-based rules and signature-based inspection of network packets. A well-managed IPS solution helps to ensure that threats are dropped at the network perimeter; an IDS provides visibility and confirmation of inside activity that is at critical network nodes.

The biggest advantage of an IPS is that it can help block an attack when it occurs; rather than simply sending an alert, it actively helps to block malicious and unwanted traffic.

However, as with an IDS, the IPS must be properly configured and tuned to be effective. Threshold settings that are too high or too low will lead to limited effectiveness of the IPS. Additionally, some concerns have been raised that IPSs may in themselves constitute a threat, because a clever attacker could send commands to numerous hosts protected by an IPS to cause them to become dysfunctional. Such a situation could have a potentially catastrophic outcome in today's typical enterprise computing environment where continuity of service is critical. In addition, IPSs can generate false positives that can create serious problems if automated responses are used.

Virtual Private Network (VPN)

A VPN is a secure private network that uses the public telecommunications infrastructure to transmit data. In contrast to a much more expensive system of owned or leased lines that can only be used by one enterprise, VPNs are used by enterprises for both extranets and wide areas of intranets. Using encryption and authentication, a VPN encrypts all data that pass between two Internet points, maintaining privacy and security. Encryption is needed to make the connection virtually private. It is important to note that VPNs by themselves are not ironclad and enterprises are cautioned against allowing remote users unrestricted access to enterprise resources once authenticated by the VPN.

Wireless Network Security

Wireless data transmission is subject to a higher risk of interception than wired traffic, in the same way that it is easier to intercept calls made from mobile phones than calls from landline telephones. There is no need to manually tap into the connection, but rather remote tools can be used to intercept the connection covertly. Wireless transmission of confidential information should be protected with strong encryption. Insecure wireless connections expose users to eavesdropping, which can lead to the exposure of confidential information, intercepted messages, or abused connections. Examples include:

- Email can be intercepted and read or changed.
- Hackers can replace a user's credential with false information that leads to the destination server rejecting the user's access attempts, thereby causing DoS.
- An unauthorized person can log on to a wireless network that is not secure and use its resources, including free connectivity to the Internet.

Wireless security standards continue to evolve. The primary security protocol for wireless today is part of the Wi-Fi Protected Access® family.[184] All Wi-Fi CERTIFIED™ devices since 2006 have implemented WPA2 which uses AES encryption (discussed later in this chapter), but has become susceptible to wireless attacks that could allow packet

---

[184] Wi-Fi Alliance, "Discover WiFi: Security," 2020, www.wi-fi.org/discover-wi-fi/security

decryption and connection hijacking among other things—especially when less than 16-character passwords are used.[185] WPA3 was released in mid-2018 and improves on WPA2 by eliminating preshared keys (PSK) and therefore is resistant to dictionary attacks.

3.4.8 Endpoint Security

A major challenge facing IT professionals is the vast number of computing devices that touch their networks. Not long ago, desktops were the prominent type of computer in enterprises. Over time, laptops became equally powerful and cost effective which enabled a paradigm shift from restricting access to executives and business professionals who traveled frequently. The technology industry has long battled with unauthorized devices, e.g., thumb drives, iPods and tablets. More recently, industry has seen a surge in mobile devices—both authorized and unauthorized—often covered by the term bring your own device (BYOD).

An endpoint is anything that touches a network to include desktops, laptops, servers, mobile devices and peripherals. Therefore, endpoint security is the protection of any device that touches a network.

3.4.9 System Hardening

System hardening is the process of implementing security controls on a computer system. It is common for most computer vendors to set the default controls to be open, allowing ease of use over security. This introduces significant vulnerabilities unless the system is hardened.

Security practitioners must understand the types and roles of accounts on each platform they are protecting. For example, Windows differentiates between files and devices, such as printers, whereas everything in UNIX is considered a file—including physical devices.

Hardening is a process that reduces vulnerability by limiting the attack vectors that might be used as points of compromise. A hardened system is one that does not store any sensitive data that are not immediately needed to support a business operation. In addition, it has all unnecessary functionality disabled, including ports, services and protocols that are not required for the intended use of the system within the enterprise environment. Many devices and systems come with guest accounts or default passwords that should be changed or disabled as part of the hardening process.[186]

The extent to which an endpoint must be hardened is driven by operating system, installed applications, system/platform use and exposure. In other words, hardening is not one size fits all. Server hardening processes are important to protect enterprise servers from potential attack.

Some common controls include:

- Authentication and authorization
- File system permissions
- Access privileges
- Logging and system monitoring
- System services
- Configuration restrictions

---

[185] Wong, W.G.; "What's the Difference Between WPA2 and WPA3?," ElectronicDesign, 31 July 2018, www.electronicdesign.com/technologies/embedded-revolution/article/21806819/whats-the-difference-between-wpa2-and-wpa3

[186] *Op cit* ISACA, *CISA Review Manual 27th Edition*

For the cybersecurity practitioner, identifying the location of critical information is imperative not only to security, but also incident response.

In UNIX, the following directories require additional consideration:

- **/etc/passwd**—Maintains user account and password information
- **/etc/shadow**—Retains the encrypted password of the corresponding account
- **/etc/group**—Contains group information for each account
- **/etc/gshadow**—Contains secure group account information
- **/bin**—Location of executable files
- **/boot**—Contains files for booting system
- **/kernel**—Kernel files
- **/sbin**—Contains executables, often for administration
- **/usr**—Include administrative commands

For Windows, the Registry is a central hierarchical database that stores configuration settings and options.[187] A hive is a logical group of keys, subkeys, and values in the registry that has a set of supporting files and backups of its data.[188]

- **HKEY_CURRENT_CONFIG**—Contains volatile information generated at boot
- **HKEY_CURRENT_USER**—Settings specific to current user
- **HKEY_LOCAL_MACHINE\SAM**—Holds local and domain account information
- **HKEY_LOCAL_MACHINE\Security**—Contains security policy referenced and enforced by kernel
- **HKEY_LOCAL_MACHINE\Software**—Contains software and Windows settings
- **HKEY_LOCAL_MACHINE\System**—Contains information about Windows system setup
- **HKEY_USERS\.DEFAULT**—Profile for Local System account

Most of the supporting files for the hives are in the %SystemRoot%\System32\Config directory. These files are updated each time a user logs on.[189]

Regardless of the variables, system hardening should entail implementing the principles of least privilege and need to know. This limits what users can *do* as well as *see,* which in turn helps to mitigate insider threats.

Most operating systems have two modes of operation—kernel mode for execution of privileged instructions for the internal operation of the system and user mode for normal activities. In kernel mode, there are no protections from errors or malicious activity and all parts of the system and memory are accessible. See **figure 3.17**. Operating systems allow controlled access to kernel mode operations through system calls that usually require privileges. These privileges are defined on a user or program basis and should be limited under the principle of least privilege. Most attacks seek to gain privileged or kernel mode access to the system to circumvent other security controls.

---

[187] Microsoft Press, *Microsoft Computer Dictionary*, 5th edition, USA, 2002
[188] Microsoft, "Registry Hives," 31 May 2018, http://msdn.microsoft.com/en-us/library/windows/desktop/ms724877%28v=vs.85%29.aspx
[189] *Op cit* ISACA, *CISA Review Manual 27th Edition*

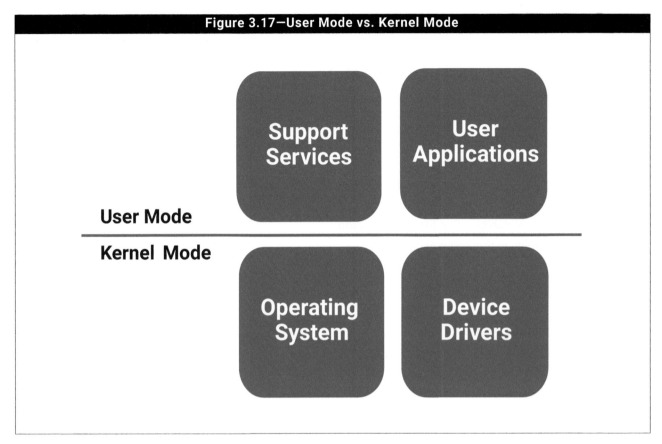

Figure 3.17—User Mode vs. Kernel Mode

The access any user has to a system is controlled through a series of mechanisms. A user's credentials define who they are and what permissions they have for accessing resources within the system.

Passwords are the standard mechanism to authenticate a user to the system and must be managed correctly to ensure they are not easily guessed or compromised. Most operating systems provide controls around passwords such as minimum length, lifetime for any particular password and how many attempts to use a password are allowed before denying access.

Another key user control is the privileges assigned to a user. These privileges must be carefully chosen and controlled to prevent misuse or compromise. Assignment of privileges should follow the principle of least privilege required for a user to do their job.

Administrators can also limit the ways in which users can access systems. For example, administrators can set logon constraints based on the time of day, the total time logged on, the source address and the number of unsuccessful logon attempts.

3.4.10 Logging, Monitoring and Detection

Monitoring, detection and logging[190] are integral parts of cybersecurity. With potential for attacks and data loss on both sides, it is necessary to monitor data and information flowing into and out of an enterprise. As this chapter illustrates, there are a number of methods and tools that an enterprise can use to detect and log potential problems. Most of these methods revolve around the central concepts of ingress, egress and data loss prevention.

---

[190] *Op cit* ISACA, *CRISC Review Manual 6th Edition*

Logging

A log is a record of events that occur within the systems and networks of an organization. Logs are one of the most valuable tools to monitor controls and detect risk, but they are often underutilized. A log should contain a record of important events that occur on a system, and should include:

- Time of the event
- Changes to permissions
- System startup or shutdown
- Login or logout
- Changes to data
- Errors or violations
- Job failures

Log reviews can identify risk-relevant events, such as compliance violations, suspicious behavior, errors, probes or scans, and abnormal activity. A failure to review the logs can result in the enterprise not being aware of an ongoing attack. Logs may be required to comply with legislation and regulatory compliance and should also be preserved for forensic analysis if needed at a later time. The cybersecurity professional may find it useful to employ analysis tools when reviewing logs to filter pertinent data.

Ensuring proper segregation of duties (SoD) and time synchronization is particularly important when it comes to log files. The ability to change system configurations should be segregated from the ability to review, modify, or delete logs to ensure that the enterprise can exercise proper oversight of administrative functions. Without time synchronization, it is extremely difficult to correlate information from different logs (server, router, firewall) to analyze the occurrence of an event.

Common challenges relating to the effective use of logs include:

- Having too many data
- Difficulty in searching for relevant information
- Improper configuration (e.g., may not be enabled or contain appropriate data)
- Modification or deletion of data before they are read (e.g., too little storage space)

Performing Active Directory® tasks often require different account types:

- **Local user**—Normal user accounts that can run most programs and access installed peripherals. Local user accounts are ideal for small office home office (SOHO) computers and other small networks.
- **Local administrator**—Local admin accounts are required to make changes on a Windows computer not attached to the domain.
- **Domain user**—Domain user accounts are found in most enterprises to allow users to access network resources. Like local user accounts, domain users cannot make most system changes on their computer.
- **Domain administrator**—This type of account is required to perform configuration changes to include adding and removing computers from the enterprise network.

Access Control Lists

To provide security authorizations for the files and facilities listed previously, logical access control mechanisms utilize access authorization tables, also referred to as access control lists (ACLs)[191] or access control tables. ACLs refer to a register of:

- Users (including groups, machines, processes) who have permission to use a particular system resource
- The types of access permitted

ACLs vary considerably in their capability and flexibility. Some only allow specifications for certain preset groups (e.g., owner, group and global), while more advanced ACLs allow much more flexibility, such as user-defined groups. Also, more advanced ACLs can be used to explicitly deny access to a specific individual or group.

With more advanced ACLs, access can be at the discretion of the policy maker (and implemented by the security administrator) or individual user, depending on how the controls are technically implemented. When a user changes a job role within an enterprise, often their old access rights are not removed before adding their new required accesses. Without removing the old access rights, you promote violation of the principles of least privilege and need-to-know or worse, a potential segregation of duties issue.

Endpoint Protection (EPP)

According to Gartner, an endpoint protection platform (EPP) is a solution deployed on endpoint devices to prevent file-based malware attacks, detect malicious activity and provide the investigation and remediation capabilities needed to respond to dynamic security incidents and alerts.[192]

EPP are an evolution from antivirus software to suites of endpoint products that typically include antivirus, data encryption, intrusion prevention and data loss protection. EPP also includes device management capabilities, lost device tracking, remote wipe, application whitelisting and endpoint patching.

3.4.11 Application Security

Insecure applications open the enterprise to external attackers who may try to use unauthorized code to manipulate the application and access, steal, modify, or delete sensitive data. Application security measures should be applied during design and development, followed by routine security countermeasures throughout the life cycle.

Best Practices

This section provides best practices for development of systems and application security.

A Tale of Two SDLCs

For many years, SDLC referred to the systems development life cycle. In recent years, however, SDLC has grown to also mean software development life cycle which creates confusion. For the purposes of this publication, the acronym SDLC is restricted to systems development life cycle—any instance of software development life cycle will be spelled out. The primary difference between system development life cycle and software development life cycle is scope. A system is a regularly interacting interdependent group of items forming a unified whole.[193] System

---

[191] *Op cit* ISACA, *CISA Review Manual 27th Edition*

[192] Gartner, "Gartner Glossary: Endpoint Protection Platform (EPP)," www.gartner.com/en/information-technology/glossary/endpoint-protection-platform-epp#20

[193] Merriam-Webster, "system," www.merriam-webster.com/dictionary/system

development life cycle involves people, processes and technology and may consist of hardware, software or both. Software development life cycle is restricted to software and therefore has narrower scope.[194] For each, it is equally important that information security be considered as early as possible.

System Development Life Cycle (SDLC)

Enterprises often commit significant resources (e.g., people, applications, facilities and technology) to develop, acquire, integrate and maintain application systems that are critical to the effective functioning of key business processes. The SDLC process (**figure 3.18**) guides the phases in the development or acquisition of a software system and, depending on the methodology, may even include the controlled retirement of the system.

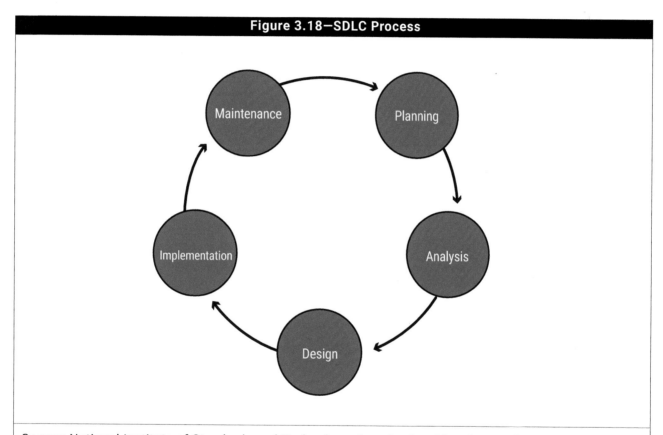

Figure 3.18—SDLC Process

Source: National Institute of Standards and Technology, *Security Considerations in the System Development Life Cycle*, Special Publication 800-64, Revision 2, USA, October 2008

The SDLC includes:

- IT processes for managing and controlling project activity
- An objective for each phase of the life cycle that is typically described with key deliverables, a description of recommended tasks and a summary of related control objectives for effective management
- Incremental steps or deliverables that lay the foundation for the next phase

The SDLC reflects a formal process to characterize design requirements and should include:

- Business requirements containing descriptions of what a system should do

---

[194] Evans, B.; "The System Development Lifecycle: A Phased Approach to Application Security," Security Intelligence, 7 January 2019, https://securityintelligence.com/the-system-development-life-cycle-a-phased-approach-to-application-security/

- Functional requirements and the use of case models describing how users will interact with a system
- Technical requirements, design specifications and coding specifications describing how the system will interact, conditions under which the system will operate and the information criteria that the system should meet
- Risk mitigation and control requirements to protect the integrity of the system, confidentiality of information stored, processed or communicated, and adequate authentication and authorization mechanisms

Security Within SDLC

The design and deployment of controls are often undertaken as a systems development project. While there are several project management techniques that can be used to manage system development projects, design and deployment of controls should always be an integral and equal part of any SDLC process.

Design Requirements

Not considering security in the design of a system or application is one of the major contributing factors to today's cybersecurity vulnerabilities, making it easier for systems to be compromised. Too often, security is an afterthought, and controls are retrofitted in an *ad hoc* way only after security weaknesses are identified. This is less than satisfactory and is often time consuming and costly to any enterprise.

Security and risk mitigation should be part of the formal design criteria in any SDLC process and start with threat and risk assessment of the proposed system, identification of controls, implementation of those controls, testing and review.

Separation of Development, Testing and Production Environments

Development and testing environments are relatively open and often have fewer access controls due to the collaborative nature of the development process. It is important to separate the development, testing and production environments to minimize a compromise or misconfiguration being introduced or cascading through the process.

It is recommended that different access controls (credentials) be used between the different environments.

Also, if production data are used in the test environment, private or personally identifiable information (PII) should be scrambled so that confidential information is not inadvertently disclosed.

OWASP Top Ten

The Open Web Application Security Project (OWASP) publishes a list of the top 10 application security risk conditions.[195] At the time of publication, the current version of the OWASP Top Ten is 2017; however, data collection has begun for a 2020 revision.

1. **Injection**—Injection flaws, such as SQL, NoSQL, OS and LDAP injection, occur when untrusted data are sent to an interpreter as part of a command or query. The attacker's hostile data can trick the interpreter into executing unintended commands or allowing access to data without proper authorization.
2. **Broken authentication**—Application functions related to authentication and session management are often implemented incorrectly, allowing attackers to compromise passwords, keys or session tokens, or to exploit other implementation flaws and assume other users' identities temporarily or permanently.
3. **Sensitive data exposure**—Many web applications and APIs do not properly protect sensitive data, such as financial and healthcare information, and/or PII. Attackers may steal or modify such weakly protected data to conduct credit card fraud, identity theft or other crimes. Sensitive data may be compromised without extra

---

[195] *Op cit* Open Web Application Security Project (OWASP)

protection (e.g., encryption at rest or in transit), and require special precautions when exchanged with the browser.

4. **XML external entities (XXE)**—Many older or poorly configured XML processors evaluate external entity references within XML documents. External entities can be used to disclose internal files using the file URI handler, internal file shares, internal port scanning, remote code execution and denial-of-service attacks.

5. **Broken access control**—Restrictions on what authenticated users are allowed to do are often not properly enforced. Attackers can exploit these flaws to access unauthorized functionality and/or data, such as access other users' accounts, view sensitive files, modify other users' data, change access rights, etc.

6. **Security misconfiguration**—Security misconfiguration is one of the most common issues. It results from insecure default configurations, incomplete or *ad hoc* configurations, open cloud storage, misconfigured HTTP headers, and verbose error messages containing sensitive information. Not only must all operating systems, frameworks, libraries and applications be securely configured, but they must be patched/upgraded in a timely fashion.

7. **Cross-site scripting XSS**—XSS flaws occur whenever an application includes untrusted data in a new web page without proper validation or escaping, or updates an existing web page with user-supplied data using a browser API that can create HTML or JavaScript. XSS allows attackers to execute scripts in the victim's browser, which can hijack user sessions, deface web sites or redirect the user to malicious sites.

8. **Insecure deserialization**—Insecure deserialization often leads to remote code execution. Even if deserialization flaws do not result in remote code execution, they can be used to perform attacks, including replay attacks, injection attacks and privilege escalation attacks.

9. **Using components with known vulnerabilities**—Components such as libraries, frameworks and other software modules run with the same privileges as the application. If a vulnerable component is exploited, such an attack can facilitate serious data loss or server takeover. Applications and APIs using components with known vulnerabilities may undermine application defenses and enable various attacks and impacts.

10. **Insufficient logging & monitoring**—Insufficient logging and monitoring, coupled with missing or ineffective integration with incident response, allow attackers to further attack systems, maintain persistence, pivot to more systems, and tamper, extract or destroy data. Most breach studies show time to detect a breach is over 200 days—and many breaches are detected by external parties, rather than internal processes or monitoring.

Application Controls

Application controls are controls over input, processing and output functions. They include methods to help ensure data accuracy, completeness, validity, verifiability and consistency, thus achieving data integrity and data reliability.

Application controls may consist of edit tests; totals; reconciliations and identification; and reporting of incorrect, missing or exception data. Automated controls should be coupled with manual procedures to ensure proper investigation of exceptions. Implementation of these controls helps ensure system integrity; that applicable system functions operate as intended; and that information contained by the system is relevant, reliable, secure and available when needed.

Application controls include:

- Monitoring of process flows outside the known good path
- Validating input
- Checking input against known bad patterns
- Thread limiting or throttling APIs
- Validating authenticity of transactions
- Validating authenticity of users

- Validating integrity of the environment the application is running in (e.g., mobile devices)
- Ensuring data integrity
- Controls to prevent abuse and fraud
- Controls to ensure integrity of the application itself (e.g., mobile devices)

To reduce application security risk, OWASP recommends that practitioners:

- Define application security requirements
- Use good application security architecture practices from the beginning of the application design
- Build strong and usable security controls
- Integrate security into the development life cycle
- Stay current on application vulnerabilities

3.4.12 Cloud Security

The NIST defines cloud computing as a "model for enabling convenient, on-demand network access to a shared pool of configurable computing resources (e.g., networks, servers, storage, applications and services) that can be rapidly provisioned and released with minimal management effort or service provider interaction."[196] This definition was adopted by the Cloud Security Alliance.

The Cloud Security Alliance (CSA) is a nonprofit organization with a mission to promote best practices for providing security assurance with cloud computing and can be considered a main source of information on this topic.

Cloud Basics

The cloud model is composed of five essential characteristics, three service models and four deployment models.[197]

Essential Characteristics

- **On-demand self-service**—A consumer can unilaterally provision computing capabilities, such as server time and network storage, as needed automatically without requiring human interaction with each service provider.
- **Broad network access**—Capabilities are available over the network and accessed through standard mechanisms that promote use by heterogeneous thin or thick client platforms (e.g., mobile phones, tablets, laptops and workstations).
- **Resource pooling**—The provider's computing resources are pooled to serve multiple consumers using a multi-tenant model, with different physical and virtual resources dynamically assigned and reassigned according to consumer demand. There is a sense of location independence in that the customer generally has no control or knowledge over the exact location of the provided resources but may be able to specify location at a higher level of abstraction (e.g., country, state or datacenter). Examples of resources include storage, processing, memory and network bandwidth.
- **Rapid elasticity**—Capabilities can be elastically provisioned and released, in some cases automatically, to scale rapidly outward and inward commensurate with demand. To the consumer, the capabilities available for provisioning often appear to be unlimited and can be appropriated in any quantity at any time.
- **Measured service**—Cloud systems automatically control and optimize resource use by leveraging a metering capability at some level of abstraction appropriate to the type of service (e.g., storage, processing, bandwidth and

---

[196] Mell, P.; T. Grance; *The NIST Definition of Cloud Computing*, National Institute of Standards and Technology, Special Publication 800-145, September 2011, https://nvlpubs.nist.gov/nistpubs/Legacy/SP/nistspecialpublication800-145.pdf
[197] *Ibid.*

active user accounts). Resource usage can be monitored, controlled and reported, providing transparency for both the provider and consumer of the utilized service.

Cloud Service Models

Cloud service models vary based on audience and include:

- **Infrastructure as a Service (IaaS)**—The IaaS model provides virtual machines, other abstracted hardware and operating systems to clients without the need for on-premise equipment. Examples include Amazon Web Services®, Microsoft Azure and Rackspace®.

- **Platform as a Service (PaaS)**—The PaaS model allows a platform for software creation and remote configuration. PaaS can be delivered through public, private or hybrid models. Examples include Amazon Elastic Beanstalk Microsoft Azure, and Google App Engine.

- **Software as a Service (SaaS)**—The SaaS model is a software distribution model made available by third parties offering office productivity, customer relationship management (CRM), and collaboration solutions. Popular examples include Salesforce®, Google® Docs, Office 365® and cloud-based video conferencing applications.

To aid understanding, it may be best to compare these to transportation[198]:

- On-premises IT infrastructure is like owning a car. When you buy a car, you are responsible for its maintenance, and upgrading means buying a new car.

- IaaS is like leasing a car. When you lease a car, you choose the car you want and drive it wherever you wish, but the car is not yours. Want an upgrade? Just lease a different car!

- PaaS is like taking a taxi. You do not drive a taxi yourself, but simply tell the driver where you need to go and relax in the back seat.

- SaaS is like going by bus. Buses have assigned routes, and you share the ride with other passengers (**figures 3.19** and **3.20**).

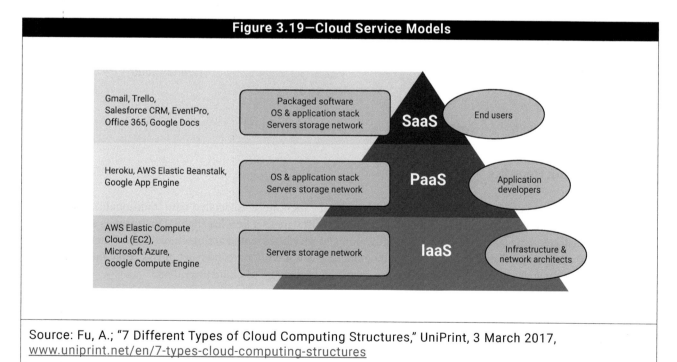

Figure 3.19—Cloud Service Models

Gmail, Trello, Salesforce CRM, EventPro, Office 365, Google Docs — Packaged software / OS & application stack / Servers storage network — **SaaS** — End users

Heroku, AWS Elastic Beanstalk, Google App Engine — OS & application stack / Servers storage network — **PaaS** — Application developers

AWS Elastic Compute Cloud (EC2), Microsoft Azure, Google Compute Engine — Servers storage network — **IaaS** — Infrastructure & network architects

Source: Fu, A.; "7 Different Types of Cloud Computing Structures," UniPrint, 3 March 2017, www.uniprint.net/en/7-types-cloud-computing-structures

---

[198] RubyGarage, "Choosing the Right Cloud Service: IaaS, PaaS, or SaaS," https://rubygarage.org/blog/iaas-vs-paas-vs-saas

Cloud Deployment Models

Cloud deployment models include (**figure 3.20**):

- **Private cloud**—The infrastructure can be used only by one single enterprise. As for community clouds, it can be deployed onsite or offsite enterprise premises. It may be owned, managed and operated by the organization, a third party, or some combination of them, and it may exist on or off premises.

- **Community cloud**—The cloud infrastructure is provisioned for exclusive use by a specific community of consumers from enterprises or interest groups (e.g., vertical industries, schools, researchers, software developers) that have shared concerns. It can be deployed onsite (within the enterprise infrastructure) or offsite (within the cloud service provider [CSP] infrastructure, also called outsourced). It may be owned, managed, and operated by one or more of the organizations in the community, a third party or some combination of them, and it may exist on or off premises.

- **Public cloud**—The infrastructure is made available to the general public (e.g., Google Apps, Amazon Elastic Compute Cloud (EC2TM), Apple® iCloud). It may be owned, managed and operated by a business, academic or government organization, or some combination of them. Public clouds are deployed within the CSP infrastructure and there is offsite to the enterprise infrastructure.

- **Hybrid cloud**—The cloud infrastructure is a composition of two or more distinct cloud infrastructures (private, community or public) that remain unique entities but are bound together by standardized or proprietary technology that enables data and application portability (e.g., cloud bursting for load balancing between clouds).

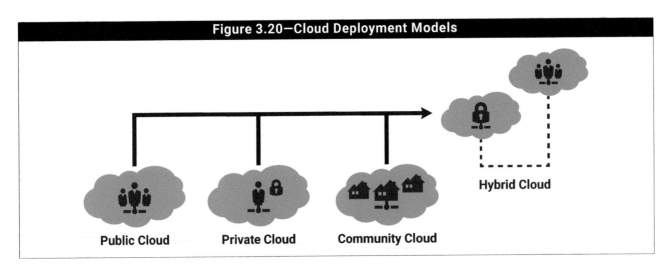

Figure 3.20—Cloud Deployment Models

Cloud Computing Benefits

Cloud computing offers enterprises a way to save on the capital expenditure associated with traditional methods of managing IT. Common platforms offered in the cloud include Software as a Service (SaaS), Platform as a Service (PaaS) and Infrastructure as a Service (IaaS). Virtualization and service-oriented architectures (SOAs) act as key enablers behind the scenes. Though attractive, cloud computing is not without its own set of risk, first and foremost of which is the safety and security of the data that are entrusted in the care of cloud providers.[199]

Widely accepted benefits include:

- Flexibility
- Scalability

[199] ISACA, "Why Cloud Computing Should be Part of Business Strategy," 1 January 2015, www.isaca.org/bookstore/bookstore-wht_papers-digital/whpccbs

- Performance
- Availability
- Collaboration
- Security

Another potential benefit is cost savings; however, this is not always the case—particularly given that an enterprise is moving from capital expenditure to operating expenditure. Although it may save money on head count in some circumstances, operations can cost considerably more.

Although cloud computing is attractive to attackers because of the massive concentrations of data, cloud defenses can be more robust, scalable, and cost-effective. ENISA provides the following top security benefits of cloud computing.[200]

- **Market drive**—Because security is a top priority for most cloud customers, cloud providers have a strong driver for increasing and improving their security practices.
- **Scalability**—Cloud technology allows for the rapid reallocation of resources, such as those for filtering, traffic shaping, authentication and encryption, and defensive measures.
- **Cost effective**—All types of security measures are cheaper when implemented on a large scale. The concentration of resources provides for cheaper physical perimeter and physical access control and easier and cheaper application of many security-related processes.
- **Timely and effective updates**—Updates can be rolled out rapidly across a homogeneous platform.
- **Audit and evidence**—Cloud computing can provide forensic images of virtual machines, which results in less downtime for forensic investigations.

  The European Network and Information Security Agency (ENISA) is an EU agency created to advance the functioning of the internal market. ENISA is a center of excellence for the European Member States and European institutions in network and information security, giving advice and recommendations and acting as a switchboard for information on good practices. Moreover, the agency facilitates contacts between European institutions, the member states, and private business and industry sectors.

Cloud Computing Risk

The challenge for cloud computing is to protect data within public and private clouds as well as ensure governance, risk management, and compliance are addressed across the full, integrated environment. NIST outlines the following top security risk for cloud infrastructure:

- **Loss of governance**—The client usually relinquishes some level of control to the cloud provider, which may affect security, especially if the service level agreements (SLAs) leave a gap in security defenses.
- **Lock-in**—It can be difficult for a client to migrate from one provider to another, which creates a dependency on a particular cloud provider for service provision. With this, clients must be concerned that their data have indeed been returned in full and removed from/destroyed by the Cloud services provider.
- **Isolation failure**—One characteristic of cloud computing is shared resources. Although not commonplace, the failure of mechanisms that separate storage, memory, routing and reputation between different tenants can create risk.
- **Compliance**—Migrating to the cloud may create a risk in the organization achieving certification if the cloud provider cannot provide compliance evidence.

---

[200] European Network and Information Security Agency (ENISA), *Cloud Computing: Benefits, risks and recommendations for information security*, Rev. B, December 2012, https://resilience.enisa.europa.eu/cloud-security-and-resilience/publications/cloud-computing-benefits-risks-and-recommendations-for-information-security

- **Management interface compromise**—The customer management interface can pose an increased risk, because it is accessed through the Internet and mediates access to larger sets of resources.

- **Data protection**—It may be difficult for clients to check the data handling procedures of the cloud provider.

- **Insecure or incomplete data deletion**—Because of the multiple tenancies and the reuse of hardware resources, there is a greater risk that data are not deleted completely, adequately or in a timely manner.

- **Malicious insider**—Cloud architects have extremely high-risk roles. A malicious insider can cause a great degree of damage.

This risk can lead to a number of different threat events. The CSA lists the following as the top cloud computing threats:[201]

- Data Breaches

- Misconfiguration and inadequate change control

- Lack of cloud security architecture and strategy

- Insufficient identity, credential, access and key management

- Account hijacking

- Insider threat

- Insecure interfaces and APIs

- Weak control plane

- Metastructure and applistructure[202] failures

- Limited cloud usage visibility

- Abuse and nefarious use of cloud services

Cloud Security Considerations

For enterprises in which security is not considered a high priority, security provided by a reputable cloud provider may be a significant improvement.[203] However, for the information security manager, security considerations are an issue that must be carefully assessed. The loss of control over sensitive data must be considered. The location of data may be an issue as well. In organizations that knowingly store and transmit data across state or national boundaries, the information security manager may need to consider myriad laws, regulations, and compliance requirements of various jurisdictions. This concern extends to the cloud provider's replication and storage of data unbeknownst to the enterprise. Requirements for handling incidents may vary from one jurisdiction to another (e.g., breach notification laws). Availability of audit logs may also be limited or nonexistent from the cloud provider, and the actual level of security may be difficult to ascertain. The relationship of cloud services and risk is shown in **figure 3.21**.

---

[201] Cloud Security Alliance, *Top Threats to Cloud Computing: Egregious Eleven*, August 2019, https://cloudsecurityalliance.org/artifacts/top-threats-to-cloud-computing-egregious-eleven

[202] An applistructure is an amalgamation of applications and technical infrastructure.

[203] *Op cit* ISACA, *CISM Review Manual 15th Edition*

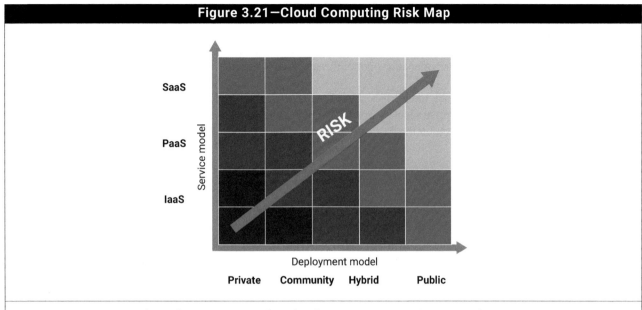

Figure 3.21—Cloud Computing Risk Map

Source: ISACA, *Controls and Assurance in the Cloud Using COBIT 5*, USA, 2014, figure 3, www.isaca.org/bookstore/cobit-5/cb5ca

Cloud Application Risk

In implementing and adapting cloud-based strategies, enterprises tend to include SaaS offerings, sometimes extending this to critical business processes and related applications. Even though these service offerings may bring business advantages, they nevertheless generate data-in-flow vulnerabilities that may be exploited by cybercriminals and through cyberwarfare. The resulting risk is exacerbated by the fact that many vendors and hardware providers for mobile devices, supply cloud-based freeware that is designed to enforce user loyalty. This is often the case for data synchronization, handling of popular file types such as music or pictures, and personal information such as email and calendar entries.

The application layer within the overall IT environment is particularly susceptible to zero-day exploits, as witnessed by many practical examples. Even major software vendors frequently update and patch their applications, but new attack vectors using such applications emerge almost daily. In terms of cybercrime and cyberwarfare, the market for zero-day exploits is a lively one, and the time span from discovery to recognition and remediation is increasing.

Likewise, the propagation of complex malware has been growing over the past several years. From a cybercrime and cyberwarfare perspective, recent specimens of malware show a higher level of sophistication and persistence than the basic varieties used by opportunistic attackers. Although software vendors are quick to address malware in terms of recognition and removal, there is a significant residual risk of malware becoming persistent in target enterprises and any enterprise can become a target.

Secondary malware attacks—where APTs make use of already installed simple malware—are often successful where the environmental conditions are conducive to user error or lack of vigilance, namely in home-user or traveling-user scenarios. In practice, removal of the primary malware (a fairly simple process) often allays any further suspicion and causes users and security managers to be lulled into a false sense of security. The secondary and very complex malware may have infiltrated the system, presenting a known and simple piece of primary malware as bait.

Cloud Best Practices

In the past, security and data privacy concerns were barriers to cloud adoption. That is no longer the case supported by a 2020 survey revealing 93% of respondents reported having a multicloud usage.[204] What is sometimes lost is the fact that the use of reputable cloud providers does not eliminate security risk.

Like the use of any third-party contract, enterprises should ensure that their CSP has a security system in place equivalent to or better than the enterprise security practice. In addition, enterprises can request audits of the cloud provider. The security audits should cover the facilities, networks, hardware, and operating systems within the cloud infrastructure.

Additional recommendations by the CSA[205] include:

- Monitor employees in the cloud
- Employ cloud data loss prevention (DLP) technologies to monitor and stop any unauthorized data exfiltration.
- Invest in solutions like cloud access security brokers (CASBs) or software-defined gateways (SDGs) to analyze outbound activities and help discover cloud usage and at-risk users and to follow behavior usage of credentialed employees to identify anomalies.
- Use a WAF to analyze all inbound connections
- Select solutions specifically designed to monitor and control all key enterprise cloud applications (enterprise resource planning, human capital management, commerce experience and supply chain management)
- Implement a Zero-Trust model across the enterprise
- Require penetration testing results from CSPs
- API hygiene

Additionally, McAfee published a comprehensive set of best practices[206] that span data protection, internal cloud security threats and partnerships. A summary follows:

- **Data Protection**—Categorize and protect data accordingly. Pay attention to who has access and their abilities (i.e., sharing). Encrypt data before putting data in the cloud.
- **Internal Cloud Security Threats**—Understand how employees are using cloud. Take measures to adjust behavior that is inconsistent with policies. Create a list of pre-approved cloud services. Endpoint security is important. Insider threats are prominent. Trust but verify.
- **Partnerships**—Compliance responsibilities do not go away when using cloud services. Leverage and extend enterprise identity services to the cloud. Seek out trustworthy partners (i.e., ISO 27001 or SAS 70 Type II certification). SLAs are critically important (must address incident response). Routinely scan cloud files for malware. Audit configurations.

3.4.13 Data Security

In recent years, data breaches have increased in frequency and severity with the average cost being US $3.92 million in 2019.[207] Reporting reveals that the top six most-breached industries are healthcare, accommodations and food services, public administration, professional services, retail and financial.[208] Data breaches are caused by both

---

[204] Flexera, *Flexera 2020 State of the Cloud Report*, https://info.flexera.com/SLO-CM-REPORT-State-of-the-Cloud-2020

[205] *Op cit* Cloud Security Alliance, *Top Threats to Cloud Computing: Egregious Eleven*

[206] McAfee, "19 Cloud Security Best Practices for 2019, " 22 August 2019, www.mcafee.com/blogs/enterprise/cloud-security/top-19-cloud-security-best-practices/

[207] Ponemon, L.; "What's New in the 2019 Cost of a Data Breach Report," Security Intelligence, 23 July 2019, https://securityintelligence.com/posts/whats-new-in-the-2019-cost-of-a-data-breach-report/

[208] Hospelhorn, S.; "Hacker Motives: Red Flags and Prevention," Varonis, 29 March 2020, www.varonis.com/blog/hacker-motives/

internal and external actors with external actors being predominantly organized criminals.[209] Beyond the hard costs associated with responding to the attack, data breaches are increasingly resulting in fines and reputational damage.

Operating systems have file systems that manage data files stored within the system and provide access controls to determine which users (or programs) have what type of access to a file. Common file accesses include creation, modification, read, write, and deletion controls.

Databases can be individually protected with control that is similar to protections applied at the system level. Specific controls that can be placed at the database level include:

- Authentication and authorization of access
- Access controls limiting or controlling the type of data that can be accessed and what types of accesses are allowed (such as read-only, read and write, or delete)
- Logging and other transactional monitoring
- Encryption and integrity controls
- Backups

The controls used to protect databases should be designed in conjunction with system and application controls and form another layer of protection in a defense-in-depth scheme.

Encryption is an effective and increasingly practical way to restrict access to confidential information while in storage. The traditional protection method—a password—has inherent weaknesses and, in many cases, is easily guessable. Access control lists (ACLs) that define who has access are also effective, but they often have to be used in conjunction with operating systems or applications. Further, ACLs cannot prevent improper use of information by systems administrators, as the latter can have total control of a computer. Encryption can fill the security gap, and it can also protect data from hackers who, by means of malicious software, can obtain systems administration rights. Encryption also helps to protect data when a computer or a disk falls into the wrong hands. Many email encryption programs can also be applied to stored data. There are also some encryption products that focus on file protection for computers and mobile smart devices. Encryption is discussed later in this chapter.

Data Classification

The information that an enterprise uses can be of varying value and importance. For example, some information may be public and require minimal protection, while other information, such as national security information, health or other personal information or trade secrets, can result in significant harm to the enterprise if inadvertently released, deleted, or modified.

It is important for an enterprise to understand the sensitivity of information and classify data based on its sensitivity and the impact of release or loss of the information.

Data classification works by tagging data with metadata based on a classification taxonomy. This enables data to be found quickly and efficiently, cuts back on storage and backup costs, and helps to allocate and maximize resources.

Classification levels should be kept to a minimum. They should be simple designations that assign different degrees of sensitivity and criticality.

Data classification should be defined in a data classification policy that provides definition of different classes of information and how each class of information should be handled and protected. In addition, the classification scheme should convey the association of the data and their supporting business processes.

[209] *Ibid.*

In some cases, local regulations may impact data classification and handling, such as those controlled by data protection acts. For example, the US Sarbanes-Oxley Act, European Union General Data Protection Regulation and Australian Privacy Principles each define which data records must be stored and for how long.

Information may also need to be reclassified based on changes to its importance. For example, prior to a product release, details of the design, pricing and other information may be confidential and need significant protection; however, after the product is announced, this information may become public and not require the same levels of protection.

Data Owners

Another important consideration for data security is defining the data owner. Although IT applies the security controls and monitoring of business data, the data do not belong to IT. Business information belongs to whoever is ultimately responsible for the business process. The owner is usually responsible for determining the data classification and, therefore, the level of protection required. The data owner may be an individual who creates the data or an organizational element that acts as a custodian of the information. The data classification process is shown in **figure 3.22**.

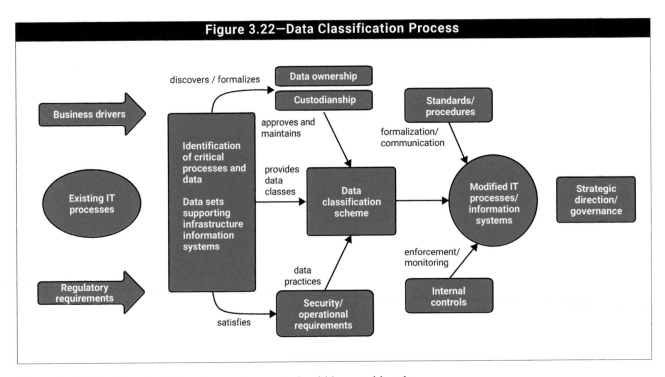

Figure 3.22—Data Classification Process

When classifying data, the following requirements should be considered:

- **Access and authentication**—Determine access requirements, including defining user profiles, access approval criteria and validation procedures.

- **Confidentiality**—Determine where sensitive data are stored and how they are transmitted.

- **Privacy**—Use controls to warn an affected user that his or her information is about to be used.

- **Availability**—Determine the uptime and downtime tolerances for different data types.

- **Ownership and distribution**—Establish procedures to protect data from unauthorized copy and distribution.

- **Integrity**—Protect data from unauthorized changes using change control procedures and automated monitoring and detection for unauthorized changes and manipulation.

- **Data retention**—Determine retention periods and preserve specific versions of software, hardware, authentication credentials and encryption keys to ensure availability.

- **Auditability**—Keep track of access, authorizations, changes and transactions.

After data classification has been assigned, security controls can be established, such as encryption, authentication and logging. Security measures should increase as the level of data sensitivity or criticality increases. The full data life cycle is shown in **figure 3.23**.

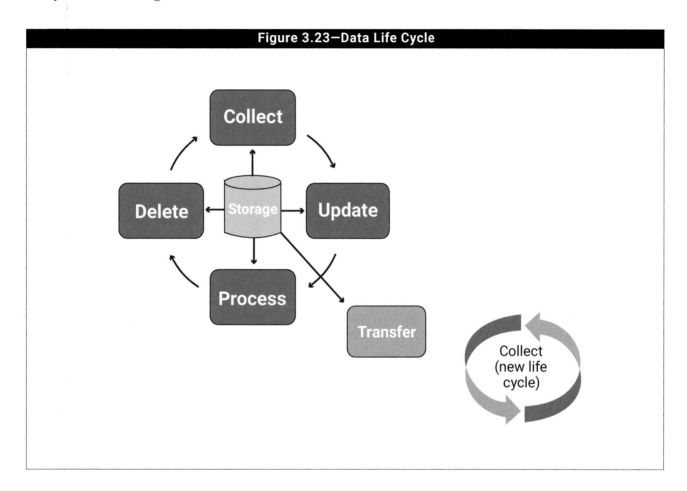

Figure 3.23—Data Life Cycle

Database Security

Database security covers a wide range of information security controls to protect the databases in an enterprise. Database security is essential because databases contain critical and sensitive information that is required to support business operations. Databases are vulnerable to types of risk, including:

- Unauthorized activity by authorized users
- Malware infections or interactions
- Capacity issues
- Physical damage
- Design flaws
- Data corruption

Database security is provided through the following:[210]

- Encryption of sensitive data in the database
- Use of database views to restrict information available to a user
- Secure protocols to communicate with the database
- Content-based access controls that restrict access to sensitive records
- Restricting administrator-level access
- Efficient indexing to enhance data retrieval
- Backups of databases (shadowing, mirroring)
- Backups of transaction journals (remote journaling)
- Referential integrity
- Entity integrity
- Validation of input
- Defined data fields (schema)
- Layered network access restrictions or segregation

Ingress, Egress and Data Loss Prevention

There are two types of attack vectors: ingress and egress (also known as data exfiltration). Ingress refers to network communications coming in, while egress refers to network communications going out. While most attack analysis concentrates on the ingress or intrusion into systems, if the adversary's goal is theft of information or data, then it is important to consider the vector or path used to remove the data from the owner's systems and networks. Data loss prevention (DLP) software is helpful in this regard. A successful data loss prevention program helps an enterprise protect its information and prevent the exfiltration of sensitive data.

Strong DLP solutions cover three primary states of information. Data at rest refers to stored data. DLP solutions must be able to log where various file types are stored. Crawler applications then explore the information on these files searching for sensitive data like social security or credit card information. These crawlers determine whether the storage location follows predefined rules.

Data in transit refers to data traveling through the network. Deep packet inspection (DPI) is used to analyze the data for sensitive content. DLP solutions can alert management and even block, quarantine or encrypt controlled information based on controls.

Finally, good DLP solutions manage data in use, which is data movement at the user workstation level. This includes sending information to printers, thumb drives, or even the copy-and-paste clipboard. DLP solutions use agent software to set rules for data use. All three information types, data at rest, data in motion and data in use, must be addressed to create a full DLP solution.

3.4.14 Configuration Management

Maintaining the security configurations of network devices, systems, applications, and other IT resources is critically important to ensure that security controls are properly installed and maintained. As enterprises grow and evolve, so does the potential for change and dysfunction. To manage such changes and minimize their potential to disrupt operations, efficiency, and profits, it is necessary to develop formal processes. These processes of configuration management can be quite complex, as they support many other activities within the enterprise.

---

[210] *Op cit* ISACA, *CISA Review Manual 27th Edition*

Implementing a configuration management process has several benefits for security including:[211]

- Verification of the impact on related items
- Assessment of risk for a proposed change
- Ability to inspect different lines of defense for potential weaknesses
- Tracking of configuration items against approved secure configuration baselines
- Insights into investigations after a security breach or operations disruption
- Version control and production authorization of hardware and software components

3.4.15 Change Management

Change management is an essential part of technology practices within an enterprise. Its purpose is to ensure that changes to processes, systems, software, applications, platforms, and configuration are introduced in an orderly, controlled manner. Controls are implemented in the form of a structured review process intended to evaluate and minimize the potential for disruption that a proposed change, maintenance activity or patch may introduce. Effective controls ensure that all changes are categorized, prioritized, and authorized. The process generally includes mechanisms for tracking and documenting changes to demonstrate accountability and compliance with best practices.

It is important to note that change management is not a standalone process; it draws upon a number of other processes and controls and may require cross functional input. Therefore, it requires a comprehensive knowledge of enterprise operations and infrastructure to be implemented effectively.

3.4.16 Patch Management

Patches are solutions to software programming errors. In many cases, security vulnerabilities are introduced by coding errors. Therefore, it is vital that software bugs that are identified as security vulnerabilities be patched as soon as possible. Most software vendors release regular software updates and patches as the vulnerabilities are identified and fixed.

Failure to apply patches to known security vulnerabilities is the most common cause of security breaches. Therefore, patching is an important part of vulnerability management, and enterprises must set up processes to identify patches that are relevant to their IT infrastructure. Once a necessary patch is identified, it should be tested to ensure it does not negatively impact operations. After the patch has been verified, it can be scheduled and installed where appropriate.

3.4.17 Encryption Fundamentals, Techniques and Applications

Encryption is the process of converting a plaintext message into a secure-coded form of text, called ciphertext. The ciphertext cannot be understood without converting back, via decryption—the reverse process—to plaintext. This is done via a mathematical function and a special encryption/decryption password called the key. In many countries, encryption is subject to governmental laws and regulations that limit the key size or define what may not be encrypted.

Encryption is part of a broader science of secret languages called cryptography, which is generally used to:

- Protect information stored on computers from unauthorized viewing and manipulation
- Protect data in transit over networks from unauthorized interception and manipulation

---

[211] ISACA, *Configuration Management: Using COBIT 5*, USA, 2013, www.isaca.org/bookstore/cobit-5/cb5cm

CYBERSECURITY
FUNDAMENTALS
An ISACA Certificate

- Deter and detect accidental or intentional alterations of data
- Verify authenticity of a transaction or document

Encryption is limited in that it cannot prevent the loss of data. It is possible to compromise encryption programs if encryption keys are not protected adequately. Therefore, encryption should be regarded as an essential, but incomplete, form of access control that should be incorporated into the enterprise overall computer security program.

Elements of Cryptographic Systems

Key elements of cryptographic systems include:

- **Encryption algorithm**—Mathematically based function or calculation that encrypts or decrypts data.
- **Encryption key**—Piece of information similar to a password that makes the encryption or decryption process unique. A user needs the correct key to access or decipher a message, because the wrong key converts the message into an unreadable form.
- **Key length**—Predetermined length for the key. The longer the key, the more difficult it is to compromise in a brute force attack where all possible key combinations are tried.

Effective cryptographic systems depend upon a variety of factors including:

- Algorithm strength
- Secrecy and difficulty of compromising a key
- Nonexistence of back doors by which an encrypted file can be decrypted without knowing the key
- Inability to decrypt parts of a ciphertext message and prevent known plaintext attacks
- Properties of the plaintext known by a perpetrator

Encryption algorithms may either be block ciphers or stream ciphers. Block ciphers encrypt and decrypt one block of text at a time, whereas stream ciphers encrypt and decrypt one byte at a time. One byte is 8 bits.

Key Systems

There are two types of cryptographic systems:

- **Symmetric key systems**—These use single, secret, bidirectional keys that encrypt and decrypt.
- **Asymmetric key systems**—These use pairs of unidirectional, complementary keys that only encrypt or decrypt. Typically, one of these keys is secret, and the other is publicly known.

Public key systems are asymmetric cryptographic systems. Most encrypted transactions over the Internet use a combination of private/public keys, secret keys, hash functions (fixed values derived mathematically from a text message), and digital certificates (that prove ownership of a public encryption key) to achieve confidentiality, message integrity, authentication and nonrepudiation by either sender or recipient (also known as a public key infrastructure [PKI]). Essentially, keys and hash values are used to transform a string of characters into a shorter or fixed-length value or key that represents the original string. This encryption process allows data to be stored and transported with reduced exposure, so data remain secure as they move across the Internet or other networks.

Symmetric (Private) Key Encryption

Symmetric key cryptographic systems are based on a symmetric encryption algorithm, which uses a secret key to encrypt the plaintext to the ciphertext and the same key to decrypt the ciphertext to the corresponding plaintext. In this case, the key is said to be symmetric because the encryption key is the same as the decryption key. An example of symmetric cryptography is shown in **figure 3.24**.

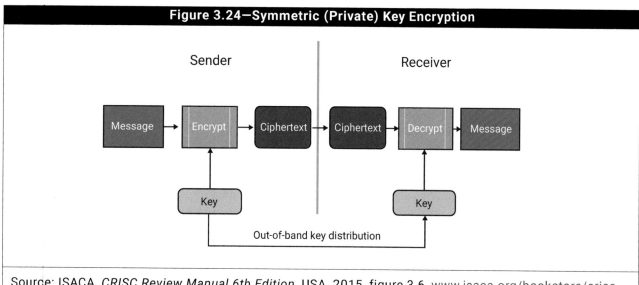

Figure 3.24—Symmetric (Private) Key Encryption

Source: ISACA, *CRISC Review Manual 6th Edition*, USA, 2015, figure 3.6, www.isaca.org/bookstore/crisc-exam-resources/crr6ed

The most common symmetric key cryptographic system used to be the data encryption standard (DES). It was the first encryption algorithm approved for public disclosure by NIST and employed keys of 56 bits (plus 8 bits used for parity checking). The bits in the plaintext are processed one 64-bit block at a time and, as such, DES was a block-cipher. [212] DES was officially deprecated in 2006 after many years of being easily brute forced.[213]

The Data Encryption Algorithm (TDEA)—more commonly referred to as Triple DES or 3DES—sought to extend the DES standard while retaining backward compatibility (it applies the DES cipher algorithm three times to each data block).[214] Triple DES provided a relatively simple method of increasing the key size of DES to protect information without the need to design a completely new block cipher algorithm and was successful in itself endeavor. 3DES was broadly used to protect websites, VPNs, and financial industries to include EMV chip cards. However, it too was broken in 2016[215] and has begun to be retired—at least by NIST.[216, 217]

Currently, Advanced Encryption Standard (AES) is widely adopted and has three key lengths – 128, 192, and 256 bits. AES is faster and stronger than 3DES, in part, due to a more complex algorithm and longer key length. AES encrypts and decrypts blocks in blocks of 128 bits. AES appears safe—for now. However, the progress of quantum computing will eventually change this.[218]

There are two main advantages to symmetric key cryptosystems such as AES:

- The user only has to know one key for both encryption and decryption.

[212] *Op cit* ISACA, *CISA Review Manual 27th Edition*

[213] Kelly, S.; "Security Implications of Using the Data Encryption Standard (DES)," The IETF Trust (2006), December 2006, www.rfc-editor.org/rfc/pdfrfc/rfc4772.txt.pdf

[214] *Op cit* ISACA, *CISA Review Manual 27th Edition*

[215] Stealthsploit, "3DES is finally actually broken!," 7 September 2016, https://stealthsploit.com/2016/09/07/3des-is-finally-actually-broken/

[216] Henry, J.; "3DES is Officially Being Retired," 3 August 2018, Cryptomathic, www.cryptomathic.com/news-events/blog/3des-is-officially-being-retired

[217] Gamey, D.; "NIST is Sunsetting Triple DES - so what will the Financial Industry do?," Control Gap, 9 April 2019, https://controlgap.com/blog/nist-is-sunsetting-triple-des-so-what-will-the-financial-industry-do

[218] Stubbs, R.; "Symmetric Encryption Algorithms - Their Strengths and Weaknesses, and the Need for Crypto-Agility," Cryptomathic, 12 March 2019, www.cryptomathic.com/news-events/blog/symmetric-encryption-algorithms-their-strengths-and-weaknesses-and-the-need-for-crypto-agility

- Symmetric key cryptosystems are generally less complicated and, therefore, use up less processing power than asymmetric techniques. They are ideally suited for bulk data encryption.

The disadvantages of this approach include:

- **Difficulty distributing keys**—Getting the keys into the hands of those with whom you want to exchange data can be a challenge, particularly in ecommerce environments where customers are unknown, untrusted entities.

- **Limitations of shared secret**—A symmetric key cannot be used to sign electronic documents or messages because the mechanism is based on a shared secret.

There are many other types of symmetric encryption algorithms that have outlived their usefulness. Governmental bodies may provide supplemental guidance for their respective area of authority. For example, NIST categorizes algorithms as deprecated, disallowed, or allowed. NIST defines deprecated as "the use of the algorithm and key length is allowed, but the user must accept some risk," whereas disallowed means that "the algorithm or key length is no longer allowed for indicated use."[219] Alternatively, vendors may provide guidance to customers. For instance, Cisco has published guidance categorizing algorithms as being legacy, quantum resistant, next generation or recommending avoidance.[220]

Asymmetric (Private) Key Encryption

Public key cryptographic systems developed for key distribution solve the problem of getting single symmetric keys into the hands of two people who do not know each other but who want to exchange information securely. Based on an asymmetric encryption process, two keys work together as a pair. One key is used to encrypt data; the other is used to decrypt data. Either key can be used to encrypt or decrypt, but once the key has been used to encrypt data, only its partner can be used to decrypt the data. The key that was used to encrypt the data cannot be used to decrypt it. Thus, the keys are asymmetric in that they are inversely related to each other.

Asymmetric keys are often used for short messages such as encrypting DES symmetric keys or creating digital signatures. If asymmetric keys were used to encrypt bulk data (long messages), the process would be very slow; this is the reason they are used to encrypt short messages, such as digests or signatures.

With asymmetric encryption, one key—the secret or private key—is known only to one person. The other key—the public key—is known by many people. In other words, a message that has been sent encrypted by the secret (private) key of the sender can be deciphered by anyone with the corresponding public key. In this way, if the public key deciphers the message satisfactorily, one can be sure of the origin of the message because only the sender (owner of the correspondent private key) could have encrypted the message. This forms the basis of authentication and nonrepudiation, because the sender cannot later claim that he or she did not generate the message.

A message that has been sent encrypted using the public key of the receiver can be generated by anyone but can only be read by the receiver. This is one basis of confidentiality. In theory, a message that has been encrypted twice, first by the sender's secret key and second by the receiver's public key, achieves both authentication and confidentiality objectives, but it is not commonly used because it could generate performance issues.

One disadvantage to using asymmetric algorithms is they are computationally intensive and slow relative to symmetric algorithms. For that reason, asymmetric cryptography is typically used only to encrypt short messages. In fact, the most common use of asymmetric algorithms is to distribute symmetric keys that can then be used by the participants for fast, secure communication, as seen in **figure 3.25**.[221]

[219] *Op cit* National Institute of Standards and Technology, "Glossary"
[220] Cisco, "Next Generation Cryptography," Cisco Security, https://tools.cisco.com/security/center/resources/next_generation_cryptography
[221] *Op cit* ISACA, *CRISC Review Manual 6th Edition*

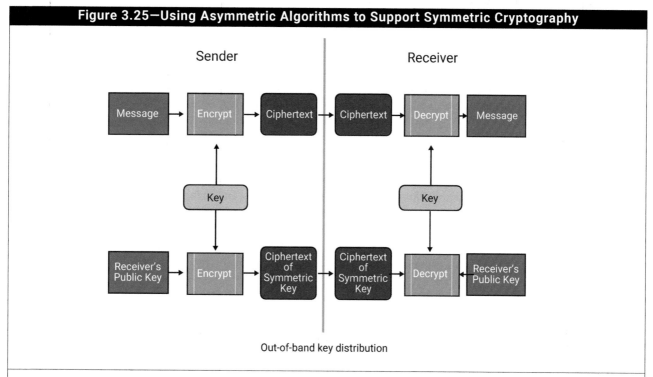

Figure 3.25—Using Asymmetric Algorithms to Support Symmetric Cryptography

Source: ISACA, *CRISC Review Manual 6th Edition*, USA, 2015, figure 3.7, www.isaca.org/bookstore/crisc-exam-resources/crr6ed

Elliptical Curve Cryptography

Although public key cryptography ensures message security, the long keys and mathematical problems it uses tend to be inefficient. A variant and more efficient form of public key cryptography is elliptical curve cryptography (ECC), which has gained prominence as a method for increasing security while using minimum resources. It is believed that ECC demands less computational power and therefore offers more security per bit. For example, an ECC with a 256-bit key offers the same security as an RSA-based system with a 3,072-bit key. ECC works well on networked computers requiring strong cryptography. However, ECC has some limitations, such as bandwidth and processing power. And, like many other public key cryptographies, ECC is able to be broken using Shor's algorithm in a quantum computing environment.

Quantum Cryptography

Quantum cryptography solves some of the existing problems associated with current cryptographic systems, specifically the random generation and secure distribution of symmetric cryptographic keys. It is based on a practical application of the characteristics of the photons (the smallest particles of light) and the physical laws governing the generation, propagation and detection of those photons. Though quantum cryptography is a highly secure form of encryption, researchers have demonstrated that quantum cryptography systems can be hacked by exploiting the physical properties of the systems themselves.

Post-Quantum Cryptography

Post-quantum cryptography, which is also referred to as quantum-proof, quantum-safe, or quantum-resistant cryptography, refers to cryptography that is thought to be secure against hacking by quantum computers. Current public key cryptographies, like elliptical curve and large-integer factorization cryptographies, can be broken using a powerful enough quantum computer. Current research in post-quantum cryptography is focusing on hash functions and existing symmetric cryptographic algorithms, which are believed to provide security against quantum computing-based attacks and attacks by traditional computers.

Applications of Cryptographic Systems

The use of cryptosystems by applications, for example in email and Internet transactions, generally involves a combination of private/public key pairs, secret keys, hash functions and digital certificates. The purpose of applying these combinations is to achieve confidentiality, message integrity, or nonrepudiation by either the sender or recipient. The process generally involves the sender hashing the message into a message digest or pre-hash code for message integrity, which is encrypted using the sender's private key for authenticity, integrity and nonrepudiation (i.e., digital signature).

Using his/her secret key, the sender then will encrypt the message. Afterward, the secret key is encrypted with the recipient's public key, which has been validated through the recipient's digital certificate and provides message confidentiality. The process on the receiving end reverses what has been done by the sender. The recipient uses his/her private key to decrypt the sender's secret key. He/she uses this secret key to decrypt the message, to expose it. If the pre-hash code has been encrypted with the sender's private key, the recipient verifies its authenticity using the public key contained in the sender's digital certificate and decrypts the pre-hash code, which provides the nonrepudiation to the recipient of the sender's message. For integrity purposes, the recipient calculates a post-hash code, which should equal the pre-hash code. Specific examples of this method or related variants are described below.

Digital Signature

A digital signature is an electronic identification of a person or entity created by using a public key algorithm. It serves as a way for the recipient to verify the integrity of the data and the identity of the sender. To verify the integrity of the data, a cryptographic hashing algorithm, called a checksum, is computed against the entire message or electronic document, which generates a small, fixed-string message, usually about 128 bits in length. This process, also referred to as a digital signature algorithm, creates a message digest (i.e., smaller extrapolated version of the original message).

Common types of message digest algorithms are SHA-256 and SHA-512. These algorithms are one-way functions, unlike private and public key encryption algorithms. The process of creating message digests cannot be reversed.

They are meant for digital signature applications where a large electronic document or string of characters, such as word processor text, a spreadsheet, a database record, the content of a hard disk, or a JPEG image has to be compressed in a secure manner before being signed with the private key. All digest algorithms take a message of arbitrary length and produce a 128-bit message digest.

The next step, which verifies the identity of the sender, is to encrypt the message digest using the sender's private key, which signs the document with the sender's digital signature for message authenticity. To decipher, the receiver would use the sender's public key, proving that the message could only have come from the sender. This process of sender authentication is known as nonrepudiation because the sender cannot later claim that they did not generate the message.

After being decrypted, the hash is recomputed by the receiver using the same hashing algorithm on the electronic document, and the receiver compares the results with what was sent, to ensure the integrity of the message. Therefore, digital signature is a cryptographic method that ensures:

- **Data integrity**—Any change to the plaintext message would result in the recipient failing to compute the same message hash.

- **Authentication**—The recipient can ensure that the message has been sent by the claimed sender since only the claimed sender has the secret key.

- **Nonrepudiation**—The claimed sender cannot later deny generating and sending the message.

- **Digital signatures and public key encryption** are vulnerable to man-in-the-middle attacks where the sender's digital signature private key and public key may be faked. To protect against such attacks, an independent sender authentication authority has been designed. The PKI performs the function of independently authenticating the validity of senders' digital signatures and public keys.

Transport Layer Security (TLS)

TLS[222] is a cryptographic protocol that provides secure communications on the Internet. TLS is a session- or connection-layered protocol widely used for communication between browsers and web servers. Besides communication privacy, it also provides endpoint authentication. The protocols allow client-server applications to communicate in a way designed to prevent eavesdropping, tampering and message forgery.

TLS involves a number of basic phases:

- Peer negotiation for algorithm support

- Public-key, encryption-based key exchange and certificate-based authentication

- Symmetric cipher-based traffic encryption

During the first phase, the client and server negotiate which cryptographic algorithms will be used. Current implementations support the following choices:

- For public-key cryptography: RSA, Diffie-Hellman, DSA or Fortezza

- For symmetric ciphers: RC4, IDEA, Triple DES or AES

- For one-way hash functions: SHA-1 or SHA-2 (SHA-256)

TLS runs on layers above the TCP transport protocol and provides security to application protocols, even if it is most commonly used with HTTP to form Secure Hypertext Transfer Protocol (HTTPS). HTTPS is similar to HTTP, just with an encrypted session via TLS (or SSL) protocols. HTTPS serves to secure World Wide Web pages for applications. In electronic commerce, more authentication may be used both in business-to-business (B-to-B) activities (for which both the client and the server are authenticated) and business-to-consumer (B-to-C) interaction (in which only the server is authenticated).

Besides TLS, SSL protocol is also widely used in real-world applications, even though its use is now deprecated as a significant vulnerability was discovered in 2014. TLS is a further development of SSL, but TLS and SSL are not interchangeable. Interoperability between SSL and TLS is impossible.

The newest version of TLS is TLS 1.3, which arrived in 2018. TLS 1.3 is faster and improves on version 1.2 by eliminating supporting for legacy encryption systems that made TLS 1.2 vulnerable to man in the middle (MITM) attacks.[223] Practitioners may happen upon even older versions but are encouraged to migrate to the newest version.

---

[222] *Op cit* ISACA, *CISA Review Manual 27th Edition*
[223] Fruhlinger, J.; "What is SSL, TLS? And how this encryption protocol works," CSO, 4 December 2018, www.csoonline.com/article/3246212/what-is-ssl-tls-and-how-this-encryption-protocol-works.html

Secure Hypertext Transfer Protocol (HTTPS)

As an application layer protocol, HTTPS transmits individual messages or pages securely between a web client and server by establishing a TLS-type connection. Using the https:// designation in the URL instead of the standard http://, HTTPS directs the message to a secure port number rather than the default web port address. This protocol uses SSL secure features but does so as a message rather than as a session-oriented protocol.

IPSec

IPSec is used for communication among two or more hosts, two or more subnets, or hosts and subnets. This IP network layer packet security protocol establishes VPNs via transport and tunnel mode encryption methods. For the transport method, the data portion of each packet—referred to as the encapsulation security payload (ESP)—is encrypted to achieve confidentiality. In the tunnel mode, the ESP payload and its header are encrypted. To achieve nonrepudiation, an additional authentication header (AH) is applied.

In establishing IPSec sessions in either mode, security associations (SAs) are established. SAs define which security parameters should be applied between the communicating parties as encryption algorithms, keys, initialization vectors, life span of keys, etc.

To increase the security of IPSec, asymmetric encryption via Internet Security Association and Key Management Protocol/Oakley (ISAKMP/Oakley) should be used because it allows the key management, use of public keys, negotiation, establishment, modification and deletion of SAs and attributes. For authentication, the sender uses digital certificates. The connection is made secure by supporting the generation, authentication, and distribution of the SAs and cryptographic keys.

Secure Shell (SSH)

SSH is a client-server program that opens a secure, encrypted command-line shell session from the Internet for remote logon. Similar to a VPN, SSH uses strong cryptography to protect data, including passwords, binary files and administrative commands, transmitted between systems on a network. SSH is typically implemented by validating both parties' credentials via digital certificates. SSH is useful in securing Telnet and FTP services. It is implemented at the application layer, as opposed to operating at the network layer (IPSec implementation).

Secure Multipurpose Internet Mail Extensions (S/MIME)

S/MIME is a standard secure email protocol that authenticates the identity of the sender and receiver, verifies message integrity, and ensures the privacy of a message's contents, including attachments.

Secure Electronic Transactions (SET)

SET was an early protocol developed jointly by VISA and MasterCard to secure payment transactions among all parties involved in credit card transactions. As an open system specification, SET is an application-oriented protocol that uses trusted third parties' encryption and digital signature processes, via a PKI of trusted third-party institutions, to address confidentiality of information, integrity of data, cardholder authentication, merchant authentication and interoperability.

Virtual Private Network (VPN)

Recall from earlier in the chapter that a VPN remains a popular mechanism for remote access to enterprise resources. A popular VPN technology is IPSec which traditionally used either DES, Triple DES, or AES encryption algorithms. Of the three, only AES is recommended due to key strength.

Common protocols for VPNs are:

- Internet Protocol Security (IPSec)
- Layer Two Tunneling Protocol (L2TP)
- Point-to-Point Tunneling Protocol (PPTP)
- OpenVPN (SSL/TLS)

Public Key Infrastructure (PKI)

If an individual wants to send messages or electronic documents and sign them with a digital signature using a public key cryptographic system, how does the individual distribute the public key in a secure way? If the public key is distributed electronically, it can be intercepted and changed. To prevent this from occurring, a framework known as a PKI is used. PKI allows a trusted party to issue, maintain, and revoke public key certificates.

PKI allows users to interact with other users and applications to obtain and verify identities and keys from trusted sources. The actual implementation of PKI varies according to specific requirements. Key elements of the infrastructure are as follows:

- **Digital certificates**—A digital certificate is composed of a public key and identifying information about the owner of the public key. The purpose of digital certificates is to associate a public key with the individual's identity to prove the sender's authenticity. These certificates are electronic documents, digitally signed by some trusted entity with its private key (transparent to users) that contains information about the individual and his or her public key. The process requires the sender to sign a document by attaching a digital certificate issued by a trusted entity. The receiver of the message and accompanying digital certificate relies on the public key of the trusted third-party certificate authority (CA) (that is included with the digital certificate or obtained separately) to authenticate the message. The receiver can link the message to a person, not simply to a public key, because of their trust in this third party. The status and values of a current user's certificate should include:
  - A distinguishing username
  - An actual public key
  - The algorithm used to compute the digital signature inside the certificate
  - A certificate validity period

- **Certificate authority**—A CA is an authority in a network that issues and manages security credentials and public keys for message signature verification or encryption. The CA attests to the authenticity of the owner of a public key. The process involves a CA making a decision to issue a certificate based on evidence or knowledge obtained in verifying the identity of the recipient. As part of a PKI, a CA checks with a registration authority (RA) to verify information provided by the requestor of a digital certificate. If the RA verifies the requestor's information, the CA can then issue a certificate. Upon verifying the identity of the recipient, the CA signs the certificate with its private key for distribution to the user. Upon receipt, the user will verify the certificate signature with the CA's public key (e.g., commercial CAs such as VeriSign™ issue certificates through web browsers). The ideal CA is authoritative (someone that the user trusts) for the name or key space it represents. A certificate always includes the owner's public key, expiration date and the owner's information. Types of CAs may include:
  - Organizationally empowered, which have authoritative control over those individuals in their name space

- Liability empowered, for example, choosing commercially available options (such as VeriSign) in obtaining a digital certificate. The CA is responsible for managing the certificate throughout its life cycle. Key elements or subcomponents of the CA structure include the certification practice statement (CPS), RAs and certificate revocation lists (CRLs).

- **Registration authority**—An RA is an authority in a network that verifies user requests for a digital certificate and tells the CA to issue it. An optional entity separate from a CA, an RA would be used by a CA with a very large customer base. CAs use RAs to delegate some of the administrative functions associated with recording or verifying some or all of the information needed by a CA to issue certificates or CRLs and to perform other certificate management functions. However, with this arrangement, the CA still retains sole responsibility for signing either digital certificates or CRLs. RAs are part of a PKI. The digital certificate contains a public key that is used to encrypt messages and verify digital signatures. If an RA is not present in the PKI structure established, the CA is assumed to have the same set of capabilities as those defined for an RA. The administrative functions that a particular RA implements will vary based on the needs of the CA but must support the principle of establishing or verifying the identity of the subscriber. These functions may include the following:

  - Verifying information supplied by the subject (personal authentication functions)

  - Verifying the right of the subject to requested certificate attributes

  - Verifying that the subject actually possesses the private key being registered and that it matches the public key requested for a certificate (generally referred to as proof of possession [POP])

  - Reporting key compromise or termination cases where revocation is required

  - Assigning names for identification purposes

  - Generating shared secrets for use during the initialization and certificate pick-up phases of registration

  - Initiating the registration process with the CA on behalf of the subject end entity

  - Initiating the key recovery processing

  - Distributing the physical tokens (such as smart cards) containing the private keys

  - Certificate revocation list (CRL)—The CRL is an instrument for checking the continued validity of the certificates for which the CA has responsibility. The CRL details digital certificates that are no longer valid because they were revoked by the CA. The time gap between two updates is critical and is also a risk in digital certificates verification.

  - Certification practice statement (CPS)—CPS is a detailed set of rules governing the CA's operations. It provides an understanding of the value and trustworthiness of certificates issued by a given CA in terms of the following:

    - The controls that an organization observes

    - The method it uses to validate the authenticity of certificate applicants

  - The CA's expectations of how its certificates may be used

Encryption Risk and Key Protection

The security of encryption methods relies mainly on the secrecy of keys. In general, the more a key is used, the more vulnerable it will be to compromise. For example, password cracking tools for today's microcomputers can brute force every possible key combination for a cryptographic hashing algorithm with a 40-bit key in a matter of a few hours.

The randomness of key generation is also a significant factor in the ability to compromise a key. When passwords are tied into key generation, the strength of the encryption algorithm is diminished, particularly when common words are used. This significantly reduces the key space combinations to search for the key. For example, an eight-character password is comparable to a 32-bit key. When encrypting keys based on passwords, a password that lacks randomness will diminish the capabilities of a 128-bit encryption algorithm. Therefore, it is essential that effective password syntax rules are applied and easily guessed passwords are prohibited.

3.5 Chapter 3 Knowledge Check

REVIEW QUESTIONS

1. Which of the following best describes the role of encryption within an overall cybersecurity program?

    A. Encryption is the primary means of securing digital assets.
    B. Encryption depends upon shared secrets and is therefore an unreliable means of control.
    C. Encryption is an essential but incomplete form of access control.

2. _____ is defined as a model for enabling convenient, on-demand network access to a shared pool of configurable resources (e.g., networks, servers, storage, applications and services) that can be rapidly provisioned and released with minimal management or service provider interaction.

    A. Software as a Service (SaaS)
    B. Cloud computing
    C. Platform as a Service (PaaS)

3. Which of the following terms designates the process of implementing security controls on a computer system?

    A. Cybersecurity
    B. System hardening
    C. Patching

4. The number and types of layers needed for defense in depth are a function of:

    A. Asset value, criticality, reliability of each control and degree of exposure
    B. Network configuration, navigation controls, user interface and VPN traffic
    C. Isolation, segmentation, internal controls and external controls

5. Match the following types of compliance documents to the appropriate descriptions.

a. Policies	1. Provide strong general recommendations such as what to do in particular circumstances
b. Standards	2. Provide details on how to comply with policies and standards
c. Procedures	3. Communicate required and prohibited activities and behaviors
d. Guidelines	4. Interpret policies in specific situations

Answers on page 154

Chapter 3 ANSWER KEY

Review Questions

1. A. Encryption is the primary means of securing digital assets.

    B. Encryption depends upon shared secrets and is therefore an unreliable means of control.

    C. Encryption is an essential but incomplete form of access control. Refer to page 144.

2. A. Software as a Service (SaaS)

    B. Cloud computing. Refer to page 132.

    C. Platform as a Service (PaaS)

3. A. Cybersecurity

    B. System hardening. Refer to page 124.

    C. Patching

4. **A. Asset value, criticality, reliability of each control and degree of exposure. Refer to page 96.**

    B. Network configuration, navigation controls, user interface and VPN traffic

    C. Isolation, segmentation, internal controls and external controls

5. Match the following types of compliance documents to the appropriate descriptions. **Refer to page 102.**

a. Policies	3. Communicate required and prohibited activities and behaviors
b. Standards	4. Interpret policies in specific situations
c. Procedures	2. Provide details on how to comply with policies and standards
d. Guidelines	1. Provide strong general recommendations such as what to do in particular circumstances

Chapter 4:

Security Operations and Response

Security Operations and Response

Security Operations and Response

4.1 Learning Objectives

After completing this chapter, learners will be able to:

1. Discuss security operations center (SOC) deployment models.
2. Identify common SOC functions, roles and responsibilities.
3. Identify vulnerability assessment tools, including open source tools and their capabilities.
4. Differentiate vulnerability scanning and penetration testing.
5. Discuss common phases of penetration testing.
6. Identify and use common cybersecurity tools.
7. Discuss components that aid cybersecurity monitoring and detection.
8. Understand incident response and handling methodologies.
9. Distinguish between an event and an incident.
10. Discuss the elements of an incident response plan (IRP).
11. Explain the basic concepts, practices, tools, tactics, techniques and procedures for processing digital forensic data.
12. Identify common antiforensic tactics and techniques.

4.2 Security Operations

It is common to hear of enterprises establishing a security operations center (SOC).[224],[225],[226] SOCs have become important; however, they are not always practical for smaller enterprises. This chapter provides an overview of SOCs; note, though, that in practice, many variables determine which activities a SOC handles. When appropriate, conclusions are made based on industry research. The remainder of this chapter is focused on providing useful information on specific activities performed by cybersecurity professionals, regardless of whether they are assigned to a formal SOC.

4.2.1 Security Operations Centers (SOC)

A SOC means different things to different people. For instance, Gartner defines a SOC as "a team, often operating in shifts around the clock, and a facility dedicated to and organized to prevent, detect, assess and respond to cybersecurity threats and incidents, and to fulfill and assess regulatory compliance."[227] Alternatively, SANS defines a SOC as "a combination of people, processes and technology protecting the information systems of an organization through: proactive design and configuration, ongoing monitoring of system state, detection of unintended actions or undesirable state, and minimizing damage from unwanted effects."[228] Other references are less rigid but share similar attributes of being centralized teams assigned to monitor, detect and remediate IT issues.[229],[230],[231]

[224] Crowley, C.; J. Pescatore; *Common and Best Practices for Security Operations Centers: Results of the 2019 SOC Survey*, SANS Institute, July 2019, www.sans.org/media/analyst-program/common-practices-security-operations-centers-results-2019-soc-survey-39060.pdf

[225] Zimmerman, C.; "Ten Strategies of a World-Class Cybersecurity Operations Center," MITRE, 2014, www.mitre.org/sites/default/files/publications/pr-13-1028-mitre-10-strategies-cyber-ops-center.pdf

[226] Gartner, "Security Operations Centers and Their Role in Cybersecurity," 12 October 2017, www.gartner.com/en/newsroom/press-releases/2017-10-12-security-operations-centers-and-their-role-in-cybersecurity

[227] *Ibid.*

[228] Crowley, C.; J. Pescatore "The Definition of SOC-cess? SANS 2018 Security Operations Center Survey," SANS, 13 August 2018, www.sans.org/reading-room/whitepapers/analyst/definition-soc-cess-2018-security-operations-center-survey-38570

[229] Rapid7, "Security Operations Center (SOC)," www.rapid7.com/fundamentals/security-operations-center/

[230] AT&T Business, "Building a security operations center (SOC)," https://cybersecurity.att.com/solutions/security-operations-center/building-a-soc

[231] Splunk, "What Is a Security Operations Center (SOC)?," www.splunk.com/en_us/data-insider/what-is-a-security-operations-center.html

For our purposes, a SOC is a formally recognized team responsible for monitoring, detecting and remediating technical security threats and protecting their critical infrastructure regardless of physical location.[232] These teams necessitate people, processes and technology, as illustrated in **figure 4.1**.

A SOC is a formally recognized team responsible for monitoring, detecting, and remediating technical security threats and protecting their critical infrastructure, regardless of its physical location.[233]

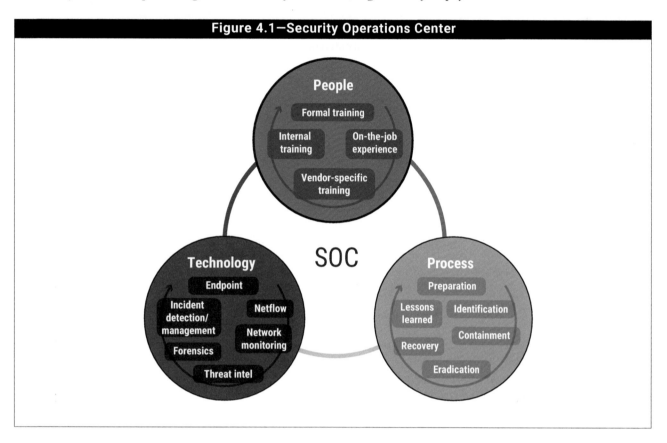

Figure 4.1—Security Operations Center

SOC Deployment Models

SOCs are deployed multiple ways with three primary categories—in-house, outsourced, and hybrid. In-house SOCs are dedicated internal teams that afford the enterprise autonomy and self-reliance. These are typically 24/7/365 operations. Outsourced SOCs are third-party services typically referred to as Managed Security Service Providers (MSSP). A hybrid SOC deployment entails the enterprise performing certain activities in-house, while outsourcing others. **Figure 4.2** illustrates SOC deployment models.

Scope of the coverage services also influences SOC deployment. For example, a SOC with large areas of responsibility may be called a Command SOC (CSOC) or a GSOC (Global SOC). Another implementation is a Distributed SOC which distributes workload dayshift workload by region. This model is sometimes referred to as follow the sun, because workload is handed off between offices in other time zones.

Lastly, a virtual SOC (VSOC) lacks a dedicated facility and typically staffed by on-call members. This type is increasing used whenever governments want trained volunteer cyberteams.

---

[232] *Op cit* AT&T Business
[233] *Op cit* ISACA, "Glossary"

A growing number of states in the United States are establishing volunteer response teams[234] using public private partnerships. Notable examples include the Michigan Civilian Cyber Corps (MiC3)[235] and the Maryland Defense Force (MDDF) Cyber Security Unit (CYSEC).[236] A global example of voluntary organizations rising to the challenge include the Estonia Defence League's Cyber Unit (EDLCU).[237]

Figure 4.2—SOC Deployment Models	
Model	**Description**
Dedicated SOC	Classic SOC with dedicated facility, dedicated full time staff, operated fully in-house. 24x7 operations.
Distributed SOC	Some full-time staff and some part-time, typically operates 8x5 in each region.
Multifunctional SOC/NOC	A dedicated facility with a dedicated team that performs the functions of a Network Operations Center (NOC) and a SOC.
Fusion SOC	A traditional SOC combined with new functions, such as threat intelligence and operational technology (OT).
Command SOC/Global SOC	Coordinates other SOCs in a global enterprise; provides threat intelligence, situational awareness and guidance.
Virtual SOC	No dedicated facility, part-time team members and usually reactive and activated by a high-profile alert or security incident. The term Virtual SOC is also sometimes used for an MSSP or managed SOC (see below).
Managed SOC/MSSP/MDR	Many enterprises are turning to Managed Security Service Providers (MSSPs) to provide SOC services on an outsourced basis. Modern offerings are called Managed Detection and Response (MDR). Managed SOCs can be outsourced completely or co-managed with in-house security staff.

MSSP ≠ MDR

A managed security service provider (MSSP) provides outsourced monitoring and management of security devices and systems. MSSPs largely exist to provide off-hours monitoring and other passive security services. Managed Detection Response (MDR) actively supports enterprises through a blended approach of technology and cyber analysis capable of intrusion detection and response.

SOC Functions

As stated earlier, the exact roles and responsibilities may vary; however, newer research reveals some industry trends to establish an appreciation of the breadth of responsibilities assigned to a typical SOC.[238]

- Security Administration
- Security Architecture
- Incident Response
- Remediation
- Compliance Support
- Security Monitoring
- Digital Forensics
- Threat Research
- Purple-teaming

---

[234] Ruiz, M.; "Bridging State-level Cybersecurity Resources," 23 October 2018, Lawfare, www.lawfareblog.com/bridging-state-level-cybersecurity-resources

[235] Michigan.gov, "Michigan Cyber Civilian Corps," www.michigan.gov/som/0,4669,7-192-78403_78404_78419---,00.html

[236] Maryland, "Maryland Defense Force," https://military.maryland.gov/mddf/Pages/default.aspx

[237] Kaitseliit, "Estonian Defence League's Cyber Unit," www.kaitseliit.ee/en/cyber-unit

SOC Roles

SOCs are typically organized with tiers and, depending on the enterprise deployment model, may have any number of area subject matter experts (SMEs) assigned to it. **Figures 4.3** through **4.5** illustrate a basic SOC team structure and responsibilities, respectively.

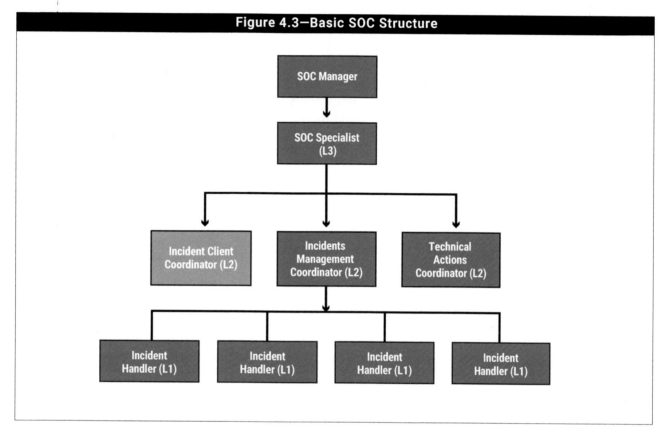

Figure 4.3—Basic SOC Structure

Figure 4.4—Typical SOC Responsibilities

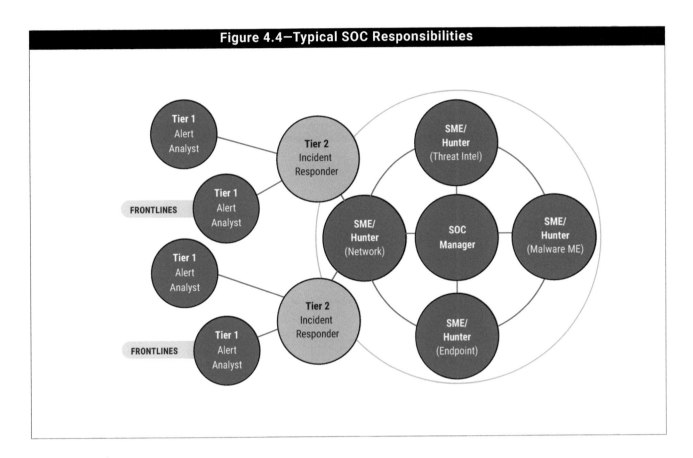

Figure 4.5—Typical SOC Roles, Qualifications and Duties

Role	Qualifications	Duties
Tier 1 Analyst Alert investigator	• System administration skills • Web programming languages, such as Python, Ruby, PHP, scripting languages • Entry-level security certifications	• Monitors SIEM alerts, manages and configures security monitoring tools • Prioritizes alerts or issues, and performs triage to confirm a real security incident is taking place
Tier 2 Analyst Incident responder	• Similar to Tier 1 analyst but with more experience, including incident response • Advanced forensics, malware assessment, threat intelligence • White-hat hacker certification or training is a major advantage	• Receives incidents and performs deep analysis, correlates with threat intelligence to identify the threat actor, nature of the attack and systems or data affected • Decides on strategy for containment, remediation and recovery, and acts on it
Tier 3 Analyst Subject matter expert/Threat hunter	• Similar to Tier 2 analyst but with more experience including high-level incidents • Experience with penetration testing tools and cross-organization data visualization • Malware reverse engineering, experience identifying and developing responses to new threats and attack patterns	• Day-to-day, conducts vulnerability assessments and penetration tests, and reviews alerts, industry news, threat intelligence and security data • Actively hunts for threats that have found their way into the network, unknown vulnerabilities and security gaps • When a major incident occurs, joins the Tier 2 analyst in responding and containing it.

Figure 4.5—Typical SOC Roles, Qualifications and Duties *(cont.)*		
Role	**Qualifications**	**Duties**
Tier 4 SOC Manager Commander	• Similar to Tier 3 analyst, including project management skills, incident response management training, strong communication skills	• Like the commander of a military unit, responsible for hiring and training SOC staff, in charge of defensive and offensive strategy • Manages resources, priorities and projects, and manages the team directly when responding to business-critical security incidents • Acts as a point of contact for the business for security incidents, compliance and other security
Security Engineer Support and infrastructure	• Degree in computer science, computer engineering or information assurance, typically combined with intermediate or advanced technical certifications	• A software or hardware specialist who focuses on security aspects in the design of information systems • Creates solutions and tools that help organizations deal robustly with disruptions of operation or malicious attack • Sometimes employed within the SOC and sometimes supporting the SOC as part of development or operations teams

4.2.2 Major Cybersecurity Areas

Lack of conformity across job titles and responsibilities represents a major professional issue in cybersecurity. NIST has made tremendous strides working with industry partners to normalize U.S. government titles and define functional areas and associated knowledge, skills and abilities. However, lack of consistent terminology—coupled with continued fragmented attempts to address the cybersecurity skills shortage—still challenges practitioners throughout the field.[239] The following list of titles and responsibilities captures a general consensus around industry roles and responsibilities. Note that it is not universal or all-inclusive.

Security Administration

Security administration[240] generally involves the installation, configuration and maintenance of servers (both hardware and software) to ensure their confidentiality, integrity and availability. Security administrators often manage security-related tools and technologies (i.e., SIEM, SOAR, firewalls) and may be responsible for access control, passwords and account creation and administration.

Security Architecture

Security architecture[241] generally involves development of system concepts, work on the capability phases of the systems development life cycle, and translation of technology and environmental conditions (e.g., law and regulation) into system and security designs and processes. Security architects are responsible for implementing, monitoring and enforcing security rules established and authorized by management,[242] and ensure that stakeholder

---

[239] ISACA, *State of Cybersecurity 2020, Part 1: Global Update on Workforce Efforts and Resources*, USA, 2020, www.isaca.org/bookstore/bookstore-wht_papers-digital/whpsc201

[240] National Initiative for Cybersecurity Careers & Studies (NICCS), "Systems Administration," https://niccs.us-cert.gov/workforce-development/cyber-security-workforce-framework/systems-administration#

[241] National Initiative for Cybersecurity Careers & Studies (NICCS), "Systems Architecture," https://niccs.us-cert.gov/workforce-development/cyber-security-workforce-framework/systems-architecture

security requirements necessary to protect the enterprise mission and business processes are adequately addressed in all aspects of enterprise architecture (including reference models, segment and solution architectures, and the resulting systems supporting those missions and business processes).

Cyberinvestigations

Cyberinvestigation[243] activities span both law enforcement (cybercrime investigators) and digital forensics (across both industry and law enforcement). Cybercrime investigators apply tactics, techniques and procedures (TTPs) using a full range of investigative tools and processes that include, but are not limited to, interview and interrogation techniques, surveillance, countersurveillance and surveillance detection, while appropriately balancing the benefits of prosecution versus intelligence gathering. Digital forensics entails collection, processing, preservation, analysis and presentation of computer-related evidence in support of network vulnerability mitigation and/or criminal, fraud, counterintelligence, or law-enforcement investigations.

Incident Response

Incident responders address crises or urgent situations within pertinent domains to mitigate immediate and potential threats.[244] They use mitigation, preparedness, and response and recovery approaches, as needed, to maximize preservation of life and property, while optimizing information security. Additionally, incident responders investigate and analyze all relevant response activities.

Analysis

Cybersecurity is by and large an analytical occupation. Cyberanalysts thrive on problem solving; they are inquisitive by nature, skilled in inferential logic and adept at finding needles in digital haystacks. An analyst is a person who analyzes or who is skilled in analysis.[245] For cybersecurity professionals, analysis aids in correlation, deconstruction and reconstruction of incidents. An analyst may have a broad, incidentwide focus, or may analyze narrow aspects of an incident, such as host artifacts, network traffic, malware or threat characteristics.

Analyst opportunities are abundant and vary greatly by country and sector. Focus areas may include cyberdefense[246], open source[247], exploitation[248], targets[249] and threats.[250] Increasingly, cybersecurity analysts are simply called SOC analysts.

Analysts may be bound to fixed analytical focus areas, although geography, industry and enterprise size may heavily influence their professional domains. The shortage of cybersecurity professionals often hits small-to-medium enterprises hardest, as they may lack the budgets to hire or retain talent (which in turn increases the types and amount of work they do).

[242] *Op cit* ISACA, "Glossary"

[243] National Initiative for Cybersecurity Careers & Studies (NICCS), "Cyber Investigation," https://niccs.us-cert.gov/workforce-development/cyber-security-workforce-framework/cyber-investigation

[244] National Initiative for Cybersecurity Careers & Studies (NICCS), "Incident Response," https://niccs.us-cert.gov/workforce-development/cyber-security-workforce-framework/incident-response

[245] Merriam-Webster, "analyst," https://www.merriam-webster.com/dictionary/analyst

[246] National Initiative for Cybersecurity Careers & Studies (NICCS), "Cyber Defense Analysis," https://niccs.us-cert.gov/workforce-development/cyber-security-workforce-framework/cyber-defense-analysis

[247] National Initiative for Cybersecurity Careers & Studies (NICCS), "All-Source Analysis," https://niccs.us-cert.gov/workforce-development/cyber-security-workforce-framework/all-source-analysis

[248] National Initiative for Cybersecurity Careers & Studies (NICCS), "Exploitation Analysis," https://niccs.us-cert.gov/workforce-development/cyber-security-workforce-framework/exploitation-analysis

[249] National Initiative for Cybersecurity Careers & Studies (NICCS), "Targets," https://niccs.us-cert.gov/workforce-development/cyber-security-workforce-framework/targets

[250] National Initiative for Cybersecurity Careers & Studies (NICCS), "Threat Analysis," https://niccs.us-cert.gov/workforce-development/cyber-security-workforce-framework/threat-analysis

In simplest terms, analysis reflects problem solving and requires the practitioner to be detail-oriented, inquisitive and observant. The cybersecurity industry has consistently overpromised and underdelivered products and/or technologies; although some products increased productivity or cybersecurity readiness, many other costly technological investments either failed to live up to their hype, or were simply inadequate relative to enterprise requirements. Workforce-development efforts tend to focus on offensive aspects of cybersecurity (e.g., ethical hacking), often perceived as sexy by many. But there is no reason to believe those types of jobs will outnumber analysis and other defensive positions in the foreseeable future, if ever.

Technological advancements in machine learning and other security analytics technologies offer promise in terms of processing large amounts of data and otherwise streamlining mundane work. However, at the end of the day, analysts are needed to investigate false positives and negatives as well as validate findings. These advanced technologies are only as good as their configuration, algorithms and rules. Here again, analyst findings are necessary inputs to fine-tune sensors and rules to enhance detection.

Large quantities of security data led to the growth of security analytics. Security analytics combines software, algorithms and analytic processes used to detect potential threats to IT systems,[251] and empowers enterprises to pivot from reactive to proactive security by leveraging data sets that enable preemptive enhancements to their cybersecurity program.[252]

Use cases for security analytics include, but are not limited to, the following:[253]

- Analyzing user behavior
- Compliance
- Detection and classification of threats
- Employee monitoring
- Insider threats
- Malware analysis and provenance
- Network traffic analysis
- Threat hunting

Security analytics data stem from multiple sources, including the tools and technologies referenced in Section 4.9 Monitoring and Detection.

Vulnerability Assessment and Management

Vulnerability assessment[254] involves anticipation, review and evaluation of threats and vulnerabilities. Vulnerabilities are continuously being discovered, and enterprises must be constantly vigilant in identifying and quickly remediating them. Common knowledge, skills and abilities (KSAs) among assessment professionals sometimes result in grouping vulnerability assessment and penetration testing together; however, there are important distinctions between the two. (Vulnerability management and penetration testing are discussed in greater detail later in this chapter.)

Vulnerability assessment and management often involve practices known as blue teaming, red teaming, and purple teaming.

---

[251] McAfee, "What is Security Analytics?," https://www.mcafee.com/enterprise/en-us/security-awareness/operations/what-is-security-analytics.html
[252] Exabeam, "Security Analytics," www.exabeam.com/siem-guide/siem-concepts/security-analytics/.
[253] Lord, N.; "What is Security Analytics? Learn about the Use Cases and Benefits of Security Analytics Tools," Digital Guardian, 12 September 2018, https://digitalguardian.com/blog/what-security-analytics-learn-about-use-cases-and-benefits-security-analytics-tools
[254] National Initiative for Cybersecurity Careers & Studies (NICCS), "Vulnerability Assessment and Management," https://niccs.us-cert.gov/workforce-development/cyber-security-workforce-framework/vulnerability-assessment-and-management

- **Blue team**—The quintessential blue team is a team of cyberdefenders charged with defending the enterprise during scheduled assessments.

- **Red team**—Red teaming is a common term to describe penetration testing. For most enterprises, red teaming is performed by external resources using adversarial TTPs, however, some larger enterprises maintain an in-house penetration-testing capability.

- **Purple team**—Purple teams facilitate cooperation between red and blue teams, and should enhance red and blue teaming, but not replace it. Some practitioners argue that purple teams are unnecessary if both red and blue teams are functioning correctly.

Threat Hunting

Threat hunting[255] is the pursuit of abnormal activity on servers and endpoints that may be signs of compromise, intrusion or exfiltration of data.[256] Threat hunting is about being proactive and looking for signs of compromise. As defenders, threat hunters reduce the time it takes to detect attackers. Threat hunting assumes that bad actors have already penetrated defenses, and threat hunters seek to find evidence of their malicious activities.

The activities (or steps) involved in threat hunting vary by source; in general, threat hunters:

- Identify target networks or systems

- Generate analytical questions (hypotheses) and seek answers

- Search for evidence to prove or disprove hypotheses

- Identify evidence and amend questions as necessary

- Report on and enhance existing detection systems

Hunt teams provide enterprises with an advanced security operations capability. Threat hunting does not make up for poor cybersecurity practices or cyberhygiene. Additionally, threat hunting is not appropriate for every enterprise. Threat hunting commonly requires robust endpoint detection and response (EDR) data, mature detection capabilities, and skilled human resources who are knowledgeable with respect to the threat landscape.[257]

4.2.3 Vulnerability Management

Vulnerability management starts by understanding the IT assets and where they reside—both physically and logically. This can be done by maintaining an asset inventory that details important information about each asset such as location (physical or logical), criticality of the asset, the organizational owner of the asset, and the type of information the asset stores or processes.

It is important to analyze vulnerabilities in the context of how they are exploited, and both vulnerabilities and exploits need to be considered in vulnerability assessments. Vulnerabilities and exploits can be identified in many ways. At a technical level, automated tools (both proprietary and open source) can be used to identify common vulnerabilities in computer and network implementations and configurations. Other vulnerability analysis tools include open source and proprietary sources such as SANS, MITRE and OWASP, software vendors, historical incidents, etc.

[255] O'Farril, R.; "Traits of a Successful Threat Hunter," ISACA Now blog, 20 August 2018, www.isaca.org/resources/news-and-trends/isaca-now-blog/2018/traits-of-a-successful-threat-hunter. See also Carbon Black, "What is Threat Hunting?," 19 April 2017, www.carbonblack.com/2017/04/19/what-is-threat-hunting; CrowdStrike, "What Is Cyber Threat Hunting?," 21 June 2019, www.crowdstrike.com/epp-101/threat-hunting/#where-does-threat-hunting-fit

[256] Gregory, P.H.; *Threat Hunting for Dummies*, Carbon Black Special Edition, Wiley, https://secure.carbonblack.com/ebook-threat-hunting-for-dummies/

[257] Chuvakin, A.; "Threat Hunting Is Not for Everyone," Informa Tech, DarkReading, 29 January 2020, www.darkreading.com/threat-intelligence/threat-hunting-is-not-for-everyone/a/d-id/1336877

Organizations need to identify and assess vulnerabilities to determine the threat and potential impact and to determine the best course of action in addressing each vulnerability. Vulnerabilities can be identified by information provided by software vendors (e.g., through the release of patches and updates) and by utilizing processes and tools that identify known vulnerabilities in the enterprise specific environment. The two most common techniques are vulnerability scanning and penetration testing.

Vulnerability Scanning

Vulnerability scanning is the process of using proprietary or open source tools to search for known vulnerabilities. Often the same tools used by adversaries to identify vulnerabilities are used by enterprises to locate vulnerabilities proactively.

There are many forms of vulnerability assessment tools. Several Linux distributions (e.g., Kali Linux) supply open source tools. Commercial tools (e.g., Core Impact, Nessus®, Nexpose®) are often used to scan IT infrastructure, web application, databases or a mix of them. The licensed updates of the vulnerability rule base fall into two categories: host-based and network-based. Naming every tool is impractical because individual needs and budgets vary.

Likewise, higher cost does not always equate to greater functionality, and tools can be found that are either free or free to try. Tools should be researched and selected based on enterprise needs and return on investment, keeping in mind that combinations of tools often provide greater insight to your network's security posture.

Vulnerability scans should be conducted regularly to identify new vulnerabilities and ensure that previously identified vulnerabilities have been properly corrected.

Vulnerability Assessment

The simplest definition of a vulnerability is an exploitable weakness that results in a loss. The method used to take advantage of a vulnerability is called an exploit. Vulnerabilities can occur in many forms and at different architectural levels (e.g., physical, operating system, application). **Figure 4.6** provides a list of common types of vulnerabilities.

Figure 4.6—Common Types of Vulnerabilities		
Type of Vulnerability	**Cause**	**Cybersecurity Examples**
Technical	Errors in design, implementation, placement or configuration	• Coding errors • Inadequate passwords • Open network ports • Lack of monitoring
Process	Errors in operation	• Failure to monitor logs • Failure to patch software
Organizational	Errors in management, decisions, planning or from ignorance	• Cross-organizational failures • Interoperability errors • Implementing new technology

Remediation

After vulnerabilities are identified and assessed, appropriate remediation can take place to mitigate or eliminate the vulnerability. Most often, remediation will be through a patch management process but may also require reconfiguration of existing controls or addition of new controls.

Reporting and Metrics

Vulnerability management includes tracking vulnerabilities and the remediation efforts to mitigate them and any risk associated with them. This provides a clear opportunity to provide good qualitative metrics to the enterprise management on the numbers and types of vulnerabilities, the potential impacts, and the effort needed to mitigate them.

4.2.4 Penetration Testing

Penetration testing is a live test of the effectiveness of security defenses through mimicking the actions of real-life attackers[258] and offers a solution to the problem of logical verification of a system's security via purposeful controlled attack. Penetration testing consists of the reconnaissance and exploitation of vulnerabilities in hardware and software caused by misconfiguration and user behavior.[259] Penetration tests are critical to operating and maintaining an effective information security program and useful for assessing system readiness, identifying gaps and evaluating vendor viability.

Penetration testing includes identifying existing vulnerabilities and using known exploit methods to:

- Confirm exposure
- Assess the level of effectiveness and quality of existing security controls
- Identify how specific vulnerabilities expose IT resources and assets
- Ensure compliance

  "Don't assume a crack is too small to be noticed, or too small to be exploited," he [Rob Joyce, former chief of the US National Security Agency Tailored Access Operations] said. "If you do a penetration test of your network and 97 things pass the test but three esoteric things fail, don't think they don't matter. Those are the ones the NSA, and other nation-state attackers will seize on" he explained. "We need that first crack, that first seam. And we're going to look and look and look for that esoteric kind of edge case to break open and crack in."[260]

Precautions

Because penetration testing simulates actual attacks, it must be planned carefully. Failure to do so may result in ineffective results, negative impact on or damage to the enterprise IT infrastructure, potential liability, or criminal prosecution. Several considerations are important prior to any penetration testing:

- Clearly define the scope of the test including what systems or networks are in and out of scope, the type of exploits that may be used, and the level of access allowed. These exploits can include network, social engineering, web, mobile application and other kinds of testing.

---

[258] *Op cit* ISACA, "Glossary"

[259] Michel, B.; "The Validity of Penetration Tests," *ISACA Journal*, vol 2, 17 April 2017, www.isaca.org/resources/isaca-journal/issues/2017/volume-2/the-validity-of-penetration-tests

[260] Zetter, K.; "NSA Hacker Chief Explains How to Keep Him Out of Your System," Wired, 28 January 2016, www.wired.com/2016/01/nsa-hacker-chief-explains-how-to-keep-him-out-of-your-system/

- Gather explicit, written permission from the enterprise authorizing the testing. This is the only accepted industry standard that distinguishes the service as authorized and legal.

- Ensure testers implement Do-no-harm procedures to ensure no assets are harmed, such as deletions, denial-of-service (DoS), or other negative impacts. However, even the best laid plans and precautions can produce unintended consequences.

- Put in place communication and escalation plans for the enterprise and testers to communicate quickly during the tests.

Penetration testing requires specialized knowledge of vulnerabilities, exploits, IT technology and the use of testing tools. It should not be performed by untrained or unqualified practitioners. Penetration tests should be carefully planned to mitigate the risk of causing a service outage, and the results require careful interpretation and elimination of false positives.

One commonly held belief is that penetration tests are not high priority because they are typically successful in finding a hole in an enterprise defense. The thought is that if an enterprise can design a successful penetration test (i.e., create/identify the vulnerability), then the money is better spent creating the fix rather than testing the vulnerability.

Penetration testing can be covert (the general IT staff do not know the testing is going to take place) so that the reactions of the enterprise to detect and respond are also tested. Also, penetration testing can be external, from outside the enterprise, or internal, starting from a system behind the enterprise firewall.[261]

Penetration Testing Methodology

Penetration testing should use a framework to deliver repeatability, consistency, and high quality in various kinds of security tests. Penetration testing frameworks include:[262]

- **PCI Penetration Testing Guide**—Provides a good introduction to testing tools

- **Penetration Testing Execution Standard**—Provides hands-on technical guidance on penetration testing

- **Penetration Testing Framework**—Provides a comprehensive guide to penetration testing and testing tools

- **NIST SP 800-15**—Technical Guide to Information Security Testing and Assessment

- **Information Systems Security Assessment Framework (ISSAF)**—Provides comprehensive penetration technical guidance

- **Open Source Security Testing Methodology Manual (OSSTMM)**—Provides a methodology for testing operational security and can support ISO 27001

Penetration Testing Common Phases

Penetration testing can be divided into four common main phases, as shown in **figure 4.7**.

[261] Chickowski, E., "Cybersecurity penetration testing explained: what is pen testing?" 30 June 2020, https://cybersecurity.att.com/blogs/security-essentials/cybersecurity-penetration-testing-explained
[262] Open Web Application Security Project, "Penetration Testing Methodologies," OWASP, https://owasp.org/www-project-web-security-testing-guide/latest/3-The_OWASP_Testing_Framework/1-Penetration_Testing_Methodologies

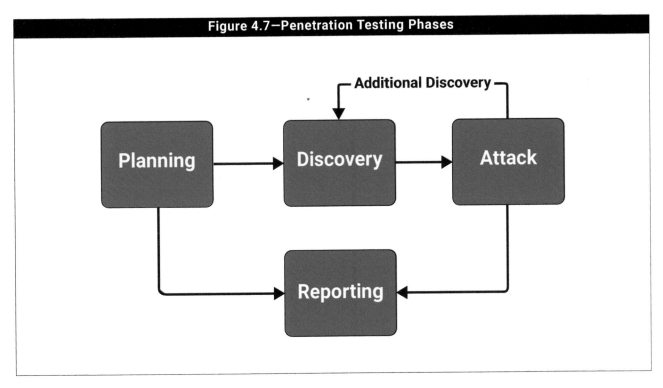

Figure 4.7—Penetration Testing Phases

The phases include:

1. **Planning**—In the planning phase, the goals are set, the scope is defined, and the test is approved and documented by management. The scope determines if the penetration test is internal or external, limited to certain types of attacks or limited to certain networks or assets.

2. **Discovery**—In the discovery phase, the penetration tester gathers information by conducting research on the enterprise and scans the networks for port and service identification. Techniques used to gather information include:

   - DNS interrogation, WHOIS queries and network sniffing to discover host name and IP address information
   - Search web servers and directory servers for employee names and contact information
   - Banner grabbing for application and service information
   - NetBIOS enumeration for system information
   - Dumpster diving and physical walk-throughs of the facilities to gather additional information
   - Use of online Internet infrastructure search tools, such as Shodan® (Shodan is the world's first search engine for Internet-connected devices, see https://www.shodan.io/), to passively profile exposed systems and services
   - Social engineering, such as posing as a help desk agent and asking for passwords, posing as a user and calling the service desk to reset passwords, or sending phishing emails

   A vulnerability assessment is also conducted during the discovery phase. This involves comparing the services, applications, and operating systems of the scanned host against vulnerability databases.

3. **Attack**—The attack phase is the process of verifying previously identified vulnerabilities by attempting to exploit them. Metasploit® hosts a public database of quality-assured exploits. They rank exploits for safe testing.

   Sometimes, exploit attempts do not provide the tester with access, but they do give the tester additional information about the target and its potential vulnerabilities. If a tester is able to exploit a vulnerability, they can install more tools on the system or network to gain access to additional systems or resources.

A payload is the piece of software that lets a user control a computer system after it has been exploited. The payload is typically attached to and delivered by the exploit. Metasploit's most popular payload is called Meterpreter, which enables a user to upload and download files from the system, take screenshots, and collect password hashes. The discovery and attack phases are illustrated in **figure 4.8**.

4. **Reporting**—The reporting phase occurs simultaneously with the other phases. An assessment plan is developed during the planning phase. Logs are kept during the discovery and attack phases. And, at the conclusion of the penetration test, a report is developed to describe the vulnerabilities identified, assign risk ratings, and provide mitigation plans.

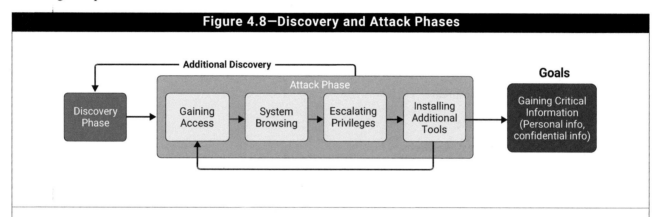

Figure 4.8—Discovery and Attack Phases

Source: Adapted from: National Institute of Standards and Technology (NIST), Special Publication 800-115, *Technical Guide to Inform Security Testing and Assessment*, September 2008, USA, Figure 5-2

4.2.5 Penetration Testing vs. Vulnerability Scanning

There are differences between penetration testing and vulnerability scanning[263] despite the fact they are complimentary functions to identify weaknesses. Below are three notable differences between the two:

- Penetration testing is a live, targeted event using highly skilled individuals leveraging well-known bad actor TTPs. The testers have no preconceived notions and use all the information that they can attain through social engineering, open source reconnaissance, and technical prowess. Penetration testing exploits vulnerabilities.

- Vulnerability scanning is automated, using numerous industry tools to find known and unknown vulnerabilities. Scanning only reports vulnerabilities often categorized by severity and risk rated with recommendations provided for remediation processes.

- Vulnerability scanning is enterprisewide, whereas penetration testing is often limited by rules of engagement (ROE) to protect core business functions.

4.2.6 DevOps and DevSecOps

DevOps[264] combines the concepts of agile development, agile infrastructure, and flexible operations to enable rapid and continuous releases and ongoing improvement in IT value creation. The DevOps movement was built out from frustration of IT groups with the dysfunction and deficient tools and processes, with the aim of making software development and operations more efficient and less painful.

DevOps breaks large projects into smaller deliverables and multiple deployments, which are easier to manage from design, to deployment and operations. Iterative and frequent deployments can be orchestrated to move seamlessly

[263] Mahmood, B.; "Vulnerability Scanning vs. Penetration Testing," Tripwire, 13 January 2020, www.tripwire.com/state-of-security/vulnerability-management/difference-vulnerability-scanning-penetration-testing/
[264] ISACA, DevOps: Process Maturity By Example, USA, 2017, www.isaca.org/bookstore/bookstore-wht_papers-digital/whpdop

from one group to the next, until they are promoted to production with minimal risk of disruptions. Small deployments are easier to debug along the development process and are stabilized after they are in operation.

Some business performance benefits of DevOps include:

- Reduced time to market
- Faster return on investment
- High performance
- Increased quality
- Customer satisfaction
- Reduced IT waste
- Improved supplier and business partner performance
- Reduction to the human factor threat

Challenges to using DevOps include:

- Misconception about what DevOps means
- Belief that DevOps is not concerned with compliance and security
- Need for automation
- Lack of skills
- Organizational culture
- Fear of change
- Silo mentality

DevOps is the natural evolution of the Agile methodology, which counters the flaws in a traditional waterfall software development life cycle (SDLC) approach. Agile improves efficiency and typically relies on popular open-source tools for a continuous integration/continuous development (CI/CD) pipeline that makes rapid feedback and deployment of code possible, which enables enterprises to achieve daily software deployments if they desire.

Although reduced time to market makes business and product teams very happy, cybersecurity professionals have concerns—vulnerable code, if not checked, can also be deployed faster.

The traditional way of security assurance cannot keep up and does not work in a CI/CD world, which sparked the DevSecOps[265] movement. DevSecOps applies the same principles to cybersecurity that DevOps applies to traditional IT processes to improve efficiency and removes manual intervention wherever possible. DevSecOps aims to shift security to the left by incorporating security assurance at every stage of the CI/CD pipeline and making it as essential a success criterion as development and testing. This shift is achieved by building and automating security into the CI/CD pipeline and requires a cultural change that must be endorsed by top-level management to succeed.

Information security professionals need to ensure that tools are compatible with CI/CD tools and can be used in a DevSecOps environment. The policies, procedures, and service level agreements (SLAs) for software security assurance should also be reviewed to ensure that they can be adapted to work in a high-speed CI/CD world.

---

[265] Ijlal, T.; "Three Strategies for a Successful DevSecOps Implementation," *ISACA Journal*, vol 4, 1 July 2019, www.isaca.org/resources/isaca-journal/issues/2019/volume-4/three-strategies-for-a-successful-devsecops-implementation

4.3 Tools and Technologies (Monitoring, Detection, Correlation)

4.3.1 Common Tools

Cybersecurity professionals use many tools[266] as part of their security routine—many of which are command line. Undoubtedly, there are dedicated security tools categorized by purpose (i.e., network analysis, vulnerability assessment, penetration testing, audits, etc.). Other tools, such as those used by IT administrators (i.e., utilities), are dual purpose for security. This section identifies essential tools that security practitioners should be familiar with.[267] Each tool includes a reference for independent learning.

- **Ping**[268]—Network connectivity tool
- **Tracert**[269]—Windows command prompt command to identify path information
- **Traceroute**[270]—Unix version of Tracert.
- **ARP**[271]—Locates the MAC address of an IP address
- **Ip**[272]—Newer version of ifconfig with additional functionality.
- **Ifconfig**[273]—Displays and configures Linux network interface. Ifconfig has been deprecated in some distributions in favor of ip.
- **Ipconfig**[274]—Windows application to attain IP address
- **Iptables**[275]—Command-line firewall for Linux
- **Hashcat**[276]—Open source password recovery tool with versions for Linux, OS X and Windows.
- **Nmap**[277]—Open source tool for network discovery and vulnerability scanning
- **Nslookup**[278]—Command-line tool to query IP addressing information
- **Netcat**—Networking utility that reads and writes data across network connections, using the TCP/IP protocol
- **Netstat**[279]—Displays detailed network status information. Netstat has been deprecated in some distributions in favor of "ss".
- **Nftables**[280]—Replaces iptables in new versions of Linux that provides firewall and network address translation functionality.
- **PuTTy**[281,282,283]—GUI version of SSH with versions for Linux, macOS, and Windows

---

[266] "SecTools.Org: Top 125 Network Security Tools," SecTools.Org, https://sectools.org/

[267] Whitfield, B.; "12 Cyber Security Tools Every IT Pro Should Have," Haking, https://hakin9.org/12-cyber-security-tools/

[268] Mitchell, B.; "How to Perform a Computer Ping Test (And When You Need To)," Lifewire, 18 November 2019, www.lifewire.com/computer-ping-test-817743

[269] Fisher, T.; "Tracert Command," Lifewire, 25 November 2019, www.lifewire.com/tracert-command-2618101

[270] Haas, J.; "Traceroute Command for Linux," Lifewire, 8 November 2019, www.lifewire.com/traceroute-linux-command-4092586

[271] Newell, G.; "A Beginners Guide to Address Resolution Protocols (ARP)," Lifewire, 20 October 2019, www.lifewire.com/beginners-guide-to-arp-4096766

[272] GeeksforGeeks, "ip command in Linux with examples," www.geeksforgeeks.org/ip-command-in-linux-with-examples/

[273] Lifewire, "Linux," www.lifewire.com/linux-command-ifconfig-4091934

[274] Mitchell, B., "ipconfig - Windows Command Line Utility," 9 March 2020, Lifewire, www.lifewire.com/ip-config-818377

[275] Brown, K.; "The Beginner's Guide to iptables, the Linux Firewall," How-To Geek, 3 July 2017, www.howtogeek.com/177621/the-beginners-guide-to-iptables-the-linux-firewall/

[276] hashcat, "hashcat," https://hashcat.net/wiki/doku.php?id=hashcat

[277] nmap.org, "News," https://nmap.org/

[278] Mitchell, B.; "What the NSLOOKUP Tool Can Tell You About Internet Domains," Lifewire, 12 November 2019, www.lifewire.com/what-is-nslookup-817516

[279] Fisher, T.; "How to Use the Netstat Command," Lifewire, 18 May 2020, www.lifewire.com/netstat-command-2618098

[280] Netfilter, "The netfilter.org "nftables" project," https://netfilter.org/projects/nftables/

[281] SSH.COM, "How to Use PuTTY on Windows," SSH Academy, www.ssh.com/ssh/putty/windows/

[282] SSH.COM, "PuTTY - Graphical Terminal & SSH Client for Linux," SSH Academy, www.ssh.com/ssh/putty/linux/

[283] SSH.COM, "PuTTY for Mac OS X," SSH Academy, www.ssh.com/ssh/putty/mac

- **Route command**—Command-line tool to view and edit IP routing tables
- **Pathping/MTR Utilities**[284]—Command-line utility beginning in Windows 2000 to identify network issues.
- **Ss**[285]—Newer version of netstat which offers benefit of displaying more TCP and state information than netstat
- **Secure Shell (SSH)**[286]—Open source program for remotely accessing endpoints
- **Wireshark**[287]—Open source protocol analyzer useful for examining live network traffic or packet capture files
- **Systernals Suite**[288]—Site of Windows troubleshooting utilities
- **Windows "God Mode"**[289]—Special folder that can be enabled for quick reference to most Windows admin tools
- **Snort®**—Open-source IDS/IPS
- **John the Ripper**[290]—Password cracker

4.3.2 Unix Commands

Cybersecurity practitioners cannot excel without proficiency with Unix and, more specifically, Linux-based systems. **Figure 4.9** is a quick reference guide of Unix commands.

Figure 4.9—UNIX Commands	
Command	**Description**
finger (userid)	Display information about a user
cat	Display or concatenate file
cd	Change directory
chmod	Change file permissions
	Note: The UNIX permissions are managed using octal notation by user, group,
cp	Copy
date	Display current date and time
diff	Display differences between text files
grep	Find string in file
ls	Directory list. Useful switches:
	−a Display all files*
	−d Display only directories
	−l Display long listing
	−u Display files by access (newest first)
	−U Display results by creation (newest first)
	Note: Unlike Windows, UNIX does not afford the opportunity to "turn on" hidden files. Referred to as dot files, these file names begin with a ".", hence the name. To view these protected system files, you must use the -a switch. [ls - a or ls - al]
man	Displays help
mkdir	Makes directory
mv	Move/rename file
ps	Display active processes

---

[284] Ellingwood, J., "How To Use Traceroute and MTR to Diagnose Network Issues," 22 October 2013, www.digitalocean.com/community/tutorials/how-to-use-traceroute-and-mtr-to-diagnose-network-issues

[285] Linux.com, "An Introduction to the ss Command," 22 January 2019, www.linux.com/topic/networking/introduction-ss-command/

[286] Ylonen, T.; "SSH (Secure Shell)," SSH Academy, www.ssh.com/ssh/

[287] SecTools.Org, "Wireshark," https://sectools.org/tool/wireshark/

[288] Microsoft, "Windows Sysinternals," 24 June 2020, https://docs.microsoft.com/en-us/sysinternals/

[289] Fisher, T.; "How to Activate GodMode in Windows," Lifewire, 18 November 2019, www.lifewire.com/god-mode-windows-4154662

[290] Openwall, "John the Ripper password cracker," www.openwall.com/john/

Figure 4.9—UNIX Commands *(cont.)*	
Command	**Description**
pwd	Displays the current directory
rm	Delete file
rmdir	Delete directory
sort	Sort data
whoami	Tells you who you are logged in as

4.3.3 Monitoring and Detection

To prepare for and identify an incident, enterprises use a myriad of security tools that ultimately collect a high volume of data. Many advocate that this data is necessary for correlation (it is), however collecting every possible event is pointless if it not processed efficiently—if at all. Security teams that must analyze and interpret this overwhelming amount of data often face log data overload or analysis paralysis. Following are important components towards a comprehensive cybersecurity response capability.

Endpoint Detection and Reporting (EDR)

Also called Endpoint Threat Detection and Response (ETDR), these tools have been around since at least 2013. EDRs are increasingly popular for their ability to detect all endpoint threats which places them light years ahead of signature-based antivirus software.[291],[292],[293]

Primary functions of EDR include:

- Monitor and collect endpoint activity data

- Analyze the collected data for threat patterns

- Provide an automated threat-driven response (i.e., remove, contain, alert)

- Forensics and analysis tools for further analysis

The additional capabilities of EDR make it much better than EPP (discussed in Chapter 2).

Threat Intelligence Platforms (TIP)

TIPs [294] are a formal name for a software product that combines and provides threat intelligence feeds to end users. Crowdstrike defines threat intelligence as data collected and analyzed by an enterprise to understand a threat actor's motives, targets and attack behaviors.[295] Threat Intelligence enables organizations to make faster, more informed security decisions and change their behavior from reactive to proactive in the fight against breaches.[296] Threat intelligence platforms help address early problems of non-standard formats and labor-intensive analysis work.

---

[291] CrowdStrike, "CrowdStrike evaluated in Gartner's Comparison of Endpoint Detection and Response Technologies and Solutions," 19 July 2016, www.crowdstrike.com/blog/gartners-comparison-of-endpoint-detection-and-response-technologies-and-solutions/

[292] Chuvakin, A.; "Named: Endpoint Threat Detection & Response," Gartner, 26 July 2013, https://blogs.gartner.com/anton-chuvakin/2013/07/26/named-endpoint-threat-detection-response

[293] McAfee, "What Is Endpoint Detection and Response?," www.mcafee.com/enterprise/en-us/security-awareness/endpoint/what-is-endpoint-detection-and-response.html

[294] CyberRisk Alliance, LLC, "What is a Threat Intelligence Platform?," SC Media, 9 April 2019, www.scmagazine.com/home/advertise/what-is-a-threat-intelligence-platform/

[295] Baker, K.; "What Is Cyber Threat Intelligence?," 12 July 2019, CrowdStrike, www.crowdstrike.com/epp-101/threat-intelligence/#definition

[296] *Ibid.*

Security Information and Event Management (SIEM)

SIEMs[297] have been around for more than a decade to help enterprises aggregate and correlate security event log data across multiple security devices. This allows security analysts to focus on a manageable list of critical events.

Security incidents are often made up of a series of events that occur throughout a network. By correlating data, SIEMs can take many isolated events and combine them to create one relevant security incident. Early SIEMs were signature based; however, technology has evolved them. Features vary by product – especially commercial SIEMs vs. open-source ones. Most modern SIEMs can use correlation rules or model profiles. SIEM capabilities encompass four steps:

- Internal data collection
- Data aggregation
- Analysis
- Alerting

SIEMs can be difficult to set up and tune properly.

Security Orchestration, Automation and Reporting (SOAR)

SOAR solutions entered the security market a few years ago and generally refer to any security solution or group of preexisting tools that allow enterprises to streamline incident response, security operations and threat and vulnerability management.[298] Like SIEMs, SOAR also ingest multiple sources of data but are reportedly better at ingesting external data sources such as threat intelligence feeds. This has made SOAR popular because security teams can orchestrate SOAR data sources (i.e., SIEM, EDR, antimalware) to automate incident response.

4.4 Incident Handling

All enterprises need to put significant effort into protecting themselves and preventing cyberattacks from causing harm or disruption. However, security controls are not perfect and cannot always eliminate all risk. Therefore, it is important that enterprises prepare for and be capable of detecting and managing their cybersecurity incidents.

4.4.1 Incident Management

Incident management is this process of identifying, analyzing and determining an organizational response to computer security incidents.[299] This section explores incident management to include incident identification, incident handling and incident response.

Incident Handling vs. Incident Response

Incident Handling differs from Incident Response (IR). Incident Response entails the technical factors required to analyze and contain an incident. Conversely, Incident Handling is broader and includes the communications, coordination, logistics, and planning required to drive resolution calmly and efficiently.

---

[297] WhoisXML API, "SOAR Versus SIEM: The Fundamental Differences," CircleID, 18 November 2019, www.circleid.com/posts/20191118_soar_versus_siem_the_fundamental_differences/

[298] Scott, A.; "SIEM vs SOAR, What's the Difference?" *The Startup*, 6 April, https://medium.com/swlh/siem-vs-soar-whats-the-difference-f81cf830fd03

[299] Department of Homeland Security, "Incident Management," Cybersecurity & Infrastructure Security Agency, www.us-cert.gov/bsi/articles/best-practices/incident-management

Responsibilities

Before SOCs became mainstream, cybersecurity response was the responsibility of Computer Security Incident Response Teams (CSIRTs). Another term often used is SIRT or Security Incident Response Team. The distinction between the two is admittedly nuanced but SIRT is broader often including the non-technical members of enterprise response to include communications teams and legal.

Outside of individual enterprises are National Computer Security Incident Response Teams (CSIRTs). A list of major CSIRTs can be viewed at https://www.first.org/members/teams/. ENISA also provides a listing of CSIRTS (only applicable to Europe); see www.enisa.europa.eu/topics/csirts-in-europe/csirt-inventory/certs-by-country-interactive-map.

Of importance, the use of the term computer emergency response team is ill-advised, because CERT® is a registered trademark owned by Carnegie Mellon University since 1997. CSIRTs may apply for authorization to use the CERT mark by contacting Carnegie Mellon University's Software Engineering Institute (SEI).[300]

Event vs. Incident

It is important to distinguish between an event and an incident because the two terms are often used synonymously, even though they have different meanings. An event is any change, error, or interruption within an IT infrastructure such as a system crash, a disk error or a user forgetting their password. The National Institute of Standards and Technology (NIST) defines an event as "any observable occurrence in a system or network."[301]

While there is general agreement on what an event is, there is a greater degree of variety in defining an incident. NIST defines an incident as "a violation or imminent threat of violation of computer security policies, acceptable use policies, or standard security practices."[302] Another commonly used definition is "the attempted or successful unauthorized access, use, disclosure, modification or loss of information or interference with system operations in an information system."[303] Many enterprises define an incident as the activity of a human threat agent. Others would include anything disruptive, including a court order for discovery of electronic information or disruption from a natural disaster.

Regardless of the exact definition used by a particular enterprise, it is important to distinguish between events that are handled in the normal course of business and incidents that require security and investigative expertise to manage.

Incident Characterization

A cybersecurity incident is an adverse event that negatively impacts the confidentiality, integrity and availability of data. Cybersecurity incidents may be unintentional, such as someone forgetting to activate an access list in a router, or intentional, such as a targeted attack by a hacker. These events may also be classified as technical or physical.

Technical incidents include viruses, malware, denial-of-service (DoS), and system failure. Physical incidents may include social engineering and lost or stolen laptops or mobile devices. There are many types of cybersecurity-related incidents, and new types of incidents emerge frequently. Reporting requirements vary by country and sector.

[300] Carnegie Mellon University, "Authorized Users of the CERT Mark," Software Engineering Institute, www.sei.cmu.edu/education-outreach/license-sei-materials/authorization-to-use-cert-mark/

[301] National Institute of Standards and Technology (NIST), *Computer Security Incident Handling Guide*, Special Publication 800-61, Revision 2, USA, August 2012

[302] NIST Special Publication SP800-61 revision 2, *Computer Security Incident Handling*, https://nvlpubs.nist.gov/nistpubs/SpecialPublications/NIST.SP.800-61r2.pdf

[303] Health IT Security, "Creating a Healthcare Security Incident Reporting Process," https://healthitsecurity.com/news/creating-a-healthcare-security-incident-reporting-process

For illustration purposes, we present reporting information from US-CERT that is mandated for all federal entities within the United States. The European Union Agency for Network and Information Security (ENISA) offers a more detailed incident reference taxonomy[304] and a threat taxonomy,[305] which evolve based on ENISA threat-landscape research.

Whenever reporting is mandated or encouraged, enterprises will likely need to category the impact, identify threat vectors and attack attributes, as shown in **figures 4.10** to **4.13**.

Figure 4.10—Impact Category Descriptions	
Impact Category	**Category Severity Levels**
Functional Impact—A measure of the impact to business functionality or ability to provide services	NO IMPACT—Event has no impact.
	NO IMPACT TO SERVICES—Event has no impact to any business or Industrial Control Systems (ICS) services or delivery to entity customers.
	MINIMAL IMPACT TO NONCRITICAL SERVICES—Some small level of impact to noncritical systems and services
	MINIMAL IMPACT TO CRITICAL SERVICES—Minimal impact but to a critical system or service, such as email or active directory.
	SIGNIFICANT IMPACT TO NONCRITICAL SERVICES—A noncritical service or system has a significant impact.
	DENIAL OF NONCRITICAL SERVICES—A noncritical system is denied or destroyed.
	SIGNIFICANT IMPACT TO CRITICAL SERVICES—A critical system has a significant impact, such as local administrative account compromise.
	DENIAL OF CRITICAL SERVICES/LOSS OF CONTROL—A critical system has been rendered unavailable.
Information Impact—Describes the type of information lost, compromised, or corrupted.	NO IMPACT—No known data impact.
	SUSPECTED BUT NOT IDENTIFIED—A data loss or impact to availability is suspected, but no direct confirmation exists.
	PRIVACY DATA BREACH—The confidentiality of personally identifiable information (PII) or personal health information was compromised.
	PROPRIETARY INFORMATION BREACH—The confidentiality of unclassified proprietary information, such as protected critical infrastructure information (PCII), intellectual property, or trade secrets was compromised.
	DESTRUCTION OF NONCRITICAL SYSTEMS—Destructive techniques, such as master boot record (MBR) overwrite, have been used against a noncritical system.
	CRITICAL SYSTEMS DATA BREACH—Data pertaining to a critical system has been exfiltrated.
	CORE CREDENTIAL COMPROMISE—Core system credentials (such as domain or enterprise administrative credentials) or credentials for critical systems have been exfiltrated.
	DESTRUCTION OF CRITICAL SYSTEM—Destructive techniques, such as MBR overwrite, have been used against a critical system.
Recoverability—Identifies the scope of the resources needed to recover from the incident	REGULAR—Time to recovery is predictable with existing resources.
	SUPPLEMENTED—Time to recovery is predictable with additional resources.
	EXTENDED—Time to recovery is unpredictable; additional resources and outside help are needed.
	NOT RECOVERABLE—Recovery from incident is not possible (e.g., sensitive data exfiltrated and posted publicly).
Source: Department of Homeland Security, "US-CERT Federal Incident Notification Guidelines," https://www.us-cert.gov/incident-notification-guidelines#attack-vectors-taxonomy	

[304] European Union Agency for Cybersecurity, *Reference Incident Classification Taxonomy*, ENISA, 26 January 2018, www.enisa.europa.eu/publications/reference-incident-classification-taxonomy/at_download/fullReport

[305] European Union Agency for Cybersecurity, "Threat Taxonomy," ENISA, September 2016, www.enisa.europa.eu/topics/threat-risk-management/threats-and-trends/enisa-threat-landscape/threat-taxonomy/view

Figure 4.11—Attack Vectors Taxonomy		
Attack Vector	**Description**	**Example**
Unknown	Cause of attack is unidentified.	This option is acceptable if cause (vector) is unknown upon initial report. The attack vector may be updated in a follow-up report.
Attrition	An attack that employs brute force methods to compromise, degrade, or destroy systems, networks, or services.	Denial of Service intended to impair or deny access to an application; a brute force attack against an authentication mechanism, such as passwords or digital signatures.
Web	An attack executed from a website or web-based application.	Cross-site scripting attack used to steal credentials, or a redirect to a site that exploits a browser vulnerability and installs malware.
Email/Phishing	An attack executed via an email message or attachment.	Exploit code disguised as an attached document, or a link to a malicious website in the body of an email message.
External/Removable Media	An attack executed from removable media or a peripheral device.	Malicious code spreading onto a system from an infected flash drive.
Impersonation/Spoofing	An attack involving replacement of legitimate content/services with a malicious substitute.	Spoofing, man in the middle attacks, rogue wireless access points, and structured query language injection attacks all involve impersonation.
Improper Usage	Any incident resulting from violation of an organization's acceptable usage policies by an authorized user, excluding the above categories.	User installs file-sharing software, leading to the loss of sensitive data; or a user performs illegal activities on a system.
Loss or Theft of Equipment	The loss or theft of a computing device or media used by the organization.	A misplaced laptop or mobile device.
Other	An attack method does not fit into any other vector	

Source: Department of Homeland Security, "US-CERT Federal Incident Notification Guidelines," https://www.us-cert.gov/incident-notification-guidelines#attack-vectors-taxonomy

Figure 4.12—Incident Attributes	
Attribute Category	**Attribute Definitions**
Location of observed activity—Where the observed activity was detected in the network	**LEVEL 1** – BUSINESS DEMILITARIZED ZONE—Activity was observed in the business network's demilitarized zone (DMZ)
	LEVEL 2 – BUSINESS NETWORK—Activity was observed in the business or corporate network of the victim. These systems would be corporate user workstations, application servers, and other non-core management systems.
	LEVEL 3 – BUSINESS NETWORK MANAGEMENT—Activity was observed in business network management systems such as administrative user workstations, active directory servers, or other trust stores.
	LEVEL 4 – CRITICAL SYSTEM DMZ—Activity was observed in the DMZ that exists between the business network and a critical system network. These systems may be internally facing services such as SharePoint sites, financial systems, or relay "jump" boxes into more critical systems.

Figure 4.12—Incident Attributes *(cont.)*	
Attribute Category	**Attribute Definitions**
Location of observed activity—Where the observed activity was detected in the network *(cont.)*	**LEVEL 5** – CRITICAL SYSTEM MANAGEMENT—Activity was observed in high-level critical systems management such as human-machine interfaces (HMIs) in industrial control systems.
	LEVEL 6 – CRITICAL SYSTEMS—Activity was observed in the critical systems that operate critical processes, such as programmable logic controllers in industrial control system environments.
	LEVEL 7 – SAFETY SYSTEMS—Activity was observed in critical safety systems that ensure the safe operation of an environment. One example of a critical safety system is a fire suppression system.
	UNKNOWN—Activity was observed, but the network segment could not be identified.
Actor characterization	The type of actor(s) involved in the incident (if known). This element is not selected by the reporting entity.
Cross-sector dependency	A weighting factor that is determined based on cross-sector analyses conducted by the DHS Office of Critical Infrastructure Analysis (OCIA). This element is not selected by the reporting entity.
Potential impact	An estimate of the overall national impact resulting from a total loss of service from the affected entity. This element is not selected by the reporting entity.
Source: Department of Homeland Security, "US-CERT Federal Incident Notification Guidelines," https://www.us-cert.gov/incident-notification-guidelines#attack-vectors-taxonomy	

Figure 4.13—Example Classification Taxonomy		
Incident Classification	**Incident Examples**	**Description**
Abusive Content	Spam	Spam or unsolicited bulk email reflects the fact that a recipient has not granted verifiable permission for the message to be sent, and that the message is sent as part of a larger collection of messages, all having a functionally comparable content.
	Harmful Speech	Discreditation or discrimination of someone (e.g., cyberstalking, racism and threats against one or more individuals)
	Child/Sexual/Violence	Child pornography, glorification of violence
Malicious Code	Virus	Software that is intentionally included or inserted in a system for a harmful purpose. A user interaction is normally necessary to activate the code.
	Worm	
	Trojan	
	Spyware	
	Dialler	
	Rootkit	
Information Gathering	Scanning	Attacks that send requests to a system to discover weak points. These also include some kind of testing processes to gather information about hosts, services and accounts. Examples: fingerd, DNS querying, ICMP, SMTP (EXPN, RCPT), port scanning
	Sniffing	Observing and recording of network traffic (wiretapping)
	Social Engineering	Gathering information from a human being in a nontechnical way (e.g., lies, tricks, bribes or threats)

Cybersecurity Fundamentals Study Guide, 3rd Edition
ISACA. All Rights Reserved.

	Figure 4.13—Example Classification Taxonomy *(cont.)*	
Incident Classification	**Incident Examples**	**Description**
Intrusion Attempts	Exploiting known vulnerabilities	An attempt to compromise a system or to disrupt any service by exploiting vulnerabilities with a standardized identifier such as CVE name (e.g., buffer overflow, backdoor, and cross-site scripting)
	Login attempts	Multiple login attempts (guessing, cracking of passwords, brute force)
	New attack signature	An attempt using an unknown exploit
Intrusions	Privileged account compromise	A successful compromise of a system or application (service). This can have been caused remotely by a known or new vulnerability, but also by an unauthorized local access. Also includes being part of a botnet.
	Unprivileged account compromise	
	Application compromise	
	Bot	
Availability	DoS	In this kind of attack, a system is bombarded with so many packets that the operations are delayed or the system crashes. DoS examples are ICMP and SYN floods, Teardrop attacks and mail-bombing. DDoS is often based on DoS attacks originating from botnets, but also other scenarios exist like DNS Amplification attacks. However, the availability also can be affected by local actions (destruction, disruption of power supply, etc.)—or by Act of God, spontaneous failures or human error, without malice or gross neglect being involved.
	DDoS	
	Sabotage	
	Outage (no malice)	
Information Content Security	Unauthorized access to information	Besides a local abuse of data and systems the information security can be endangered by a successful account or application compromise. Furthermore, attacks are possible that intercept and access information during transmission (wiretapping, spoofing or hijacking). Human/configuration/software error can also be the cause.
	Unauthorized modification of information	
Fraud	Unauthorized use of resources	Using resources for unauthorized purposes including profit-making ventures (e.g., the use of e-mail to participate in illegal profit chain letters or pyramid schemes)
	Copyright	Offering or installing copies of unlicensed commercial software or other copyright protected materials (Warez)
	Masquerade	Type of attack in which one entity illegitimately assumes the identity of another in order to benefit from it
	Phishing	Masquerading as another entity in order to persuade the user to reveal a private credential
Vulnerable	Open for abuse	Open resolvers, world readable printers, vulnerability apparent from Nessus etc scans, virus signatures not up to date, etc.
Other	All incidents which do not fit in one of the given categories should be put into this class	If the number of incidents in this category increases, it is an indicator that the classification scheme must be revised.
Test	Meant for testing	Meant for testing
Source: ENISA Reference Incident Classification Taxonomy, Jan 2018, Table 3: Detailed Reference Taxonomy vs Common Taxonomy for LE and CSIRTs, https://www.enisa.europa.eu/publications/reference-incident-classification-taxonomy		

Incident Handling Checklist

The following table from NIST SP 800-61 rev. 2 (**figure 4.14**) illustrates major steps associated with handing a cybersecurity incident. Regardless of the checklist used by an enterprise, incident handlers should know they serve as guides and their work may not always occur in order.

Figure 4.14—Incident Handling Checklist		
Action		Completed
Detection and Analysis		
1.	Determine whether an incident has occurred	
1.1	Analyze the precursors and indicators	
1.2	Look for correlating information	
1.3	Perform research (e.g., search engines, knowledge base)	
1.4	As soon as the handler believes an incident has occurred, begin documenting the investigation and gathering evidence	
2.	Prioritize handling the incident based on the relevant factors (functional impact, information impact, recoverability effort, etc.)	
3.	Report the incident to the appropriate internal personnel and external organizations	
Containment, Eradication and Recovery		
4.	Acquire, preserve, secure, and document evidence	
5.	Contain the incident	
6.	Eradicate the incident	
6.1	Identify and mitigate all vulnerabilities that were exploited	
6.2	Remove malware, inappropriate materials, and other components	
6.3	If more affected hosts are discovered (e.g., new malware infections), repeat the Detection and Analysis steps (1.1, 1.2) to identify all other affected hosts, then contain (5) and eradicate (6) the incident for them	
7.	Recover from the incident	
7.1	Return affected systems to an operationally ready state	
7.2	Confirm that the affected systems are functioning normally	
7.3	If necessary, implement additional monitoring to look for future related activity	
Postincident Activity		
8.	Create a follow-up report	
9.	Hold a lessons-learned meeting (mandatory for major incidents, optional otherwise)	
Source: NIST SP 800-61 rev. 2, Computer Security Incident Handling Guide, August 2012, https://nvlpubs.nist.gov/nistpubs/SpecialPublications/NIST.SP.800-61r2.pdf		

4.4.2 What is Incident Response?

Incident response is a formal program that prepares an entity for an incident. Incident response phases are shown in **figure 4.15**. Incident response generally includes:

1. **Preparation**—To establish roles, responsibilities, and plans for how an incident will be handled

2. **Detection and analysis capabilities**—To identify incidents as early as possible and effectively assess the nature of the incident

3. **Investigation capability**—To identify an adversary, if required

4. **Mitigation and recovery procedures**—To contain the incident, reduce losses and return operations to normal

5. **Post-incident analysis**—To determine corrective actions that prevent similar incidents in the future

Figure 4.15—Incident Response Phases

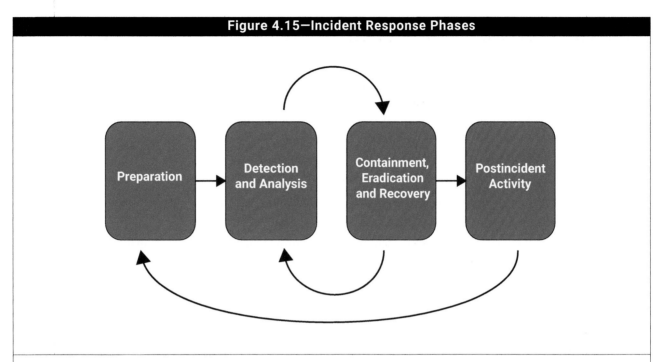

Source: Adapted from: National Institute of Standards and Technology (NIST), *Computer Security Incident Handling Guide*, Special Publication 800-61, Revision 2, Figure 3-1. Incident Response Life Cycle, USA, August 2012, https://resources.sei.cmu.edu/asset_files/WhitePaper/2018_019_001_524597.pdf

Purpose of Incident Response

Waiting until an incident occurs to figure out what to do is a recipe for disaster. Adequate incident response planning and implementation allows an enterprise to respond to an incident in a systematic manner, which is more effective and timelier. Organizations that do not plan for a cybersecurity incident will suffer greater losses for a more extended period of time. The current trend shows an increase in incident occurrences. These attacks are becoming more sophisticated and are resulting in escalating losses.

In addition, many national regulations and international standards require the development of incident response capabilities. Compliance regulations provide strict requirements for security policies and incident response planning.

Elements of An Incident Response Plan (IRP)

A common approach to developing an IRP is a six-phase model of incident response including preparation, identification, containment, eradication, restoration, and follow-up:[306]

1. **Preparation**—This phase prepares an enterprise to develop an IRP prior to an incident. Sufficient preparation facilitates smooth execution. Activities in this phase include:

    a. Establishing an approach to handle incidents

    b. Establishing policy and warning banners in information systems to deter intruders and allow information collection

    c. Establishing communication plan to stakeholders

    d. Developing criteria on when to report an incident to authorities

---

[306] *Op cit* ISACA, *CISM Review Manual, 15th Edition*

e. Developing a process to activate the incident management team

f. Establishing a secure location to execute the IRP

g. Ensuring equipment needed is available

2. **Identification**—This phase aims to verify if an incident has happened and to find out more details about the incident. Reports on possible incidents may come from information systems, end users, or other organizations. Not all reports are valid incidents, as they may be false alarms or may not qualify as an incident. Activities in this phase include:

a. Assigning ownership of an incident or potential incident to an incident handler

b. Verifying that reports or events qualify as an incident

c. Establishing chain of custody during identification when handling potential evidence

d. Determining the severity of an incident and escalating it as necessary

3. **Containment**—After an incident has been identified and confirmed, the incident management team (IMT) is activated and information from the incident handler is shared. The team will conduct a detailed assessment and contact the system owner or business manager of the affected information systems/assets to coordinate further action. The action taken in this phase is to limit the exposure. Activities in this phase include:

a. Activating the IMT/IRT to contain the incident

b. Notifying appropriate stakeholders affected by the incident

c. Obtaining agreement on actions taken that may affect availability of a service or risk of the containment process

d. Getting the IT representative and relevant virtual team members involved to implement containment procedures

e. Obtaining and preserving evidence

f. Documenting and taking backups of actions from this phase onward

g. Controlling and managing communication to the public by the public relations team

4. **Eradication**—When containment measures have been deployed, it is time to determine the root cause of the incident and eradicate it. Eradication can be done in many ways: restoring backups to achieve a clean state of the system, removing the root cause, improving defenses and performing vulnerability analysis to find further potential damage from the same root cause. Activities in this phase include:

a. Determining the signs and cause of incidents

b. Locating the most recent version of backups or alternative solutions

c. Removing the root cause. In the event of worm or virus infection, it can be removed by deploying appropriate patches and updated antivirus software.

d. Improving defenses by implementing protection techniques

e. Performing vulnerability analysis to find new vulnerabilities introduced by the root cause

5. **Recovery**—This phase ensures that affected systems or services are restored to a condition specified in the service delivery objectives (SDO) or business continuity plan (BCP). The time constraint up to this phase is documented in the recovery time objective (RTO). Activities in this phase include:

a. Restoring operations as defined in the SDO

b. Validating that actions taken on restored systems were successful

c. Getting involvement of system owners to test the system

d. Facilitating system owners to declare normal operation

6. **Lessons learned**—At the end of the incident response process, a report should always be developed to share what has happened, what measures were taken and the results after the plan was executed. Part of the report should contain lessons learned that provide the IMT and other stakeholders valuable learning points of what

could have been done better. These lessons should be developed into a plan to enhance the incident management capability and the documentation of the IRP. Activities in this phase include:

a. Writing the incident report

b. Analyzing issues encountered during incident response efforts

c. Proposing improvement based on issues encountered

d. Presenting the report to relevant stakeholders

Incident Coordination

An incident responder may need to coordinate with others both internally and externally.[307] These may include other incident response teams (especially when portions of enterprise security are outsourced), law enforcement agencies, Internet service providers, stakeholders, and customers. **Figure 4.16** illustrates coordination at different phases of the incident response life cycle.

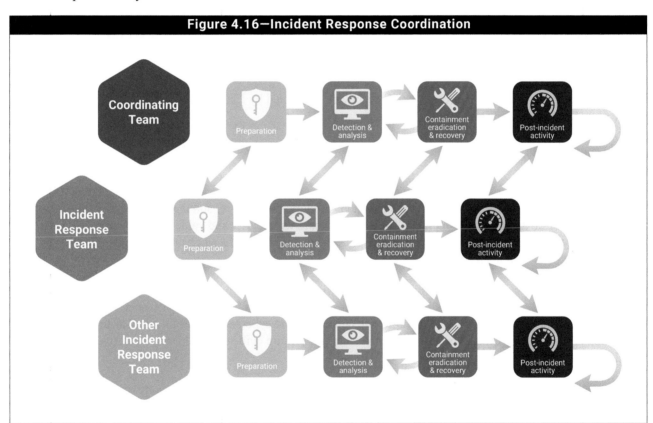

Figure 4.16—Incident Response Coordination

Source: National Institute of Standards and Technology (NIST), *Computer Security Incident Handling Guide*, Special Publication 800-61, Revision 2, Figure 4-1. Incident Response Life Cycle, USA, August 2012, figure 4.1, https://nvlpubs.nist.gov/nistpubs/SpecialPublications/NIST.SP.800-61r2.pdf

Managing cybersecurity issues requires coordination between many entities—public and private, local, regional, and global—because cybersecurity is closely tied to the security of the Internet, enterprise and home networks, and information security. This is complicated at times by matters of national security, such as not openly discussing critical infrastructure weaknesses, or enterprises that must protect intellectual property and competitive edge. Therefore, a basic framework for information sharing and incident coordination is needed to provide assurance to stakeholders that cybersecurity issues are being addressed. In the United States, member-driven organizations called Information Sharing and Analysis Centers (ISAC) help to fill this void.

4.5 Forensics

4.5.1 Investigations

Cybersecurity incident investigations include the collection and analysis of evidence with the goal of identifying the perpetrator of an attack or unauthorized use or access. This may overlap with, but is distinctly separate from, the technical analysis used in incident response where the objective is to understand the nature of the attack, what happened, and how it occurred.

The goals of an investigation can conflict with the goals of incident response. Investigations may require the attack or unauthorized access to continue while it is analyzed and evidence is collected, whereas remediation may destroy evidence or preclude further investigation. Enterprise management must be an integral part of making decisions between investigating and remediation.

Investigations may be conducted for criminal activity (as defined by governmental statutes and legislation), violations of contracts or violations of enterprise policies. Cybersecurity investigators may also assist in other types of investigations where computers or networks were used in the commission of other crimes, such as harassment where email was used.

An investigation may take place entirely in-house or may be conducted by a combination of in-house personnel, service providers, and law enforcement or regulators.

4.5.2 Evidence Preservation

It is very important to preserve evidence in any situation. Most enterprises are not well equipped to deal with intrusions and electronic crimes from an operational and procedural perspective, and they respond to it only when the intrusion has occurred and the risk is realized. The evidence loses its integrity and value in legal proceedings if it has not been preserved and subject to a documented chain of custody. This happens when the incident is inappropriately managed and responded to in an ad hoc manner.

The evidence of a computer crime exists in the form of log files, file time stamps, contents of memory, etc. Other sources include browser history, contact lists, cookies, documents, hidden files, images, metadata, temporary files, and videos. While not comprehensive, it helps provide context for the cybersecurity professional as to how much information is available to responders. The ability to locate and capture evidence is dependent on data type, investigators' skills and experience, and tools.

Rebooting the system or accessing files could result in such evidence being lost, corrupted or overwritten. Therefore, one of the first steps taken should be copying one or more images of the attacked system. Memory content should also be dumped to a file before rebooting the system. Any further analysis must be performed on an image of the system and on copies of the memory dumped—not on the original system in question.

In addition to protecting the evidence, it is also important to preserve the chain of custody. Chain of custody refers to documenting, in detail, how evidence is handled and maintained, including its ownership, transfer, and modification. This is necessary to satisfy legal requirements that mandate a high level of confidence regarding the integrity of evidence.

For evidence to be admissible in a court of law, the chain of custody needs to be maintained accurately and chronologically. The chain of evidence essentially contains information regarding:

- Who had access to the evidence (chronological manner)
- The procedures followed in working with the evidence (such as disk duplication, virtual memory dump)

- Proof that the analysis is based on copies that are identical to the original evidence (could be documentation, checksums, time stamps)

4.5.3 Legal Requirements

Investigations have clearly defined legal requirements, and these vary from country to country. Only trained investigators working with legal counsel should undertake investigations. Some legal issues that may be applicable include:

- Evidence collection and storage
- Chain of custody of evidence
- Searching or monitoring communications
- Interviews or interrogations
- Law enforcement involvement
- Labor, union and privacy regulation

These and other legal considerations are evolving when applied to cyberspace and vary, sometimes significantly, from jurisdiction to jurisdiction. Failure to perform an investigation in compliance with the appropriate legal requirements may create criminal or civil liabilities for the investigator and enterprise or may result in an inability to pursue legal remedies.

Many attacks are international in scope and navigating the different (and sometimes conflicting) legal issues can be challenging, adding complexity to cybersecurity investigations. In some countries, private individuals and enterprises are not permitted to carry out investigations and require law enforcement.

By definition, digital forensics is the "process of identifying, preserving, analyzing and presenting digital evidence in a manner that is legally acceptable in any legal proceedings (i.e., a court of law)."[308] Computer forensics includes activities that involve the exploration and application of methods to gather, process, interpret and use digital evidence that help to substantiate whether an incident happened, such as:

- Providing validation that an attack occurred
- Gathering digital evidence that can later be used in judicial proceedings

Any electronic document or data can be used as digital evidence, provided there is sufficient manual or electronic proof that the contents of digital evidence are in their original state and have not been tampered with or modified during the process of collection and analysis.

It is important to use industry-specified best practices, proven tools and due diligence to provide reasonable assurance of the quality of evidence. It is also important to demonstrate integrity and reliability of evidence for it to be acceptable to law enforcement authorities. For example, if the cybersecurity practitioner boots a computer specialist of containing stored information that might represent evidence in a court case, the practitioner cannot later deny that they wrote data to the hard drive because the boot sequence writes a record to the drive. This is the reason industry-accepted tools are used to take a true copy of the drive, which is then used in the investigation.

Four major considerations are in the chain of events regarding evidence in digital forensics (**figure 4.17**):

- **Identify**—Refers to the identification of information that is available and might form the evidence of an incident.

---

[308] McKemmish, D.R.; *Computer and Intrusion Forensics*, Artech House, USA, 2003

- **Preserve**—Refers to the practice of retrieving identified information and preserving it as evidence. The practice generally includes the imaging of original media in presence of an independent third party. The process also requires being able to document chain-of-custody so that it can be established in a court of law.

- **Analyze**—Involves extracting, processing and interpreting the evidence. Extracted data can be unintelligible binary data after it has been processed and converted into human readable format. Interpreting the data requires an in-depth knowledge of how different pieces of evidence may fit together. The analysis should be performed using an image of media and not the original.

- **Present**—Involves a presentation to the various audiences such as management, attorneys, court, etc.

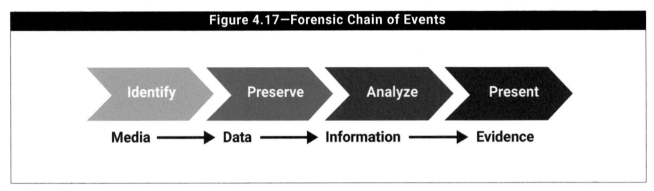

Figure 4.17—Forensic Chain of Events

Acceptance of the evidence depends on the manner of presentation (it should be convincing), qualifications of the presenter and credibility of the process used to preserve and analyze the evidence.

4.5.4 Data Protection

To prevent sought-after information from being altered, all measures must be in place. It is important to establish specific protocols to inform appropriate parties that electronic evidence will be sought and to not destroy it by any means. Infrastructure and processes for incident response and handling should be in place to permit an effective response and forensic investigation if an event or incident occurs.

4.5.5 Data Acquisition

All information and data required should be transferred into a controlled location; this includes all types of electronic media such as fixed disk drives and removable media. Each device must be checked to ensure that it is write-protected. This may be achieved by using a device known as a write-blocker. It is also possible to get data and information from witnesses or related parties by recorded statements. By volatile data, investigators can determine what is currently happening on a system. This kind of data includes open ports, open files, active processes, user logons and other data present in RAM. This information is lost when the computer is shut down.

4.5.6 Imaging

Imaging is a process that allows one to obtain a bit-for-bit copy of data to avoid damage of original data or information when multiple analyses may be performed. The imaging process is made to obtain residual data, such as deleted files, fragments of deleted files and other information present, from the disk for analysis. This is possible because imaging duplicates the disk surface, sector by sector. With appropriate tools, it is sometimes possible to recover destroyed information (erased even by reformatting) from the disk surface.

Cybersecurity Fundamentals Study Guide, 3rd Edition

4.5.7 Extraction

This process consists of identification and selection of data from the imaged data set. This process should include standards of quality, integrity and reliability. The extraction process includes software used and media where an image was made. The extraction process can include different sources such as system logs, firewall logs, intrusion detection system (IDS) logs, audit trails and network management information.

4.5.8 Interviews

Interviews are used to obtain prior indicators or relationships, including telephone numbers, IP addresses, and names of individuals, from extracted data.

4.5.9 Ingestion/Normalization

This process converts the information extracted to a format that can be understood by investigators. It includes conversion of hexadecimal or binary data into readable characters or a format suitable for data analysis tools. It is possible to create relationships from data by extrapolation, using techniques, such as fusion, correlation, graphing, mapping or time lining, which can be used in the construction of the investigation hypothesis.

4.5.10 Reporting

The information obtained from digital forensics has limited value when it is not collected and reported in the proper way. A report must state why the system was reviewed, how the computer data were reviewed, and what conclusions were made from this analysis. The report should achieve the following goals:[309]

- Accurately describe the details of an incident
- Be understandable to decision makers
- Be able to withstand a barrage of legal scrutiny
- Be unambiguous and not open to misinterpretation
- Be easily referenced
- Contain all information required to explain conclusions reached
- Offer valid conclusions, opinions or recommendations when needed
- Be created in a timely manner.

The report should also identify the enterprise, sample reports, and restrictions on circulation (if any), and include any reservations or qualifications that the assurance professional has with respect to the assignment.

4.5.11 Digital Forensic Tools

Forensic tools have four categories:

- **Computer**—Examine nonvolatile digital media. Due to the number of tools on the market, specific tools are not discussed in this guide. Vendors base their computer tools on different platforms (i.e., Windows, Linux, etc.). Most tools are propriety; however, open source options do exist. Similarly, some tools are restricted to law enforcement and/or government agencies. Ultimately, business requirements determine tool selection.
- **Memory**—Used to acquire and analyze volatile memory.

---

[309] Mandia, K.; M. Pepe; C. Prosise; *Incident Response & Computer Forensics, 2nd Edition*, McGraw Hill/Osborne, USA, 2003

- **Mobile device**—Consists of software and hardware components. Due to the large number of devices, manufacturers, and intended scope, specific tools are not be discussed in this guide. Cables perform similar to write blockers for computer forensics.
- **Network**—Monitoring and analysis of network traffic. Options range from command-line tools previously mentioned to high-end deep packet inspection appliances.

Additionally, there are various support applications that can be used. One example is VMware®—virtualization software that allows users to run multiple instances of operating systems on a physical PC or server.

4.5.12 Timelines

Timelines are chronological graphs where events related to an incident can be mapped, to look for relationships in complex cases. Timelines can provide simplified visualization for presentation to management and other nontechnical audiences.

4.5.13 Antiforensics/Obfuscation

Programmers develop antiforensics tools to make it difficult or impossible for investigators to retrieve information during an investigation. There are numerous ways that people can hide information.

Antiforensics tactics, techniques, and procedures (TTPs) include:

- Securely deleting data
- Overwriting metadata
- Preventing data creation
- Encrypting data
- Encrypting network protocols
- Hiding data in slack space or other unallocated locations
- Hiding data or a file within another file (steganography)

4.6 Chapter 4 Knowledge Check

REVIEW QUESTIONS

1. Which element of an incident response plan (IRP) involves obtaining and preserving evidence?

   A. Identification
   B. Containment
   C. Eradication

2. Which of the following are legal issues that may affect investigations? (Select all that apply.)

   A. Evidence collection and storage
   B. Chain of custody of evidence
   C. Searching or monitoring communications
   D. Interviews or interrogations
   E. Education or training
   F. Labor, union and privacy regulation

3. NIST defines a(n) _____ as a "violation or imminent threat of violation of computer security policies, acceptable use policies, or standard security practices."

   A. Event
   B. Threat
   C. Incident

4. Vulnerability management begins with an understanding of IT assets and their locations, which can be accomplished by:

   A. Vulnerability scanning
   B. Penetration testing
   C. Maintaining an asset inventory

5. Put the steps of the penetration testing phase into the correct order.
   A. Attack
   B. Discovery
   C. Reporting
   D. Planning

Answers on page 190

Chapter 4 ANSWER KEY

Review Questions

1. A. Identification
    B. Containment. Refer to page 182.
    C. Eradication

2. **A. Evidence collection and storage. Refer to page 185.**
    B. Chain of custody of evidence. Refer to page 185.
    C. Searching or monitoring communications. Refer to page 185.
    D. Interviews or interrogations. Refer to page 185.
    E. Education or training
    F. Labor, union and privacy regulation. Refer to page 185.

3. A. Event
    B. Threat
    C. Incident. Refer to page 175.

4. A. Vulnerability scanning
    B. Penetration testing
    C. Maintaining an asset inventory. Refer to page 164.

5. D. Planning
    B. Discovery
    A. Attack
    C. Reporting

    Refer to page 168.

Glossary

A

Acceptable use policy—A policy that establishes an agreement between users and the enterprise that defines, for all parties, the ranges of use that are approved before gaining access to a network or the Internet

Access control list (ACL)—An internal computerized table of access rules regarding the levels of computer access permitted to logon IDs and computer terminals

Scope Notes: Also referred to as access control table

Access rights—The permission or privileges granted to users, programs or workstations to create, change, delete or view data and files within a system, as defined by rules established by data owners and the information security policy

Accountability—The ability to map a given activity or event back to the responsible party

Advanced Encryption Standard (AES)—A public algorithm that supports keys from 128 bits to 256 bits in size

Advanced persistent threat (APT)—An adversary that possesses sophisticated levels of expertise and significant resources that allow it to create opportunities to achieve its objectives by using multiple attack vectors, including cyber, physical and deception. Typically, APT objectives include establishing and extending footholds within the IT infrastructure of the targeted organizations for purposes of exfiltrating information, or undermining or impeding critical aspects of a mission, program or organization; or positioning itself to carry out those objectives in the future. The advanced persistent threat pursues its objectives repeatedly, over an extended period, adapts to defenders' efforts to resist it and is determined to maintain the level of interaction that is needed to execute its objectives.

Source: NIST SP 800-39

Adversary—A threat agent

Adware—A software package that automatically plays, displays or downloads advertising material to a computer after the software is installed on it or while the application is being used

Scope Notes: In most cases, this is done without any notification to the user or without the user's consent. The term adware may also refer to software that displays advertisements, whether or not it does so with the user's consent; such programs display advertisements as an alternative to shareware registration fees. These are classified as adware in the sense of advertising supported software, but not as spyware. Adware in this form does not operate surreptitiously or mislead the user, and it provides the user with a specific service.

Analog—A transmission signal that varies continuously in amplitude and time and is generated in wave formation

Scope Notes: Analog signals are used in telecommunications

Antimalware—A widely used technology to prevent, detect and remove many categories of malware, including computer viruses, worms, Trojans, keyloggers, malicious browser plug-ins, adware and spyware

Antivirus software—An application software deployed at multiple points in an IT architecture. It is designed to detect and potentially eliminate virus code before damage is done and repair or quarantine files that have already been infected.

Application layer—In the Open Systems Interconnection (OSI) communications model, the application layer provides services for an application program to ensure that effective communication with another application program in a network is possible.

Architecture—Description of the fundamental underlying design of the components of the business system, or of one element of the business system (e.g., technology), the relationships among them, and the manner in which they support enterprise objectives

Asset—Something of either tangible or intangible value that is worth protecting, including people, information, infrastructure, finances and reputation

Asymmetric key (public key)—A cipher technique in which different cryptographic keys are used to encrypt and decrypt a message

Scope Notes: See public key encryption.

Attack—An actual occurrence of an adverse event

Attack mechanism—A method used to deliver the exploit. Unless the attacker is personally performing the attack, an attack mechanism may involve a payload, or container, that delivers the exploit to the target.

Attack vector—A path or route used by the adversary to gain access to the target (asset)

Scope Notes: There are two types of attack vectors: ingress and egress (also known as data exfiltration).

Audit trail—Data in the form of a logical path linking a sequence of events, used to trace the transactions that have affected the contents of a record

Source : ISO

Authentication—1. The act of verifying identity, i.e., user, system

Scope Notes: Can also refer to the verification of the correctness of a piece of data.

2. The act of verifying the identity of a user, the user's eligibility to access computerized information

Scope Notes: Authentication is designed to protect against fraudulent logon activity. It can also refer to the verification of the correctness of a piece of data.

Authenticity—Undisputed authorship

Availability—Ensuring timely and reliable access to and use of information

B

Backdoor—A means of regaining access to a compromised system by installing software or configuring existing software to enable remote access under attacker-defined conditions

Bandwidth—The range between the highest and lowest transmittable frequencies. It equates to the transmission capacity of an electronic line and is expressed in bytes per second or Hertz (cycles per second).

Bastion—System heavily fortified against attacks

Biometrics—A security technique that verifies an individual's identity by analyzing a unique physical attribute, such as a handprint

Block cipher—A public algorithm that operates on plaintext in blocks (strings or groups) of bits

Botnet—A term derived from robot network; a large automated and distributed network of previously compromised computers that can be simultaneously controlled to launch large-scale attacks, such as a denial-of-service attack, on targeted victims

Boundary—Logical and physical controls to define a perimeter between the organization and the outside world

Bring your own device (BYOD)—An enterprise policy used to permit partial or full integration of user-owned mobile devices for business purposes

Brute force—A class of algorithms that methodically try all possible combinations until a solution is found

Brute-force attack—Methodically trying all possible combinations of passwords or encryption keys until the correct one is found

Buffer overflow—Occurs when a program or process tries to store more data in a buffer (temporary data storage area) than it was intended to hold

Scope Notes: Because buffers contain a finite amount of data, the excess data can overflow into adjacent buffers, corrupting or overwriting the valid data held in them. Although it may occur accidentally through programming error, buffer overflow is an increasingly common type of security attack on data integrity. In buffer overflow attacks, the extra data may contain codes designed to trigger specific actions, in effect sending new instructions to the attacked computer that can damage user files, change data or disclose confidential information.

Business continuity plan (BCP)—A plan used by an enterprise to respond to disruption of critical business processes; depends on the contingency plan for restoration of critical systems

Business impact analysis/assessment (BIA)—Evaluating the criticality and sensitivity of information assets; An exercise that determines the impact of losing the support of any resource to an enterprise, establishes the escalation of that loss over time, identifies the minimum resources needed to recover and prioritizes the recovery of processes and the supporting system

Scope Notes: This process also addresses:

- Income loss
- Unexpected expense
- Legal issues (regulatory compliance or contractual)
- Interdependent processes
- Loss of public reputation or public confidence

C

Certificate (Certification) authority (CA)—A trusted third party that serves authentication infrastructures or enterprises and registers entities and issues them certificates

Certificate revocation list (CRL)—An instrument for checking the continued validity of the certificates for which the certification authority (CA) has responsibility

Scope Notes: The CRL details digital certificates that are no longer valid. The time gap between two updates is very critical and is also a risk in digital certificates verification.

Chain of custody—The process of evidence handling from collection to presentation that is necessary to maintain the validity and integrity of evidence

Scope Notes: Includes documentation of who had access to the evidence and when, and the ability to identify that evidence is the exact item that was recovered or tested. Lack of control over evidence can lead to it being discredited. Chain of custody depends on the ability to verify that evidence could not have been tampered with. This is accomplished by sealing off the evidence, so it cannot be changed, and providing a documentary record of custody to prove that the evidence was, at all times, under strict control and not subject to tampering.

Checksum—A checksum value is generated by an algorithm and associated with an input value and/or whole input file. The checksum value can be used to assess its corresponding input data or file later and verify that the input has not been maliciously altered. If a subsequent checksum value no longer matches the initial value, the input may have been altered or corrupted.

Chief information security officer (CISO)—The person in charge of information security within the enterprise

Chief security officer (CSO)—The person usually responsible for all physical and digital security matters in an enterprise

Cipher—An algorithm to perform encryption

Ciphertext—Information generated by an encryption algorithm to protect the plaintext and that is unintelligible to the unauthorized reader

Cleartext—Data that is not encrypted. Also known as plaintext.

Cloud computing—Convenient, on-demand network access to a shared pool of resources that can be rapidly provisioned and released with minimal management effort or service provider interaction

Compartmentalization—A process for protecting very-high value assets or in environments where trust is an issue. Access to an asset requires two or more processes, controls or individuals.

Compliance—Adherence to, and the ability to demonstrate adherence to, mandated requirements defined by laws and regulations, as well as voluntary requirements resulting from contractual obligations and internal policies

Compliance documents—Policies, standards and procedures that document the actions that are required or prohibited. Violations may be subject to disciplinary actions.

Computer forensics—The application of the scientific method to digital media to establish factual information for judicial review

Scope Notes: This process often involves investigating computer systems to determine whether they are or have been used for illegal or unauthorized activities. As a discipline, it combines elements of law and computer science to collect and analyze data from information systems (e.g., personal computers, networks, wireless communication and digital storage devices) in a way that is admissible as evidence in a court of law.

Computer security incident response team (CSIRT)—Technical team responsible for addressing security incidents

Confidentiality—Preserving authorized restrictions on access and disclosure, including means for protecting privacy and proprietary information

Configuration management—The control of changes to a set of configuration items over a system life cycle

Containment—Actions taken to limit exposure after an incident has been identified and confirmed

Control—The means of managing risk, including policies, procedures, guidelines, practices or organizational structures, which can be of an administrative, technical, management or legal nature

Scope Notes: Also used as a synonym for safeguard or countermeasure.

See also Internal control.

Countermeasure—Any process that directly reduces a threat or vulnerability

Critical infrastructure—Systems whose incapacity or destruction would have a debilitating effect on the economic security of an enterprise, community or nation

Criticality—The importance of a particular asset or function to the enterprise, and the impact if that asset or function is not available

Cross-site scripting (XSS)—A type of injection, in which malicious scripts are injected into otherwise benign and trusted websites

Scope Notes: Cross-site scripting (XSS) attacks occur when an attacker uses a web application to send malicious code, generally in the form of a browser-side script, to a different end user. Flaws that allow these attacks to succeed are quite widespread and occur anywhere a web application uses input from a user within the output it generates without validating or encoding it.

Source: OWASP

Cryptography—The study of mathematical techniques related to aspects of information security, such as confidentiality, data integrity, entity authentication and data origin authentication

Cryptosystem—General term referring to a set of cryptographic primitives that are used to provide information security services. Most often, the term is used in conjunction with primitives providing confidentiality, i.e., encryption.

Cybersecurity—The protection of information assets by addressing threats to information processed, stored and transported by internetworked information systems

Cybersecurity architecture—Describes the structure, components and topology (connections and layout) of security controls within the IT infrastructure of an enterprise

Scope Notes: The security architecture shows how defense-in-depth is implemented and how layers of control are linked, and is essential to designing and implementing security controls in any complex environment.

Cyberwarfare—Activities supported by military organizations with the purpose to threat the survival and well-being of society/foreign entity

D

Data classification—The assignment of a level of sensitivity to data (or information) that results in the specification of controls for each level of classification. Levels of sensitivity of data are assigned according to predefined categories as data are created, amended, enhanced, stored or transmitted. The classification level is an indication of the value or importance of the data to the enterprise.

Data Encryption Standard (DES)—A legacy algorithm for encoding binary data that was deprecated in 2006. DES and its variants have been replaced by the Advanced Encryption Standard (AES).

Data exfiltration—Unauthorized acquisition of data from any network or endpoint

Data leakage—Unauthorized transmission of data from an organization either electronically or physically

Data owner—The individual(s) who has responsibility for the integrity, accurate reporting and use of computerized data

Data retention—Refers to the policies that govern data and records management for meeting internal, legal and regulatory data archival requirements

Database—A collection of data, often with controlled redundancy, organized according to a schema to serve one or more applications. The data are stored so that they can be used by different programs without concern for the data structure or organization. A common approach is used to add new data and to modify and retrieve existing data. See Archival database.

Decentralization—The process of distributing computer processing to different locations within an enterprise

Decryption—A technique used to recover the original plaintext from the ciphertext so that it is intelligible to the reader. The decryption is a reverse process of the encryption.

Decryption key—A digital piece of information used to recover plaintext from the corresponding ciphertext by decryption

Defense in depth—The practice of layering defenses to provide added protection. Defense in depth increases security by raising the effort needed in an attack. This strategy places multiple barriers between an attacker and enterprise computing and information resources.

Demilitarized zone (DMZ)—A small, isolated network that serves as a buffer zone between trusted and untrusted networks

Scope Notes: A DMZ is typically used to house systems, such as web servers, that must be accessible from both internal networks and the Internet.

Denial-of-service attack (DoS)—An assault on a service from a single source that floods it with so many requests that it becomes overwhelmed and is either stopped completely or operates at a significantly reduced rate

Digital certificate—Electronic credentials that permit an entity to exchange information securely via the Internet using the public key infrastructure (PKI)

Digital forensics—The process of identifying, preserving, analyzing and presenting digital evidence in a manner that is legally acceptable in any legal proceedings

Digital signature—An electronic identification of a person or entity using a public key algorithm that serves as a way for the recipient to verify the identity of the sender, integrity of the data and proof of transaction

Disaster—An emergency event of such great magnitude that it overwhelms the capacity to respond and takes considerable time from which to recover

Disaster recovery plan (DRP)—A set of human, physical, technical and procedural resources to recover, within a defined time and cost, an activity interrupted by an emergency or disaster

Discretionary access control (DAC)—Logical access control filters that may be configured or modified by the users or data owners

DMZ—See Demilitarized zone.

Domain name system (DNS)—A hierarchical database that is distributed across the Internet that allows names to be resolved into IP addresses (and vice versa) to locate services, such as web and email servers

Due care—The level of care expected from a reasonable person of similar competency under similar conditions

Due diligence—The performance of those actions that are generally regarded as prudent, responsible and

necessary to conduct a thorough and objective investigation, review and/or analysis

E

Eavesdropping—Listening a private communication without permission

Egress—Network communications going out

Elliptical curve cryptography (ECC)—An algorithm that combines plane geometry with algebra to achieve stronger authentication with smaller keys compared to traditional methods, such as RSA, which primarily use algebraic factoring

Scope Notes: Smaller keys are more suitable to mobile devices.

Encapsulation Security Payload (ESP)—Protocol, which is designed to provide a mix of security services in IPv4 and IPv6. ESP can be used to provide confidentiality, data origin authentication, connectionless integrity, an antireplay service (a form of partial sequence integrity),and (limited) traffic flow confidentiality. (RFC 4303).

Scope Notes: The ESP header is inserted after the IP header, and before the next-layer protocol header (transport mode) or before an encapsulated IP header (tunnel mode).

Encryption algorithm—A mathematically based function or calculation that encrypts/decrypts data; may be block or stream ciphers.

Encryption key—A piece of information, in a digitized form, used by an encryption algorithm to convert the plaintext to the ciphertext

Eradication—When containment measures have been deployed after an incident occurs, the root cause of the incident must be identified and removed from the network

Event—Something that happens at a specific place and/or time

Evidence—1. Information that proves or disproves a stated issue

2. Information that an auditor gathers in the course of performing an IS audit; relevant if it pertains to the audit objectives and has a logical relationship to the findings and conclusions it is used to support

Scope Notes: Audit perspective

Exploit—Method used to take advantage of a vulnerability

F

File transfer protocol—Protocol used to transfer files over a Transmission Control Protocol/Internet Protocol (TCP/IP) network. Default port number is 21.

Firewall—A system or combination of systems that enforces a boundary between two or more networks, typically forming a barrier between a secure and an open environment such as the Internet

Freeware—Software available free of charge

G

Gateway—A physical or logical device on a network that serves as an entrance to another network (e.g., router, firewall or software)

Governance—The method by which an enterprise ensures that stakeholder needs, conditions and options are evaluated to determine balanced, agreed-on enterprise objectives are achieved. It involves setting direction through prioritization and decision making, and monitoring performance and compliance against agreed-on direction and objectives.

Governance, risk management and compliance (GRC)—A business term used to group the three closely related disciplines responsible for operations and the protection of assets.

Guideline—A description of a particular way of accomplishing something that is less prescriptive than a procedure

H

Hacker—An individual who attempts to gain unauthorized access to a computer system

Hash function—1. An algorithm that maps or translates one set of bits into another (generally smaller) so that a message yields the same result every time the algorithm is executed using the same message as input

2. Fixed values derived mathematically from a text message

Hashing—Using a hash function (algorithm) to create hash values or checksums that validate message integrity

Hijacking—An exploitation of a valid network session for unauthorized purposes

Honeypot—A specially configured server, also known as a decoy server, designed to attract and monitor intruders in a manner so that their actions do not affect production systems

Horizontal defense in depth—Controls are placed in various places in the path to access an asset (this is functionally equivalent to concentric ring model)

Human firewall—A person prepared to act as a network layer of defense through education and awareness

Hypertext Transfer Protocol (HTTP)—A communication protocol used to connect to servers on the World Wide Web. Its primary function is to establish a connection with a web server and transmit hypertext markup language (HTML), extensible markup language (XML) or other pages to client browsers.

Hypertext Transfer Protocol Secure (HTTPS)—A protocol for accessing a secure web server, whereby all data transferred are encrypted. Standard port number is 443.

I

IEEE—Pronounced I-triple-E; IEEE is an organization composed of engineers, scientists and students. Best known for developing standards for the computer and electronics.

IEEE 802.11—A family of specifications developed by the Institute of Electrical and Electronics Engineers (IEEE) for wireless local area network (WLAN) technology. 802.11 specifies an over-the-air interface between a wireless client and a base station, or between two wireless clients.

Imaging—A process that allows one to obtain a bit-for-bit copy of data to avoid damage of original data or information when multiple analyses may be performed

Scope Notes: The imaging process is made to obtain residual data, such as deleted files, fragments of deleted files and other information present, from the disk for analysis. This is possible because imaging duplicates the disk surface, sector by sector.

Impact—Magnitude of loss resulting from a threat exploiting a vulnerability

Impersonation—An entity that mimics a system, process or person in an attempt to manipulate the user into an action that can cause an unexpected or unwanted event to a system

Incident—A violation or imminent threat of violation of computer security policies, acceptable use policies, guidelines or standard security practices

Incident response—The response of an enterprise to a disaster or other significant event that may significantly affect the enterprise, its people or its ability to function productively. An incident response may include evacuation of a facility, initiating a disaster recovery plan (DRP), performing damage assessment and any other measures necessary to bring an enterprise to a more stable status.

Incident response plan— Also called IRP. The operational component of incident management.

Scope Notes: The plan includes documented procedures and guidelines for defining the criticality of incidents, reporting and escalation process, and recovery procedures.

Information security—Ensures that, within the enterprise, information is protected against disclosure to unauthorized users (confidentiality), improper modification (integrity) and nonaccess when required (availability). Information security deals with all formats of information – paper documents, digital assets, intellectual property in people's minds, and verbal and visual communications.

Information security program—The overall combination of technical, operational and procedural measures and management structures implemented to provide for the confidentiality, integrity and availability of information based on business requirements and risk analysis

Information systems (IS)—The combination of strategic, managerial and operational activities involved in gathering, processing, storing, distributing and using information and its related technologies

Scope Notes: Information systems are distinct from information technology (IT) in that an information system has an IT component that interacts with the process components.

Infrastructure as a Service (IaaS)—Offers the capability to provision processing, storage, networks and other fundamental computing resources, enabling the customer to deploy and run arbitrary software, which can include operating systems (OSs) and applications

Ingestion—A process to convert information extracted to a format that can be understood by investigators

Scope Notes: See also Normalization.

Ingress—Network communications coming in

Inherent risk—The risk level or exposure without taking into account the actions that management has taken or might take (e.g., implementing controls)

Injection—A general term for attack types that inject code that is then interpreted/executed by the application

Source: OWASP

Intangible asset—An asset that is not physical in nature

Scope Notes: Examples include intellectual property (patents, trademarks, copyrights and processes), goodwill and brand recognition

Integrity—The guarding against improper information modification or destruction, and includes ensuring information nonrepudiation and authenticity

Intellectual property—Intangible assets that belong to an enterprise for its exclusive use. Examples include patents, copyrights, trademarks, ideas and trade secrets.

International Standards Organization (ISO)—The world's largest developer of voluntary International Standards

Internet Control Message Protocol (ICMP)—A set of protocols that allow systems to communicate information about the state of services on other systems

Scope Notes: For example, ICMP is used in determining whether systems are up, maximum packet sizes on links, whether a destination host/network/port is available. Hackers typically use (abuse) ICMP to determine information about the remote site.

Internet Protocol (IP)—Specifies the format of packets and the addressing scheme

Internet Protocol (IP) packet spoofing— An attack using packets with the spoofed source Internet packet (IP) addresses

Scope Notes: This technique exploits applications that use authentication based on IP addresses. This technique also may enable an unauthorized user to gain root access on the target system.

Internet service provider (ISP)—A third party that provides individuals and enterprises with access to the Internet and a variety of other Internet-related services

Interrogation—Used to obtain prior indicators or relationships, including telephone numbers, IP addresses and names of individuals, from extracted data

Intruder—Individual or group gaining access to the network and its resources without permission

Intrusion detection—The process of monitoring the events occurring in a computer system or network to detect signs of unauthorized access or attack

Intrusion detection system (IDS)—Inspects network and host security activity to identify suspicious patterns that may indicate a network or system attack

Intrusion prevention—A preemptive approach to network security used to identify potential threats and respond to them to stop, or at least limit, damage or disruption

Intrusion prevention system (IPS)—A system designed to not only detect attacks, but also prevent the intended victim hosts from being affected by the attacks

Investigation—The collection and analysis of evidence with the goal to identify the perpetrator of an attack or unauthorized use or access

IP address—A unique binary number used to identify devices on a TCP/IP network. May be IP version 4 or 6.

IP Authentication Header (AH)—Protocol used to provide connectionless integrity and data origin authentication for IP datagrams and to provide protection against replays (RFC 4302)

Scope Notes: AH ensures data integrity with a checksum that a message authentication code, such as MD5, generates. To ensure data origin authentication, AH includes a secret shared key in the algorithm that it uses for authentication. To ensure replay protection, AH uses a sequence number field within the IP authentication header.

IP Security (IPSec)—A set of protocols developed by the Internet Engineering Task Force (IETF) to support the secure exchange of packets

K

Kernel mode—Used for execution of privileged instructions for the internal operation of the system. In kernel mode, there are no protections from errors or malicious activity and all parts of the system and memory are accessible.

Key length—The size of the encryption key measured in bits

Key risk indicator (KRI)—A subset of risk indicators that are highly relevant and possess a high probability of predicting or indicating important risk

Scope Notes: See also Risk indicator.

Keylogger—Software used to record all keystrokes on a computer

L

Legacy system—Outdated computer systems

Likelihood—The probability of something happening

Local area network (LAN)—Communication network that serves several users within a specified limited geographic area

Log—1. To record details of information or events in an organized record-keeping system, usually sequenced in the order in which they occurred

2. An electronic record of activity (e.g., authentication, authorization and accounting)

Logical access—Ability to interact with computer resources granted using identification, authentication and authorization

Logical access controls—The policies, procedures, organizational structure and electronic access controls designed to restrict access to computer software and data files

M

Malicious software—See Malware.

Malware—Short for malicious software. Designed to infiltrate, damage or obtain information from a computer system without the owner's consent. Examples of malware include computer viruses, worms, Trojan horses, spyware and adware.

Man-in-the-middle attack (MITM)—An attack strategy in which the attacker intercepts the communication stream between two parts of the victim system and then replaces the traffic between the two components with the intruder's own, eventually assuming control of the communication

Mandatory access control (MAC)—Logical access control filters used to validate access credentials that cannot be controlled or modified by normal users or data owners

Media access control (MAC) address—A 48-bit unique identifier assigned to network interfaces for communications on the physical network segment

Message digest—A cryptographic hash function takes an input of an arbitrary length and produces an output (also known as a message digest) that is a standard-sized binary string. The output is unique to the input in such a way that even a minor change to the input results in a completely different output. Modern cryptographic hash functions are also resistant to collisions (situations in which different inputs produce identical output); a collision, while possible, is statistically improbable. Cryptographic hash functions are developed so that input cannot be determined readily from the output. See Hash.

Message digest algorithm—One-way functions that serve as a way for the recipient to verify data integrity and sender identity. Common message digest algorithms are MD5, SHA256 and SHA512.

Miniature fragment attack—Using this method, an attacker fragments the IP packet into smaller ones and pushes it through the firewall, in the hope that only the first of the sequence of fragmented packets would be examined and the others would pass without review.

Mobile device—A small, handheld computing device, typically having a display screen with touch input and/or a miniature keyboard and weighing less than two pounds

Monitoring policy—Rules outlining or delineating the way in which information about the use of computers, networks, applications and information is captured and interpreted

Multifactor authentication—A combination of more than one authentication method, such as token and password (or personal identification number [PIN] or token and biometric device)

N

Need-to-Know—Principled approach of controlling what someone can see. Employees are only given access to data, systems or spaces that are necessary to do their job.

NetBIOS—A program that allows applications on different computers to communicate within a local area network (LAN)

Network address translation (NAT)—A methodology of modifying network address information in IP

datagram packet headers while they are in transit across a traffic routing device for the purpose of remapping one IP address space into another

Network basic input/output system—See NetBIOS.

Network segmentation—A common technique to implement network security that segments an enterprise network into separate zones that can be separately controlled, monitored and protected

Network traffic analysis—Identifies patterns in network communications

Scope Notes: Traffic analysis does not need to have the actual content of the communication but analyzes where traffic is taking place, when and for how long communications occur and the size of information transferred.

Nonrepudiation—The assurance that a party cannot later deny originating data; provision of proof of the integrity and origin of the data and that can be verified by a third party

Scope Notes: A digital signature can provide nonrepudiation.

Normalization—The elimination of redundant data

O

Obfuscation—The deliberate act of creating source or machine code that is difficult for humans to understand

Open Systems Interconnect (OSI) model—A seven-layer conceptual model that describes functions of computer network or telecommunication systems

Open Web Application Security Project (OWASP)—An open community dedicated to enabling organizations to conceive, develop, acquire, operate and maintain applications that can be trusted

Operating system (OS)—A master control program that runs the computer and acts as a scheduler and traffic controller

Scope Notes: The operating system is the first program copied into the computer memory after the computer is turned on; it must reside in memory at all times. It is the software that interfaces between the computer hardware (disk, keyboard, mouse, network, modem and printer) and the application software (word processor, spreadsheet email) which also controls access to the devices, is partially responsible for security components and sets the standards for the application programs that run in it.

Outsourcing—A formal agreement with a third party to perform IS or other business functions for an enterprise

P

Packet—Protocol data unit that is routed from source to destination in a packet-switched network

Scope Notes: A packet contains both routing information and data.

Packet filtering—Controlling access to a network by analyzing the attributes of the incoming and outgoing packets and either letting them pass, or denying them, based on a list of rules

Password—A protected, generally computer-encrypted string of characters that authenticate a computer user to the computer system

Password cracker—A tool that tests the strength of user passwords by searching for passwords that are easy to guess. It repeatedly tries words from specially crafted dictionaries and often also generates thousands (and in some cases, even millions) of permutations of characters, numbers and symbols.

Patch—Fixes to software programming errors and vulnerabilities

Patch management—An area of systems management that involves acquiring, testing and installing multiple patches (code changes) to an administered computer system to maintain up-to-date software and often to address security risk

Scope Notes: Patch management tasks include maintaining current knowledge of available patches, deciding what patches are appropriate for particular systems, ensuring that patches are installed properly, testing systems after installation and documenting all associated procedures, such as specific configurations required. A number of products are available to automate patch management tasks. Patches are sometimes ineffective and can sometimes cause more problems than they fix. Patch management experts suggest that system administrators take simple steps to avoid problems, such as performing backups and testing patches on noncritical systems prior to installations. Patch management can be viewed as part of change management.

Payload—A piece of malicious software that lets an attacker control a compromised computer system. The payload is typically attached to and delivered by an exploit.

Penetration testing—A live test of the effectiveness of security defenses through mimicking the actions of real-life attackers

Personal identification number (PIN)—A type of password (i.e., a secret number assigned to an individual) that, in conjunction with some means of identifying the individual, serves to verify the authenticity of the individual

Scope Notes: PINs have been adopted by financial institutions as the primary means of verifying customers in an electronic funds transfer (EFT) system.

Phishing—A type of electronic mail (email) attack that attempts to convince a user that the originator is genuine, but with the intention of obtaining information for use in social engineering

Scope Notes: Phishing attacks may take the form of masquerading as a lottery organization advising the recipient or the user's bank of a large win; in either case, the intent is to obtain account and personal identification number (PIN) details. Alternative attacks may seek to obtain apparently innocuous business information, which may be used in another form of active attack.

PIN—See Personal identification number (PIN)

Platform as a Service (PaaS)—Offers the capability to deploy onto the cloud infrastructure customer-created or -acquired applications that are created using programming languages and tools supported by the provider

Policy—A document that communicates required and prohibited activities and behaviors

Port—A process or application-specific software element serving as a communication endpoint for the transport layer IP protocols (UDP and TCP)

Port scanning—The act of probing a system to identify open ports

Principle of least privilege (PoLP)—Principled approach of controlling what someone can do. Extension of need-to-know, whereby individuals are only granted the least amount of system access necessary to perform their jobs.

Privacy—The right of an individual to trust that others will appropriately and respectfully use, store, share and dispose of his/her associated personal and sensitive information within the context, and according to the purposes for which it was collected or derived

Probe—Inspect a network or system to find weak spots

Procedure—A document containing a detailed description of the steps necessary to perform specific operations in conformance with applicable standards. Procedures are defined as part of processes.

Protocol—The rules by which a network operates and controls the flow and priority of transmissions

Proxy server—A server that acts on behalf of a user

Scope Notes: Typical proxies accept a connection from a user, make a decision as to whether the user or client IP address is permitted to use the proxy, perhaps perform additional authentication, and complete a connection to a remote destination on behalf of the user.

Public key encryption—A cryptographic system that uses two keys: one is a public key, which is known to everyone, and the second is a private or secret key, which is only known to the recipient of the message. See also Asymmetric Key.

Public key infrastructure (PKI)—A series of processes and technologies for the association of cryptographic keys with the entity to whom those keys were issued

R
Recovery—The phase in the incident response plan that ensures that affected systems or services are restored to a condition specified in the service delivery objectives (SDOs) or business continuity plan (BCP)

Recovery point objective (RPO)—Determined based on the acceptable data loss in case of a disruption of operations. It indicates the earliest point in time that is acceptable to recover the data. The RPO effectively quantifies the permissible amount of data loss in case of interruption.

Recovery time objective (RTO)—The amount of time allowed for the recovery of a business function or resource after a disaster occurs

Registration authority (RA)—An authority in a network that verifies user requests for a digital certificate and tells the certificate authority (CA) to issue it

Regulation—Rules or laws defined and enforced by an authority to regulate conduct

Regulatory requirements—Rules or laws that regulate conduct and that the enterprise must obey to become compliant

Remediation—Actions taken to mitigate or eliminate the vulnerability after vulnerabilities are identified and assessed

Removable media—Any type of storage device that can be removed from the system while it is running

Replay—The ability to copy a message or stream of messages between two parties and replay (retransmit) them to one or more of the parties

Residual risk—The remaining risk after management has implemented a risk response

Resilience—The ability of a system or network to resist failure or to recover quickly from any disruption, usually with minimal recognizable effect

Return on investment (ROI)—A measure of operating performance and efficiency, computed in its simplest form by dividing net income by the total investment over the period being considered

Return-oriented programming attacks—An exploit technique in which the attacker uses control of the call stack to indirectly execute cherry-picked machine instructions immediately prior to the return instruction in subroutines within the existing program code

Risk—The combination of the likelihood of an event and its impact

Risk acceptance—Decision to accept a risk, made according to the risk appetite and risk tolerance set by senior management where the enterprise can assume the risk and absorb any losses

Risk assessment—A process used to identify and evaluate risk and its potential effects

Scope Notes: Risk assessments are used to identify those items or areas that present the highest risk, vulnerability or exposure to the enterprise for inclusion in the IS annual audit plan.

Risk assessments are also used to manage the project delivery and project benefit risk.

Risk avoidance—The process for systematically avoiding risk, constituting one approach to managing risk

Risk management—1. The coordinated activities to direct and control an enterprise with regard to risk

Scope Notes: In the International Standard, the term "control" is used as a synonym for "measure." (ISO/IEC Guide 73:2002)

2. One of the governance objectives. Entails recognizing risk; assessing the impact and likelihood of that risk; and developing strategies, such as avoiding the risk, reducing the negative effect of the risk and/or transferring the risk, to manage it within the context of the enterprise's risk appetite.

Scope Notes: COBIT 5 perspective

Risk mitigation—The management of risk through the use of countermeasures and controls

Risk reduction—The implementation of controls or countermeasures to reduce the likelihood or impact of a risk to a level within the organization's risk tolerance

Risk tolerance—The acceptable level of variation that management is willing to allow for any particular risk as the enterprise pursues its objectives

Risk transfer—The process of assigning risk to another enterprise, usually through the purchase of an insurance policy or by outsourcing the service

Scope Notes: Also known as risk sharing

Risk treatment—The process of selection and implementation of measures to modify risk (ISO/IEC Guide 73:2002)

ROI—See Return on Investment.

Root cause analysis—A process of diagnosis to establish the origins of events, which can be used for learning from consequences, typically from errors and problems

Rootkit—A software suite designed to aid an intruder in gaining unauthorized administrative access to a computer system

Router—A networking device that can send (route) data packets from one local area network (LAN) or wide area network (WAN) to another, based on addressing at the network layer (Layer 3) in the open systems interconnection (OSI) model

Scope Notes: Networks connected by routers can use different or similar networking protocols. Routers usually are capable of filtering packets based on parameters, such as source addresses, destination addresses, protocol and network applications (ports).

RSA—A public key cryptosystem developed by R. Rivest, A. Shamir and L. Adleman used for both encryption and digital signatures

Scope Notes: The RSA has two different keys, the public encryption key and the secret decryption key. The strength of the RSA depends on the difficulty of the prime number factorization. For applications with high-level security, the number of the decryption key bits should be greater than 512 bits.

S

Safeguard—A practice, procedure or mechanism that reduces risk

Secure Electronic Transaction (SET)—A standard that will ensure that credit card and associated payment order information travels safely and securely between the various involved parties on the Internet

Secure Multipurpose Internet Mail Extensions (S/MIME)—Provides cryptographic security services for electronic messaging applications, including authentication, message integrity and nonrepudiation of origin (using digital signatures), and privacy and data security (using encryption), to provide a consistent way to send and receive MIME data (RFC 2311)

Secure Shell (SSH)—Network protocol that uses cryptography to secure communication, remote command line login and remote command execution between two networked computers

Secure Sockets Layer (SSL)—A protocol that is used to transmit private documents through the Internet

Scope Notes: The SSL protocol uses a private key to encrypt the data that are to be transferred through the SSL connection.

Security model—An engineering model informed by policies that specify how a system will enforce security

Security perimeter—The boundary that defines the area of security concern and security policy coverage

Segregation of duty (SoD)—See Segregation/separation of duties (SoD).

Sensitivity—A measure of the impact that improper disclosure of information may have on an enterprise

Separation of duty (SoD)—See Segregation/separation of duties (SoD).

Service delivery objective (SDO)—Directly related to the business needs, SDO is the level of services to be reached during the alternate process mode until the normal situation is restored.

Service level agreement (SLA)—An agreement, preferably documented, between a service provider and the customer(s)/user(s) that defines minimum performance targets for a service and how they will be measured

Sniffing—The process by which data traversing a network are captured or monitored

Social engineering—An attack based on deceiving users or administrators at the target site into revealing confidential or sensitive information

Software as a service (SaaS)—Offers the capability to use the provider's applications running on cloud infrastructure. The applications are accessible from various client devices through a thin client interface, such as a web browser (e.g., web-based email).

Source routing specification—A transmission technique where the sender of a packet can specify the route that packet should follow through the network

Spam—Computer-generated messages sent as unsolicited advertising

Spear phishing—An attack designed to entice specific individuals or groups to obtain important information, where social engineering techniques are used to masquerade as a trusted party to obtain important information, such as passwords from the victim

Spoofing—Faking the sending address of a transmission in order to gain illegal entry into a secure system

Spyware—Software whose purpose is to monitor a computer user's actions (e.g., websites visited) and report these actions to a third party, without the informed consent of that machine's owner or legitimate user

SQL injection—Results from failure of the application to appropriately validate input. When specially crafted user-controlled input consisting of SQL syntax is used without proper validation as part of SQL queries, it is possible to glean information from the database in ways not envisaged during application design.

Source: MITRE

Stateful inspection—A firewall architecture that tracks each connection traversing all interfaces of the firewall and makes sure they are valid

Statutory requirements—Laws created by government institutions

Symmetric key encryption—System in which a different key (or set of keys) is used by each pair of trading partners to ensure that no one else can read their messages. The same key is used for encryption and decryption. See also Private Key Cryptosystem.

System hardening—A process to eliminate as much security risk as possible by removing all nonessential software programs, protocols, services and utilities from the system

T

Target—Person or asset selected as the aim of an attack

Telnet—Network protocol used to enable remote access to a server computer

Scope Notes: Commands typed are run on the remote server.

Threat—Anything (e.g., object, substance, human) that is capable of acting against an asset in a manner that can result in harm

Scope Notes: A potential cause of an unwanted incident (ISO/IEC 13335)

Threat agent—Methods and things used to exploit a vulnerability

Scope Notes: Examples include determination, capability, motive and resources.

Threat event—Any event during which a threat element/actor acts against an asset in a manner that has the potential to directly result in harm

Threat vector—The path or route used by the adversary to gain access to the target

Timelines—Chronological graphs where events related to an incident can be mapped to look for relationships in complex cases

Scope Notes: Timelines can provide simplified visualization for presentation to management and other nontechnical audiences.

Token—In security systems, a physical device that is used to authenticate a user, typically in addition to a username and password; in programming languages, a single element of the language

Topology—The physical layout of how computers are linked together

Scope Notes: Examples of topology include ring, star and bus.

Transmission Control Protocol (TCP)—A connection-based Internet protocol that supports reliable data transfer connections

Scope Notes: Packet data are verified using checksums and retransmitted if they are missing or corrupted. The application plays no part in validating the transfer.

Transmission Control Protocol Internet Protocol (TCP/IP)—Provides the basis for the Internet; a set of communication protocols that encompass media access, packet transport, session communication, file transfer, electronic mail (email), terminal emulation, remote file access and network management

Transport Layer Security (TLS)—A cryptographic protocol that provides secure communications, endpoint security and privacy on the Internet

Triple DES (3DES)—A block cipher created from the Data Encryption Standard (DES) cipher by using it three times. 3DES was broken in 2016.

Trojan horse—Purposefully hidden malicious or damaging code within an authorized computer program

Tunnel—The paths that the encapsulated packets follow in an Internet virtual private network (VPN)

Tunnel mode—Used to protect traffic between different networks when traffic must travel through intermediate or untrusted networks. Tunnel mode encapsulates the entire IP packet with and AH or ESP header and an additional IP header.

Two-factor authentication—The use of two independent mechanisms for authentication (e.g., requiring a smart card and a password); typically the combination of something you know, are or have

U

Uniform resource locator (URL)—The string of characters that form a web address

User Datagram Protocol (UDP)—A connectionless Internet protocol that is designed for network efficiency and speed at the expense of reliability

User mode—Used for the execution of normal system activities

User provisioning—A process to create, modify, disable and delete user accounts and their profiles across IT infrastructure and business applications

V

Value—The relative worth or importance of an investment for an enterprise, as perceived by its key stakeholders, expressed as total life cycle benefits net of related costs, adjusted for risk and (in the case of financial value) the time value of money

Vertical defense-in depth—Controls are placed at different system layers—hardware, operating system, application, database or user levels

Virtual local area network (VLAN)—Logical segmentation of a LAN into different broadcast domains

Scope Notes: A VLAN is set up by configuring ports on a switch, so devices attached to these ports may communicate as if they were attached to the same physical network segment, although the devices are located on different LAN segments. A VLAN is based on logical rather than physical connections.

Virtual private network (VPN)—A secure private network that uses the public telecommunications infrastructure to transmit data

Scope Notes: In contrast to a much more expensive system of owned or leased lines that can only be used by one enterprise, VPNs are used by enterprises for both extranets and wide areas of intranets. Using encryption and authentication, a VPN encrypts all data that pass between two Internet points, maintaining privacy and security.

Virtualization—The process of adding a guest application and data onto a virtual server, recognizing that the guest application will ultimately be removed from this physical server

Virus—Piece of code that can replicate itself and spread from one computer to another. It requires intervention or execution to replicate and/or cause damage.

See Bomb, Trojan horse and worm.

Virus signature—The file of virus patterns that are compared with existing files to determine whether they are infected with a virus or worm

Voice-over Internet Protocol (VoIP)—Also called IP Telephony, Internet Telephony and Broadband Phone, a technology that makes it possible to have a voice conversation over the Internet or over any dedicated Internet Protocol (IP) network instead of over dedicated voice transmission lines

Volatile data—Data that change frequently and can be lost when the system power is shut down

Vulnerability—A weakness in the design, implementation, operation or internal control of a process that could expose the system to adverse threats from threat events

Vulnerability analysis—A process of identifying and classifying vulnerabilities

Vulnerability scanning—An automated process to proactively identify security weaknesses in a network or individual system

W

Web server—End-point hardware or software that serves web pages to users

Wi-Fi Protected Access (WPA)—A class of security protocols used to secure wireless (Wi-Fi) computer networks

Wide area network (WAN)—A computer network connecting multiple offices or buildings over a larger area

Wireless local area network (WLAN)—Wireless communication network that serves several users within a specified limited geographic area

Worm—A programmed network attack in which a self-replicating program does not attach itself to programs, but rather spreads independently of users' action

WPA2—Wireless security protocol that supports 802.11i encryption standards to provide greater security. This protocol uses advanced encryption standards (AES) and temporal key integrity protocol (TKIP) for stronger encryption.

WPA3—Wireless security protocol released mid-2018 that improves on WPA2 by eliminating preshared key (PSK), which is susceptible to dictionary attacks

Write blocker—A device that allows the acquisition of information on a drive without creating the possibility of accidentally damaging the drive

Z

Zero-day exploit—A vulnerability that is exploited before the software creator/vendor is even aware of its existence. May also refer to known flaws that do not have a patch available.